The Consummate Trainer
A Practitioner's Perspective

Ora A. Spaid

A Reston Book, Prentice-Hall
Englewood Cliffs, NJ 07632

Library of Congress Cataloging-in-Publication Data

Spaid, Ora.
  The consummate trainer.

  "A Reston book."
  1. Employees, Training of.   I. Title
HF5549.5.T7S647   1986   658.3'1243   85-30120
ISBN 0-8359-1003-2

Editorial/production supervision and
interior design by Camelia Townsend

10   9   8   7   6   5   4   3   2   1

PRINTED IN THE UNITED STATES OF AMERICA

To the late Dr. Curtis D. MacDougall,
for learning that lasted.

Contents

Preface

This book seeks to stimulate excellence in the practice of training by using pragmatic experience for a trainer-to-trainer discussion of the approaches and techniques that lift performance above competence to excellence.

The Model of the consummate trainer is used to give focus to the goal of excellence, by describing the likely characteristics and behavior of such a trainer. To further narrow the focus, the scope of the book is limited to the design, development, and delivery of training—leaving out such important functions as consultant, counselor, researcher, and manager. The book's concern is primarily for the trainer, rather than the learner, and the trainer is treated as a real person with strengths and weaknesses, human feelings and attitudes, fallible but striving to excel. By using practical experience as an information base, the many valuable contributions to the field in theory and research are not denigrated, but stress is given to that empirical reality in which trainers and training are tested and succeed or fall short.

The book is essentially the experience of one practitioner. While such a viewpoint is restricted, in my own learning of the craft I was always helped immeasurably by those reports that relate the observations of some practicing trainer—how he did this, why, the problems she faced, what to look out for, what works best—frank information from one who has done it. It seemed to me that a practitioner's perspective on what seems to produce superior training could be useful as a guide for the new trainer and as provocative shop talk for the veteran.

Plan of the Book

The book is divided into four major parts: The Person, The Field, The Approach, and The Product. A final chapter covers The Trainer of the Future.

The part on The Person begins the definition of the consummate trainer, deals with some basic qualifications for trainers and what the field appears to regard as excellence, considers some requirements of the trainer as a team member, and offers some suggestions for learning the craft.

The part about The Field is a forthright examination of the environment in which the trainer performs—its changes, pitfalls, problems, demands, competing technologies, and influences that encourage or discourage excellence.

In The Approach, adult learning theory is critically appraised, what seems to work with adults is discussed along with some ways to adopt the learner's perspective and a mode for resolving the conflict between process and content.

The major portion of the book is devoted to The Product, using a plan for training production that groups activities under Define, Design, Develop, and Deliver. Each group is the subject of a long chapter, with extensive how-to treatment of a broad range of tasks.

Numerous examples of training products and processes are added at the conclusion of chapters to illustrate the content covered. Each major part of the book ends with a Checkpoint, a series of questions based upon the foregoing content intended as much to provide opportunity for disagreement with the author's assertions as to use as a self-assessment device.

Declarations and Disclaimers

This book is somewhat unconventional in several ways. One is my attitude toward you. In describing this as a trainer-to-trainer discussion, I hope it will be just that; the kind of bull session you have over a drink with others in the trade, where you can be honest. I want to deal with you as a colleague and a fully human being with intelligence and ambition to advance, not above irritation or mistakes, with a boss to satisfy and bills to pay, too much to do and not enough time, pride in what you do and some humor to smooth the rough places.

I'm counting on some sophistication from you so that this book doesn't have to be a primer; I don't want to insult your intelligence. On the other hand, what is simplistic to some is sophisticated to others. You know the problem: where do you aim your stuff?

You won't find any section on How To Read This Book, because you'll read it your way, without advice from me. I expect to voice some candid opinions and make some unqualified generalizations, but I expect also that you will disagree when you do. I trust you can discriminate for yourself what you can accept and where you think I am a lost ball in the high weeds.

By titling this book *The Consummate Trainer*, I do not mean to claim that standing for myself. But not having achieved that status does not preclude me from striving for it or dealing with it. My 17 years in the craft have given me ample opportunity for serious reflection on excellence but that experience is limited and I will not address any training activity that I have not directly experienced. My reference to training as a craft or trade is not pejorative. Quite the contrary; I use those terms in the respectful sense of, say, the actor who speaks of "practicing my craft."

As far as gender terms are concerned, I will be using the desexing system of alternative pronouns; "she" and "he" used interchangeably, as well as alternating "him" and "her." This is to avoid the awkwardness of "he or she" or "he/she." Some may find alternative pronouns uncomfortable, too, but I am told this approach is emerging as the preferred one.

Some terms—like "participant," "trainee," 'trainer," and "practitioner" are inevitably overused. But there are no suitable alternatives.

You will find no footnotes or references; I will acknowledge debts I owe to other authors in the text. I also promise no paradigms or matrixes or Rube Goldberg flow charts or decision trees. Just one small model, with acronym—the Content Finders-Keepers Process (CFKP)—which you are free to forget.

One more caveat: it is my considered opinion that training sometimes takes itself too seriously. A bit of whimsy is needed now and then to humanize and demythologize. So keep your tongue in your cheek; that's where mine is.

The Flight of Your Life

In training, it is customary to begin with a warm-up exercise of some sort to help people get acquainted and loosened up for what lies ahead. Custom also prescribes that you declare your objectives at the outset, so everyone will know what is coming and what will be gained from it.

In that tradition, I offer a flight of fantasy as a beginning. Its objective is to stretch and warm up your mental muscles so you can endure the unorthodox approach that is in store. At the conclusion, you will be able to determine whether or not you need to read the rest of the book.

Imagine that you are a trainer employed by a consulting firm that does a lot of contract work for the government. You consider yourself a pretty good trainer—even exceptional compared to some you have seen—but you wonder sometimes if they don't expect a little too much from you.

Like now. Your boss comes walking in, smiling, breaching his usual practice by coming to your office instead of summoning you to his, and drops a Request for Proposal on your desk, announcing: "Now, *here* is one for you. This is the kind you get once in a lifetime."

You glance down at the thick stack of paper. The title *is* astonishing.

NATIONAL AERONAUTICS AND SPACE ADMINISTRATION

Request for Proposal (RFP)

A Demonstration to Provide
Pre- and In-Mission Training
for Passenger-Observers
on Space Shuttle Mission 86–3

Uncertain, you ask, "Does this mean what I think it means?"

His grin broadens. "How would you like to train people to fly in space?"

The idea seems preposterous. "I thought NASA did that kind of training itself. They did for that senator and the schoolteacher."

He doesn't seem astonished. "Maybe they're getting ready to farm it out. They could be planning for the day when there will be passengers on every shuttle and they don't want to have to train everyone that goes up. I don't know."

"Are you serious about bidding this?"

His smile fades, as it does when new business is the subject. "A lot will depend on what you think. You'll have to be the lead on this. It could be a big contract, but the competition will be fierce."

"Yeah," is all you can say, as you start leafing through the package.

"Well, read it," he says, "and let me know what you think. Sooner the better because we'll have to get ready for the bidder's conference."

But what do I, what do we, know about space?, you start to ask, but he has left. It's a silly question anyhow. You've been around long enough to know that consulting shops live by the axiom: If the money is there, we can do anything. What was it one astronaut said to the other while they were sitting in the capsule waiting for launch: "Think what a marvel of free enterprise this is. Hundreds of contractors put it together—every one the lowest bidder."

MISS PIGGY AS A PARTICIPANT?

The objectives you'd been trying to write will have to wait, so you can dig into the RFP. Following your habit, first you rip out the boilerplate pages and put them aside, then get a fresh legal pad to write down the questions that will occur to you as you read.

The summary answers your first question: What does NASA mean by passenger/observers?

"The era of space travel has reached a turning point," it begins. In the early phase, manned orbital flight was limited to carefully selected, highly trained astronauts. In the next phase, scientists and technicians— the RFP calls them "nonastronaut space workers"—were added to carry out numerous experiments and measurements possible only in a gravity-free environment. Now, the time has come for civilian passengers to join the space transportation system.

Here are the specifics: Three to five passengers will be selected by NASA to represent a cross section of age, sex, race, and nationality drawn from the disciplines and fields involved in space—meteorology, communications, oceanography, land use, geology, health care, gravity-free manufacturing, water resources, and so on.

Medical screening and training for which special equipment is needed will be done by NASA. The rest of the preparation is to be conducted by the contractor, as an experiment/demonstration of training requirements, anticipating future flights when nonastronauts will assume routine roles. The training plan and its implementation will be evaluated by a separate contractor.

You are writing as you read. "Needs assessment. How?" you jot down. "External evaluator. Who?" Then, the enormity of it creeps up on you and you can't help musing. Imagine, a workplace in space. On a space vehicle. Not Star Wars or something in the next century; this is now. Almost as a relief from the wonder of it, a ludicrous thought comes to mind—the image of Miss Piggy and the others in that space-ship shot and the wail of the unseen announcer above: "Pigs innn spaaaacce."

ALL THE COMFORTS OF HOME

How long are they allowing for this training? You ruffle through the RFP's schedule of reports and deliverables—lots of deliverables—and tot up almost a year's time; preflight briefing is slated for Day 320. Is that continuous time? How do you get these civilian passengers together?

You skip through the Work Statement for some details. You find answers to some of your questions, amid the space-age nomenclature—circularization, orbit insertion, avionics, atmospheric re-entry, Long Duration Exposure Facility, rehydratables, gimbaled.

Some of it is reassuring: space vehicle occupants now feel only three G's of pressure on liftoff; a mere 1.5 G's on re-entry. Repeated mention of "shirt-sleeve comfort" in the cabin. No EVAs—extra vehicular activities or space walks—required of passengers. Split-level cabin with closed circuit television, audio cassettes of one's choosing, exercise equipment, even playing cards with retainers to keep them from floating away. The more you read, the more the impression grows: this isn't so bad. It might be fun.

You didn't find anything about the length of the mission, so you backtrack and come across this:

The chief trainer will accompany the passengers on the mission, conduct in-progress training aboard, and carry out a thorough debriefing of passengers after the mission is completed.

Wait a minute.

Training *them* to go off in space is one thing, but . . . Go along? Could you pass the physical? What would the family say? This isn't just a trip to Kansas City after all. What if you got air sick?

DECISIONS, DECISIONS

The phone rings. It's B.G. "Well, what do you think?"

"I don't know yet. I've got a lot of questions. I didn't expect you'd want to know so soon."

"That's all right. Why I called, I am setting up a meeting tomorrow around 10:00 A.M. Several of us will go over the questions that are going to come up."

You blanch. "That's pretty quick. I wanted to do a lit search and . . . B.G., did you know that the lead trainer is supposed to go along on the flight?"

"No. Really?" He sounds almost delighted. "That's interesting. Well, 10 in the morning then." He hangs up.

For a solid five minutes you just sit there, staring at the RFP, out the window, at the phone, at the spider plant, at nothing. Slowly, the shock subsides and your mind admits some positives. It might not be so bad; it sure would be a first.

You look at the pad, almost three pages of questions. Raw, random queries, usually only a reminder word.

"Jargon," reads the pad. All that space language. Does NASA have a glossary?

"What are the pass/obs supposed to do in flight?" Just observe? Any structure to their observations?

"NASA wants objectives. What kind? How specific?" your notes read. Is anybody going to measure them, or is this another case of having objectives to have objectives?

"What criteria for success?" Survival, just getting back alive?

"Confined quarters." What about cabin fever and anxiety? Any interpersonal relations stuff needed?

The more you go over your questions, the more they multiply. Methodology? What is in-progress training? How about public relations? Those first passengers in space will get besieged by the media.

You're at that stage where it is all an unmanageable mess—the ferment of beginning. You know it will get sorted out, but it takes time, gestation.

This time, your mind doesn't seem to grab hold. It's that matter of going along on the mission; makes it too personal.

B.G. will want to know tomorrow what you recommend about trying for the contract. Sounds as though he has already made up his mind to go for it.

You'd better give the RFP another reading. Better get coffee. It's going to be a long night.

What you have just read was fiction, although not at all far-fetched. The day of passenger travel in space is here.

Suppose *you* were presented a challenge like that. What would you do?

Think of it, not just being the first trainer in space, but the demands on your skills, the strangeness of the material, the competencies to be covered, the methodology to be used, the problems, the details.

Certainly, it would be the flight of your life. But your life, and that of others, might depend upon your performance as a trainer. Could you handle it? Could you say to the boss: "Yes, let's go for it?"

If you could, then you must be the consummate trainer.

If not, if you're not quite there yet, read on.

————————INTRODUCTION CHECKPOINT————————

At the end of each major part of this book is a Checkpoint, an opportunity to mull over some of the material from previous chapters. The purpose of these Checkpoints is threefold:

1. To give you a chance to react critically to what has been presented— to challenge and disagree, to recall your own experience that may be contrary. When you agree, these Checkpoints may re-enforce your own view, or remind you of better reasons for agreeing than those given.
2. To help you discover your own standards of excellence, by asking you to make judgments that come from your own sense of what is good or bad, better or worse, thus sharpening your awareness of what contributes to excellence in training.
3. To encourage you to fix your own philosophy of training, the rationale that undergirds all that you do; to know where you stand.

The process followed in the Checkpoints is simple. I will present an Item—a statement, method, issue, or procedure—drawn from the preceeding material. You are asked to make a Judgment on that Item, rating it sometimes, comparing it to your own experience at other times. Then, space is provided for you to set down your Reasons for the Judgment you have made.

Item-Judgment-Reasons—that is the process.

The Reasons are important, because they require you to explore your own thinking. If you disagree with an Item, or have something better to offer, you can nail down your position by giving Reasons for it. If you disagree, you will know your Reasons why.

The response devices used in the Checkpoints are mostly simplified Likert scales, occasionally a straightforward question. Here is a sample:

1. *Item:* The Introduction called "The Flight of Your Life" presented a hypothetical chance for you to train the first passengers to fly on a Space Shuttle mission. It would require the utmost in training skill.

   Judgment: Do you think you could handle it?

Yes		Maybe		No
1	2	3	4	5

   Reasons:

Part
ONE

THE PERSON

The Consummate
Trainer

When you were in school, did you ever have a truly exceptional teacher, the kind that stands out in your mind above all others?

If you were unusually blessed, you might have had several, but one or two of these outstanding teachers seems to be life's allotment for most of us.

It might have been a professor you had in college, a demanding curmudgeon, or a kindly Mr. Chips, someone you remember as much for his eccentricities as for his scholarship. Or, perhaps she was the patient guide of your formative years, leading you gently into new worlds, your favorite teacher, so beloved she was almost a legend.

When you recall that teacher, chances are you remember *the person*, not anything you learned from the person. But as you think more about it, you can find in yourself the intangibles of that teacher's influence—attitudes, standards, an approach to learning, an appreciation of knowledge.

The mark of a great teacher is learning that lasts, what the teacher gives us that becomes part of us, long after we may have forgotten where it came from.

It can be useful to trace back over the schooling of your past and see which teachers return to your consciousness. Who were they? What did they have, what did they give that makes you remember them?

LEARNING TO LEAD, NOT FOLLOW

The one who comes instantly to my mind was my major professor in college, Dr. Curtis D. MacDougall, for thirty years a fiesty presence at Northwestern University's Medill School of Journalism. Dr. Mac was what sophomores would describe as a colorful character, a tall, bespectacled man in a rumpled suit and askewed tie whose unkempt appearance was true to his disdain for convention. His credentials, however, were impeccable: solid experience as reporter and editor, unquestioned scholarship that he kept current, standing in his field—his books are standard texts in many journalism schools. He also had fierce convictions and a record of leftist political activities that kept the school's administrators in continuous dither and him in hot water. We never knew whether or not the person sitting next to us in class was an FBI agent; it was the Joe McCarthy era and they constantly tried to nail Mac as a communist. He wasn't; as he once said, "I thought it (communism) was just as dogmatic as any other point of view and I've always been fiercely independent." He was always boycotting something or running for some office. Once he was stoned by a mob in downstate Illinois while campaigning for the U.S. Senate on the Progressive Party ticket headed by Henry Wallace. Still, as the *Chicago Tribune* recently noted: " . . . none of his highly controversial political activity has ever affected his reputation as a great teacher of journalism."

Dr. Mac was not an idealogue in the classroom. He cared not *what* you thought but *that* you thought, and could defend what you thought. One of my classmates was so far to the right we thought him a fascist. He repeatedly took Mac on in heated exchanges, but he drew consistently high grades because he earned them.

Dr. MacDougall drenched us with knowledge in the classroom and then put us out in the field in long-day labs where at some time we covered every news beat in the city of Chicago and returned to write news stories that day and features and editorials before the next class. We competed with the then four newspapers in Chicago and if we missed any story they had, we flunked that day because Mac wanted us to lead the field, not follow it. He demanded quality so insistently that his expectations soon became our own. He required us to read omnivorously, to clip and collect; habits that never let go. Long after we left school, when we heard from him, he was still prompting, wanting to know what we were reading, asking for samples of our work.

Remind you of anyone you know? Maybe someone not merely memorable for a novel personality, but someone whose teachings are traceable to what you know now, to how you perform now. His contribution clings, like the barking of a flying instructor I had in the old Army Air Corps, who chewed on me so ferociously from the rear cockpit that, as he said: "When you're up there by yourself, you'll still hear me yelling at you." I couldn't tell you his name now, but I can still hear him roar: "Put your flaps down, you idiot!"

WHERE ARE THE GREAT TRAINERS?

Here's an interesting question: When you ran down the list of people from whom you have learned most, were there any trainers on the list? Probably not. For one thing, I have been discussing great *teachers*, not trainers.

Still, if some trainer had had a significant impact on you, you might have at least considered that one. The irony is that trainers can be just as responsible for learning that lasts; they have a better bag of tricks, a more extensive methodology, than the traditional reading/lecture/lab mode still relied upon by many teachers. Training has just not found a niche yet for the equivalent of the great teacher. Training has its gurus, but their reputations rest more on their writings or theories or models than on the shaping of a constituency of students.

By definition, training is more short term than teaching; it doesn't expose the learner to numerous class sessions over semesters of time for long-term impact. Nor is the trainer the dominant figure in the classroom that the teacher is, or shouldn't be. Sometimes the trainer's best work, in structure and design for instance, is not apparent.

Unfortunately, the hierarchical system within which the trainer works seems to downgrade the on-line trainer. Status is found in the move up to administrator of training or out to the beckoning rewards of consulting practice. As the field has grown and reached out to enlarge its turf by encompassing all the specialties now gathered under the rubric of human resources development, training has been outgrown, relegated to entry status. And by diminishing training, the system has acted to discourage quality.

The sad state of our nation's educational system reported by national study commissions is largely a fall-off of competence in teaching, suggesting that the downgrading of the status of teachers has diminished quality. Remedies calling for merit pay or a "great teacher" program seem like sudden recognition of the importance of the teacher in the classroom.

Who will teach, who will train our citizens for their new roles in our changing society, if we continue to denigrate the contribution of those who are most directly involved with those who need to learn?

Excellence in both teaching *and* training may be needed as never before.

THE MOST RELIABLE MOTIVATION

The rewards for excellence in training are primarily inherent. If being "just a trainer," albeit a first-rate one, does not pay off as much as it should in rank and appreciation, there are returns that are personal and satisfying. Often, they are informal and unexpected. The remarks between trainees that you overhear in the hall during the coffee break: "She really knows her stuff," or "Hey, this guy is great." The novice trainer who seeks you out, rather than someone else, for help with a sticky design problem. Learning that the innovative exercise you developed has been surreptitiously borrowed and used by others. The glow you feel when a colleague you have tried to emulate drops by "to try something out on you." Of course, when some training journal wants to interview you, then you know you have arrived.

These sweet tastes of success are intoxicating, even habit forming, but not as sustaining, I submit, as the gut-deep sense of refreshment that comes when you have met your own standards. You do a piece of training; it is good, and you *know* it is good, even before it receives the confirmation of others. That kind of performance doesn't depend on some evaluation form. Naturally, that inner taskmaster that rewards you also punishes you when you fall beneath your own expectations, or waste your potential.

To hold that being proud of what you do counts more than money or recognition is corny, I'll admit. Nevertheless, pride in performance, the sense of craftsmanship, putting on a class act—whatever worn phrase is used—is in truth the most reliable motivation for success.

THE CONSUMMATE TRAINER DEFINED

The enigma for trainers is not that they don't *want* to strive for superiority, but that the definition of excellence is so murky. Training has trouble enough trying to identify competency, let alone excellence.

You might already be the consummate trainer, or close to being one, if you just knew what one is. I shall attempt such desiderata, in the spirit of the redoubtable Robert F. Mager, in his dictum: "If you can't tell one when you see one, you may end up without a leg to stand on."(Goal Analysis, Fearon Publishers, Belmont, California, 1972)

How can you tell "the consummate trainer" from all the others? Let's try defining one. The dictionary defines "consummate" as "complete in every detail, extremely skilled and accomplished, of the highest excellence."

We can't use the dictionary for the definition of "trainer," because Webster wasn't privy to the modern distinction between training and education. Without venturing into the question of whether training is education or the ever-changing definition of terms, I wish to use the narrowest definition of "training" and "trainer" for sharper focus. For this book's purposes, "training" is the planned provision of intentional, short-term learning activities, using a broad range of methodology and including participation by learners, to enable them to acquire specific skills, knowledge, or attitudes for direct and immediate use. A "trainer" is one who engages in the design, development, and delivery of training. To focus even further, by "training" I do not mean human resources development, or organizational development, or the management of training, or consulting. I mean strictly training, *doing* training.

Within these limits then, the consummate trainer is one who is extremely skilled and accomplished and whose performance is of the highest excellence in every detail of the design, development, and delivery of training.

Rather neat academic definition. Only trouble is, it doesn't help much to know one when you see one. More is needed.

Before going further in describing this thoroughbred of training, let me say that my description is not ultimately important. *Yours* is the one that matters. Identifying the elements of quality is an exercise in subjectivity. If a certain trainer was touted to you as "the best," you'd probably want to see that trainer in action to judge for yourself. Your own inner criteria are even more influential when describing quality as a goal to be achieved.

To strive for a goal, you have to accept it as your own. So the only standard of performance you will really answer to is your own. My purpose in putting up my description of the consummate trainer is to give you raw material with which to arrive at your own. Think of what you read here as starter material—options, points to consider, stimulations, even irritations—on the entire repertoire of the trainer. I expect you to sift and sort, to dismiss or accept, to make up your own mind. You'd do this anyhow without any prompting from me, but I wish to declare that as my intention.

One more caveat: To set high goals is fine, but to set unreachable goals is silly. I like to think of trainers as perfectible, but not perfect. I have always been miffed by those listings of trainer traits that read like something out of the Boy Scout manual—trustworthy, loyal, brave, clean, and reverent. Or those job specifications used in recruiting that lay down such divine qualifications that they only need to add: "able to walk on water." Even the best of trainers are human, fallible, limited. In fact, some imperfections may enhance a trainer's capability. A fallible trainer can more readily identify with fallible trainees, for instance. My description of the consummate trainer does not anticipate that any human being can fulfill all of these requirements at all times, but the best trainers fit this description most of the time.

CHARACTERISTICS OF THE CONSUMMATE TRAINER

The consummate trainer:

Has experience in virtually all tasks and techniques of the entire range of training methodology and can carry out these activities at an accept-

able level of proficiency, but prefers and performs some of them exceptionally well.

You name it—needs assessment, objectives, curriculum design, topic research, handbooks, conference management, lectures, group work, case study, simulations, slide shows, flip charts, training films, programmed instruction, video tape, computer assisted instruction, teleconference, evaluation—he has done it. She has done more of some things than others, but she has tried her hand at almost everything. He can do an acceptable job on any assignment, but finds some tasks arduous, some simply boring. She *likes* facilitating and her groups always move better than others. He's a marvel at simulations.

Orchestrates the parts of training with an acute awareness of the impact of the whole.

She visualizes training from the viewpoint of the receiver of it, plans and designs from that perspective, so that the separate pieces link and flow and build to a desired end. She is aware that all that happens, whether it is her part or that done by others or whether it is major or minor, contributes to the learning experience.

Is flexible and versatile and open to change, from one training session to another and from one subject to the next.

He does not repeat himself with Johnny-One-Note frequency, always coming back to the same design, the same method, no matter what the subject is or who the trainees are. He responds to a new training problem with the solution which fits that problem. He can present the same training piece again and again, but it is always fresh, because he adapts it to the needs of each new audience.

He does not change for the sake of changing, but because some new factor indicates the need for change.

Takes risks and can submerge ego for the good of the group and the training.

She knows that to be good you may have to be bad first. She is strong enough to court failure and doesn't panic in the early stages when things are messy and unclear. She will suffer embarrassment to break through strangeness. She can put aside her own pride to see pride increase in the learner.

Can generate excitement in training, through a sense of drama.

The consummate trainer is sensitive to the excitement of new knowledge and skill acquired by the learner. He searches the content for that which stimulates and employs methods that generate suspense, the counterpoint of one force against another, and the wonder that comes in discovery.

He tries to avoid the dull, linear unfolding of subject matter, undue abstraction, and impersonality. He does not mistake complexity for profundity. He draws the trainee personally into the subject and gives life to learning.

Has a sense of humor, which is applied to self as well as to others.

She doesn't take herself too seriously, can recoup from a blunder by making fun of herself. Her humor is not scheduled and limited to jokes and stories, but is spontaneous and infuses a training session with good spirit.

She believes that learning can be fun.

Does own homework and keeps on learning.

Not only does he keep current with the literature of the field, but he searches out opportunities to observe new practices and to learn from trainees and colleagues out of a thirsty curiosity.

He prepares thoroughly for training, but does not let his preparation destroy his spontaneity.

Exhibits patience, with learners and with self.

The consummate trainer allows participants to participate. She does not regard a question as an interruption and permits trainees to have their share of air time. She does not invent excuses to keep the floor, can shut up, get out of the way, and let the learners learn.

She can accept as human and legitimate her own frustrations and irritations, can feel anger and annoyance toward trainees without guilt and without losing her cool. She doesn't have to like everybody. She can tolerate her bad sessions and balance them with good ones.

She is not afraid to enjoy her success when it comes.

Has enough independence and toughness of mind not to be overcome by fads and untested theories.

He is not caught up by every new trend that swirls through the literature of training, retains a healthy skepticism and can await the test of time. He is not taken in by cant or pseudoscientific jargon and cuts through sophistry to seek what is applicable and effective.

The consummate trainer has faith in his own empirical judgment and uses it as his guide. He has guts enough to challenge fads, even when his stand is not supported by others.

He also retains skepticism of his own ideas, is aware of his own limitations, and is not afraid to admit his ignorance. He does not fake when he is not sure.

Respects wisdom, as not knowledge alone or experience alone, but each informing the other.

She does not perceive all that the subject expert says as gospel, nor does she believe that the practitioner of long experience is free from error, but probes for the ground between that holds wisdom.

She reaches beyond the simple grasp of knowledge or skill and points trainees toward the place where learning enriches their lives and work.

This depiction of the consummate trainer is not a complete portrait. These characteristics are perceptions of how the extraordinary trainer differs from the ordinary. Alas, they are still only generalizations and abstractions, not specific or vivid enough for us to recognize the consummate trainer if we see one.

This is only the beginning. All that comes afterward is intended to give more color and definition to the portrait, so that when it is finished, you can see whether or not you recognize yourself.

The Best in the Business

To fill out the portrait of the consummate trainer a little further, I thought it might help to get an idea of what people in the business regard as excellence in a trainer. So I asked some of them.

I picked the names of twenty persons from the Membership Directory of the American Society for Training and Development (ASTD) whose titles sounded like they were training administrators or had seen a lot of trainers in action. Although I didn't attempt to pick a scientific sample, the twenty persons are with private firms and public organizations and institutions in twelve large, small, and medium sized cities in seven states.

I wrote each a letter, explaining what I was doing and asking the question: Who is the best trainer you have known? I defined what I meant by "best trainer." Then I telephoned them (placing the usual five or six calls before finally reaching one), and asked for their answers. I was primarily interested in what they said when I asked, why did you pick that person? I tried to keep my end of the conversation open-ended so the responses would be spontaneous, but I pressed for specifics on the "best trainer's" background, methods, use of materials, and anything unique.

NOT ALWAYS AS EXPECTED

My respondents said a lot of things about their choices that could be expected, but there were some surprises. Despite the general down-playing of platform skills in training rhetoric, these people were quick with glowing terms to describe their choices as first class speakers—"dramatic," "energetic," "anecdotal," "enthusiastic," "positive," and "interesting." A few caught themselves putting so much stress on lecturing and added some qualifier; "Actually, he uses very little lecture;" or "She uses all kinds of other methods, too." Too late; it came through loud and clear that a "best trainer" is often a spellbinding speechifier.

It was evident, at least from this small sampling, that the route to the top was not necessarily through formal education in training. Some of the "best trainers" had doctorates, but frequently in an indirectly related and sometimes entirely different field of study. Many had post graduate degrees, some of them master's in human resources development, but a surprising number had no more than short-course or workshop preparation in training. Three of them had no college at all.

Nor does it appear that an outgoing, people-pleasing personality is essential for success in training. Some of the best were acknowledged to be "not very likable," "tough to the point of being unfriendly," and "so full of conviction, he's almost deadly." Respect is not limited to the lovable.

RAPPORT RATES HIGHEST

I was not interested in a statistical survey and descriptors of these trainers that someone thought of as best ranged all over the map, so generalizations are hazardous. What I had hoped would emerge were some common factors that could be attributed to most superior trainers. And maybe a clearer picture of this creature I have called the consummate trainer. I got the former, but not the latter.

Rising above all else as the characteristic mentioned most often was what could be described as respect for or rapport with participants. Again and again, the best trainers were described as people who were keenly in touch with learners, engaged to the point of enjoyment. "In sync with trainees," "able to connect," "an active listener," "creates a relaxed atmosphere," "interactive," "rewarding and interested" are terms that were used. This talent includes the ability and sensitivity to adjust and adapt to the needs and concerns of the participant group. "He is able to find what is on the group's mind and adjust his content to it." "She is a sponge with people the way she reads the environment." It was obvious, too, that this attitude toward learners is genuine, not put on.

Another pervasive conclusion that came across is that each of these trainers selected as best possesses a forceful personality. I hesitate to call it charisma, because that term is so overblown, but each one seems to have *something*, a presence, a dynamism, a little magic.

Different trainers may use different methods on different subjects with different trainee groups, but the same puissant imprint of the trainer is left. It is not style exactly, but it gives style its essence. It is not overpowering dominance, because it is sometimes exerted in very indirect ways. It is what my informants struggled to convey about the persons they had selected; that they talked around and about and couldn't quite nail down, but communicated in their infectious appreciation.

I have noticed this almost indefinable quality in trainers. Some can take a dull piece of content and make it sizzle. Some can send people out of their sessions *having learned* while other trainers doing the same sessions the same way merely send them out. To say that whatever this quality is, some have it and others haven't may be simplistic; but there is no doubt that certain superlative trainers make a difference, which is most readily detected by the people they train.

Perhaps this is a natural quality that comes out of the kind of persons these "best trainers" are. My respondents invariably described them as "intelligent," "knowledgeable," "versatile," and "creative." Some were lauded for their range: "He can handle all levels, all subjects, from technical to management;" or, "She's at home from sales to the shop floor." One was termed "a Renaissance man," and another "a man for all seasons." Willingness to change, a sense of humor, continuing growth, and sincerity were also mentioned.

As far as methods used by these leading trainers, nothing unusual. They were said to employ a variety of techniques—exercises, games, role plays, visuals, handouts, action plans—but I heard no reports of inventive methodology or new technology. On the contrary, I got the impression that these "best trainers" may not excel in design. Many used standard-brand training packages, or materials designed by others. One comment, intended to be favorable, was that "he tailors materials from off the shelf to the company."

LEADING BY COMMUNICATING

Communications skill ranks high in the repertoire of a top trainer. Besides prowess as a lecturer, there were numerous references to "clarity" and "simplicity" and the ability "to make things understandable." Leading a group was a part of communications; not facilitation precisely, more the guidance of a stand-up trainer who uses group work effectively for internalization. "He pushes the group, stretches them," said one person. "She instills confidence by a synergistic process." "He is not threatened by feedback" and "he loves interaction." "She insists that the group take the training seriously; that they do their homework . . . and she follows up religiously."

These trainers seemed to have that remarkable capacity to lead a group without dampening its spontaneity. One was a military trainer who started his classes with a discussion on the trainees' day-to-day work, then applied what they said to the content of the course. He also "knew his stuff solid," was "highly organized" and had a photographic memory. He had been a truck driver before he was tapped to attend the Air Force trainers school because of his "natural abilities." His direction of the trainees was like that of another of whom it was said: "He knows where he wants to go, and he gets you there, and you hardly know it."

INDEPENDENCE AND INDIVIDUALITY

As you might expect, there were some unusual individuals among the "best trainers." One steadfastly refused promotion to vice-president of his company. "He has made peace with himself," his boss said, "and he wants to stay in training." In the eighteen years this man had been with this big firm, he had tried his hand at virtually every training chore, was considered one of the company's most creative people, the kind that the manager called in for help when faced with a tough problem.

There was one outstanding trainer who would have nothing whatever to do with professional associations.

One self-assured woman named herself as the best trainer she knew—and made a convincing case for her choice.

The only sour note in my minisurvey came from a training manager of a sizable bank who told me he couldn't select any of the several trainers who worked for him as the best because he had never been in any of their sessions to observe their work!

QUALITY IS STILL QUALITY

Asking some leaders in the business to describe the superior trainer may be too limited an enterprise to gain much guidance on what excellence is or what it takes to achieve it. The clutter of attributes was too scattered, and some had a predictable ring. What my respondents didn't talk about may have been significant. Nothing was said about trainers hot for high technology; none had computers in the classroom; no far-out fads or avant-garde theories were being espoused. And the people I contacted are with organizations that have resources and reputations for progress in training.

The question I posed called for personal judgments and did not go directly to the matter of learning, to the effectiveness of those "best trainers." Even so, I am tempted to believe that the skills and knowledge that the field of training still holds in highest regard are not all that different from what they have been for some years, despite the great growth and change in the field of training.

One thing seems plain: the *trainer* is still the most important enabler of learning, and will not soon be replaced.

The Basic Qualifications

If somebody asked you if you have the qualifications to be a trainer, you'd probably say yes—with appropriate modesty, of course. After all, you are one, or have been one, or are going to become one—or you wouldn't be reading this book.

But if you went out on the street and stopped ten people and asked them that same question, you'd be surprised how many of them would also say yes. I know; out of curiosity, I did it.

Their answers didn't come easily. I had a lot of explaining to do, that I wasn't selling anything or passing out religious tracts or that I wasn't talking about them becoming a school teacher. With some, I cut the question down to: Do you think you'd be qualified to train somebody to do something?

After a good deal of giggling and humming and hawing, six out of ten of them allowed that, yes, they thought they could do that. One lady was quite positive. "Sure," she said, "I trained my dog to speak."

So there you have it, the supreme test. If you can train your dog to speak, you are qualified to train. And if you can get that dog to sit up, shake hands, roll over and play dead, you are the consummate trainer.

I jest, of course, but this silly survey makes a point. Many people believe that training is a pretty easy thing to do, that it doesn't take a lot of smarts or preparation to train. The anybody-can-train syndrome.

The syndrome afflicts more than people on the street. Every day somewhere in the training universe, some bright, ambitious, hard working employee gets tapped on the shoulder and told to go see the boss about a new assignment to do some training. The employee knows the job well, or is very skilled in the task, so the assumption is made that he can train others to do it. With maybe a little bit of preparation.

Or, there's this expert on some subject who has a dazzling academic pedigree and a list of publications a mile long. Let's get her to train our people, some manager suggests, with nary a thought about whether the expert has a smidgen of training skill.

The anybody-can-train syndrome makes it hard to set up any basic qualifications for trainers, or standards for competence or excellence. It scoffs at the notion that trainers might need to be trained and falls back on the good old sink-or-swim philosophy.

The fact is, nonetheless, that not anybody can train, at least not effectively. Some can and some can't; some have the qualifications and some don't.

QUALIFICATIONS: A STICKY WICKET

The rub is to define the basic qualifications a person should possess to have a reasonable chance to be an effective trainer. From the basic qualifications can come measurements of competence and excellence. Without some base line, trainers who are judged to be effective or superior are always open to the questions: compared to what? who says so?

The advancement of training demands the development of some set of qualifications for trainers that can be commonly accepted, but that is a very sticky wicket, indeed.

In the not-too-distant past, qualifications lists were so unworldly in their requirements that few mortals need apply; thrown together by organizations seeking grants or contracts for training to impress the funding agency with the high calibre of trainers they would recruit, or conjured up by academics high on theory.

Serious efforts to describe what a trainer ought to be and do have been hampered by a perplexing confusion in terminology. Some studies draw up long lists of the tasks that trainers perform, call the tasks "competencies," and make the quantum leap in assumption that the ability to perform some or several or all or many of the assorted tasks is equal to qualification as a trainer. The term "standard," traditionally used to describe minimal requirements of a job at entry or mastery level, gets used in a vague, qualitative sense, as in "setting high standards." In its more precise usage, the term "qualification" refers to capacity possessed by a person, but the term sometimes attaches to the tasks of the job.

Understandably, the focus is on the job, on training, with less attention to the person, the trainer. For instance, the "results" of training—that is, what happens with trainees—are often used as evidence of trainer competence. Such dependence upon the presumed connection between means and ends may be questionable. Results are usually determined by some form of learning evaluation, which may or may not be reliable. Results are not always attributable to the performance of the trainer. People have been known to learn in spite of the trainer, just as some fail to learn no matter how competent the trainer's performance may be.

The obligation to come up with measured results in training appears to reflect management's insistence upon cost effectiveness, that unchallenged American depiction of value. Yet much learning is not quantifiable, and much training goes unmeasured, or is judged by those unreliable happiness quotients known as participant evaluations.

As if all this were not complication enough, consider these further complexities:

- Training is done in a staggering diversity of settings, under widely varying conditions, with a broad spectrum of trainees.

- The content to be covered by training ranges from personal growth to computer literacy, from management to driving a bus.

- The performance of the trainer, himself, is seldom measured. And what the trainer does not do is sometimes as important as what she does do.

- Examining tasks puts such emphasis on the parts that the whole may get lost. How the parts are orchestrated for united impact is an important measure of training effectiveness.

- Even with the best set of trainer qualifications available, measurement is primarily by self-assessment, a grading that is always open to the vagaries of introspection.

Considering all these difficulties, the American Society for Training and Development, the Ontario Society for Training and Development, and other agencies and associations that have labored to forge a universally applicable set of trainer competencies deserve profound appreciation—and sympathy. In 1983, after two years of work by a thousand people, ASTD brought out its landmark study, *Models for Excellence*. It is a remarkable achievement, if only for the sheer fortitude required to take on the entire, diverse training and development field and extract the essential roles, competencies, and outcomes, and reduce them to simply defined and sensible form. Moreover, the study sought to define not only competence, but excellence, by providing examples of performance expected at the basic, intermediate, and advanced levels. If that were not enough, ASTD has striven to keep the document current by identifying competencies of increasing importance over the ensuing five years.

The ASTD competencies will be useful in many ways, not the least of which will be to identify the distinctive body of knowledge prerequisite to professional status for training.

My appreciation of ASTD's accomplishment is based on a meager attempt of my own to draw up a list of trainer qualifications. This was before any such list worthy of a second look was in existence, but I was not trying to make any contribution to the field; I was merely trying to solve a problem.

THE CREDIBILITY TRAP

I was working for a consulting firm in Washington, D.C., under contract with the U.S. Department of Justice to transfer new and improved practices that evolved from criminal justice research to officials in that field in workshops held around the country. We used training teams made up of experts in the content specialty we were working on mixed with one or two training specialists. The Department was big on using nationally recognized experts—researchers from the universities and practitioners from the field, judges, police chiefs, wardens, public officials, and so on. The justification was that these Big Names would gain us credibility for the technology we were trying to transfer.

We soon got caught in a credibility trap.

The credibility trap is the fallacious assumption that a person who *knows* the subject can train in it, or that one who *does* it can transfer that experience in training.

One of our experts was far and away the most eminent in his subject, but he got painfully negative evaluations from workshop participants because they just couldn't make out what he was talking about. One police executive who was acknowledged as an innovative leader bored his listeners to death with his parochial war stories. When it came to small-group work, some of the experts couldn't resist sneaking in some more lecturing.

As the problem persisted, I began to examine that unexamined matter of credibility. I came to some conclusions:

One person's credibility is another's triviality.

Who does the recognizing of the "nationally recognized" expert? Some training groups are blatantly contemptuous of experts. For some, credibility is front-line service by someone who has "paid his dues." Experts, themselves, will sometimes not-so-politely cut down other experts.

Credibility is sustained by performance, not reputation.

Maintaining credibility in a training session is a little like a speaker trying to live up to an effusive introduction. The higher the tout, the bigger the bomb if the performance doesn't live up to the reputation.

Specialists can be overspecialized.

Some substance specialists are expert on only a tiny corner of the content. They can get so overfocused on their narrow perspective that they are unable to synthesize other viewpoints, and thus become irrelevant.

Practitioners can be provincial.

Choosing people with "practical" experience to train is a calculated risk. Many can't universalize their experience for application beyond their own practice. They can antagonize others, who wonder why they don't get equal air time to tell their experiences.

It takes a thief may catch a quarrel.

The conventional wisdom that an audience will listen best and believe most if the speaker is one of their own kind—the it-takes-a-thief-to catch-a-thief rationale—is generally true. But not always. Trainees are just as likely—more likely if things get hot—to shoot down one of their peer group than someone outside. It's the hazard of familiarity breeds contempt.

Enough sour experiences brought the feds around to listen to my harping about the need for training skill in our content specialists. They were aware of the need but not sure what to do about it. Then I realized that they didn't know what I meant by training skill, because I hadn't defined it very well. They were willing to look for specialists with training skill, but what should they look for?

QUALIFICATION FACTORS

I got busy. First, I searched the literature for listings of trainer qualifications and came up almost empty. The few I found were those trainer-should-be-able-to-do-anything-and-everything kind, but they were raw material. By selecting and refining items from the lists, and adding numerous ones of my own, I came up with a starter set of qualifications. These I circulated to members of our training staff, asking them to rank order the items, by forced judgment, and add any factors they thought had been overlooked.

A remarkable consensus resulted in the ranking of factors. I reworked the list and circulated it again, to confirm the findings. Later, I circulated the list among the feds, to see if their perceptions of the qualifications of a trainer were different from those of trainers. They weren't, except for a greater emphasis on platform skills and research.

After that, we used this checklist as guidance in the selection of experts and practitioners for our training teams. There was no hard application of these qualification factors in making decisions, but the project officers began to look for training skills, and they had a better idea of what to look for. The checklist may have served most in consciousness raising. We also began giving our specialists short train-the-trainer sessions before sending them out on the road.

The checklist was published in a couple of newsletters and I developed some instruments to use it for self-assessments done in training-skills workshops.

If you are willing to accept the limited purpose and narrow use of this checklist, you may find it useful in sharpening your own awareness of the basic qualifications of a trainer. And if you go in for self-assessments, you can practice on this list until you get a better one.

TRAINER QUALIFICATIONS

A Checklist

Empirical Factors

1. Perspective of the field for which training is being conducted, as evidenced by the capacity to take a universal rather than provincial view; to see beyond the narrow scope of own experience.
2. Variety of experience, such as serving in different positions in an organization or in different communities or agencies.
3. Effectiveness of experience, such as programs developed, procedures or innovations implemented, advancement.
4. Direct experience in the field, such as being a staff member or executive in an organization from which trainees will come.
5. Awareness of mission, objectives, nomenclature, problems, interactions, and internal operations of organizations and agencies from which trainees will come.

Theoretical factors

6. Synthesis of theoretical and empirical; combining experience and learning into usable application in the field; concepts adopted for implementation.
7. Previous training or teaching conducted in the subject, either short-term, as in seminars or workshops, or long-term, as in university courses.
8. Innovative contributions to the field in the form of new concepts, special designs, systems applications, legislation, model practices.
9. Writings in the field, including books, articles, contributions to journals, symposia, reports, or specialty publications.
10. Research conducted, such as experimental or demonstration studies, design of programs, feasibility studies, position or concept papers, literature reviews or evaluations.

Personal Factors

11. Professional maturity; openness to diverse individuals and groups; not excessively defensive to critical evaluations; willing to take risks to facilitate group effectiveness; sense of humor.
12. Concern for quality, as shown in thoroughness of effort, willingness to revise and improve, facility to accommodate to change, desire for best possible product.
13. Relevancy; mindful of practical application of content in the setting of the trainees; can translate theory into practice.
14. Ability to conceptualize; not bound by own experience, open to enlarge training effectiveness by fitting particular data into larger concepts; capacity for abstract thought.
15. Dependability; can be expected to meet deadlines; prompt and conscientious about appearance at meetings and training sessions; completes assignments.

Design Factors

16. Problem solving capacity, including the ability to define and describe problems so that they can be addressed and separate the generic from the superficial; separates training needs from nice-to-know concepts.
17. Knowledge of learning theory, particularly how adults learn.
18. Familiarity, if not experience, with a wide range of training methods;

capacity to select the method most effective for content involved and to predict effectiveness.

19. Sense of training strategy, such as capacity to foresee training problems and address them in design; awareness of process of change and evolution in learning; sensitivity to pace, flow, and time in design, and linkage of one curriculum unit to another.

20. Research capability; knowledge of sources for independent research, gathering data through literature search, interview, and observation; judgment in determining most salient information.

Development Factors

21. Awareness of needs of training population as primary focus in materials development; produces materials that are on target and within capacity of trainees and time limits of training.

22. Capacity for industry; willing to work independently to develop training units as assigned; produces assignments completely and on time.

23. Sensitivity to considerations such as participant mix, level and interest of groups, influence of climate and room arrangements; clear instructions for tasks, roles of other team members, pretesting and pretiming of tasks and exercises.

24. Willingness to review work as required for improvement, to use alternative methods; to experiment.

25. Capacity for development of multimedia materials, including audio visual and visual aids, writing of cases, exercises, or role plays, rough design for flip charts, posters and slides, gathering of handout material.

Delivery Factors

26. Respect for participants in training; acceptance of diverse ethnic, racial, sexual, and occupational groups and individuals; appreciation of different viewpoints and experiences; mindful of limitations of trainer's role and viewpoint; treatment of participants as adults.

27. Facilitation skill; ability to lead discussions, to allow group to function without undue trainer domination, to reenforce positive contributions by trainees and to deal diplomatically with disrupters; skill in advancing groups and individuals by questioning; ability to keep group on subject or task; sensitive to anxieties of participants.

28. Communications skill; able to make presentations using language free of jargon or academese; capacity to adjust presentation to level

and interest of group; use of humor and illustration; discipline to avoid long and repetitious presentations.

29. Recognition that effective training delivery is engrossing and enjoyable; conducts training to entertain as well as inform; believes that training need not be dull to be effective.

30. Collegiality; willingness to serve as member of a team by assisting others in mundane, housekeeping chores, such as changing room arrangements, operating projector, greeting participants, distributing materials; serves as support to other trainers.

TRAINER QUALIFICATIONS

Factor Weighting Scale

Read each factor in the first category of Trainer Qualifications (Empirical). Then pose the following question on each factor and select your answer from the scale below. Enter the score on the scale for your answer in the space beside the number of each factor. Repeat the same process for each category.

How important is possession of this factor by the trainer to the learning of people being trained?

4 Very Important
2 Important
1 Not Very Important
0 Not Important

Empirical	*Personal*	*Development*
1. _____	11. _____	21. _____
2. _____	12. _____	22. _____
3. _____	13. _____	23. _____
4. _____	14. _____	24. _____
5. _____	15. _____	25. _____

Theoretical	*Design*	*Delivery*
6. _____	16. _____	26. _____
7. _____	17. _____	27. _____
8. _____	18. _____	28. _____
9. _____	19. _____	29. _____
10. _____	20. _____	30. _____

TRAINER QUALIFICATIONS

Self Assessment Scale

Read each factor of the first category of Trainer Qualifications and answer the following question for each factor. Enter the score which corresponds to your answer in the space beside the number of each factor. Repeat for each category.

To what degree do I possess the qualification described in this factor?

5   High Degree
3   Medium Degree
1   Low Degree
0   Not At All

Empirical	*Personal*	*Development*
1. _____	11. _____	21. _____
2. _____	12. _____	22. _____
3. _____	13. _____	23. _____
4. _____	14. _____	24. _____
5. _____	15. _____	25. _____

Theoretical	*Design*	*Delivery*
6. _____	16. _____	26. _____
7. _____	17. _____	27. _____
8. _____	18. _____	28. _____
9. _____	19. _____	29. _____
10. _____	20. _____	30. _____

TRAINER QUALIFICATIONS

Factor and Qualification Rating

To calculate your Factor and Trainer Qualification Rating, enter the factor weight for each item under FW, then enter your self assessment score for each item under SA. Multiply the score for FW by the score for SA to derive your factor rating for each item and enter in the FR space.

Complete this process for all items in each category. Then add up the total of all FR scores for each category to derive your category rating (designated as ER, TR, PR, DsR, DvR, or DIR). Finally, enter all your category totals in the appropriate space at the bottom of this page and add up all category scores to arrive at your Trainer Qualification Rating.

Empirical			*Personal*			*Development*		
FW	SA	FR	FW	SA	FR	FW	SA	FR

1. ___ × ___ = ___   11. ___ × ___ = ___   21. ___ × ___ = ___
2. ___ × ___ = ___   12. ___ × ___ = ___   22. ___ × ___ = ___
3. ___ × ___ = ___   13. ___ × ___ = ___   23. ___ × ___ = ___
4. ___ × ___ = ___   14. ___ × ___ = ___   24. ___ × ___ = ___
5. ___ × ___ = ___   15. ___ × ___ = ___   25. ___ × ___ = ___

ER Total ___   PR Total ___   DvR Total ___

Theoretical			*Design*			*Delivery*		

6. ___ × ___ = ___   16. ___ × ___ = ___   26. ___ × ___ = ___
7. ___ × ___ = ___   17. ___ × ___ = ___   27. ___ × ___ = ___
8. ___ × ___ = ___   18. ___ × ___ = ___   28. ___ × ___ = ___
9. ___ × ___ = ___   19. ___ × ___ = ___   29. ___ × ___ = ___
10. ___ × ___ = ___   20. ___ × ___ = ___   30. ___ × ___ = ___

TR Total ___   DsR Total ___   DIR Total ___

Category Totals
ER ___
TR ___
PR ___
DsR ___
DvR ___
DIR ___

Trainer Qualification Rating
TQR _____

The Trainer as
Team Player

Staging a training conference with a team is not far from show business. If you've ever played the airport motel circuit with a training troupe, you know what I mean.

Team members are the cast and the team leader is director. There are many workers behind the scenes—secretaries, the people in accounting, artists, librarians, the mailroom gang. Much planning goes into mounting the production—research, budgeting, requisition writing, assignments, details, details, meetings, meetings, meetings.

You don't start with a script, but you end up with one. Team members design the production, each improvising, contributing, and contending—like the British adaptation of Nicholas Nickleby. There are sets to be made—room arrangements, lighting, charts, lobby signs. Playbills in the form of manuals and handouts. Props like easels, projectors, monitors, chalkboards. Logistics such as location selection, notices to the audience, transportation, accommodations. Parts are learned, walked through, revised, rehearsed. Temperaments are tolerated, laggards chastised, and egos soothed.

Each curriculum piece is a scene; several become an act. They must fit together, flow, hopefully build and generate suspense, to a satisfying denouement. Maybe you try it out in a pilot before a test audience.

Comes the day you open and butterflies are frequent. The shipment of handbooks doesn't arrive and panic hovers until it does. The director looks grim. The audience is wary, strange, and cold. Introductions are ponderous and the humor during housekeeping announcements is limp. Then, your star goes on and does her state-of-the-art soliloquy. The participants stir, laugh in the right places, get over that I-dare-you-to-move-me look. The production spurts, coughs, catches, and starts to roll. The audience warms up, participates.

By the last day, when certificates are awarded, everybody knows and loves each other. Even stale jokes are hilarious. Messy group work, hard chairs, up-staging speeches are forgotten. The trainees leave happy; relieved if not fulfilled.

When the evaluations are collected, they are seized with the frenzy of actors reading opening-night reviews. Each team member scans them for ratings and comments on his role. If they are good, shouts and smiles; if not, silence. You strike the set and all go out for a drink.

AGONY AND ECSTASY

Training like that can be exhilarating. It can lift you so high it takes you days to come down. Solo performances are flat by comparison. Working with a team can also be as frustrating, abrasive, and exhausting as training can get.

For learners, training done by a team has decided benefits. Several trainers provide a broad range of knowledge and skill, diversity of views, and variety of personalities. The change of pace from one trainer to another prevents overexposure to anyone and reduces boredom and fatigue. Using several trainers reduces the trainer-to-trainee ratio, improving group work and allowing some tutoring of individuals. I'd say the ideal ratio is one trainer to eight trainees; anything over one to fifteen gets out of hand.

Not every trainer has what it takes to train with a team. Some aren't team players; they can't make the sacrifices for the good of the group. And there's no place for prima donnas on a training team.

One organization I was with brought in agency directors to be trainers. They had an awful time fitting into a team because they were accustomed to being the bosses over others. Teachers sometimes have the same trouble; they are so used to going unchallenged by passive students in the fiefdom of the classroom that they are uncomfortable being one among equals.

Given time for the rough edges to wear smooth, most people who have not previously experienced the intense interaction of a team can adjust. But a few never make it.

In a way, all training is teamwork. Even if the trainer goes into the training room alone, countless others have contributed to her delivery. Content or methodology may be bought or borrowed from others. Data for design may be collected by others. All those support staff people we take for granted are indirect members of the team. Even managers. Their participation may not be so noticeable but it shouldn't be ignored. It has always miffed me that secretaries, who labor long and vitally for the cause, are so seldom permitted to witness the end-product of their labors—to simply sit in on a training session. Managers can fulfill their oversight responsibilities far more effectively by occasional visits to the training room. In one training organization I knew about, the managers intentionally stayed away from training sessions, rationalizing that their presence would be an interference. But performance got sloppy and uneven, so they changed their policy and made monitoring, sometimes ceremonial visits when training was going on, coordinated with the team leader. They were surprised to find that those visits were welcomed; the trainers realized that management cared, and performance began to shape up.

HOW A TEAM WORKS BEST

I strongly believe that a team works best when its members take responsibility for the full cycle of design, development, and delivery. I have never understood how some large companies with extensive training operations almost completely divorce curriculum development from delivery. Recently, I had a conversation with the training manager of such a firm and he admitted that the separation was a mistake. It's a waste of resources, for starters, because the trainers who deliver are going to tear down the curriculum they've been handed and reshape it into something of their own. When the one who designs the curriculum doesn't deliver any of it—doesn't face the music—he can't see and *feel* what is wrong with it. Critiques and evaluation reports can't convey the corrections needed. If it bombs, it ought to blow up in his face.

Sometimes, there are legitimate reasons for a division of labor. If curriculum and materials designed by others must be used, then the delivering trainers are justified in as much redesign as necessary to make it their own and relevant to their trainees.

I have served as design consultant to teams and found it good practice to participate in at least two deliveries, sometimes doing a piece or two with the trainer who was going to inherit delivery. That way, there's no argument over midcourse corrections; you both know what's wrong.

The best assurance of coordination of design and delivery is to have a strong design person on the team. A team should be a mix of strengths and specialties—content specialists and facilitators, someone sharp on methodology, a top-notch presenter. It helps to have a solid substance person, the quiet, thoughtful kind with the view of the Big Picture, and someone who has that natural knack of really getting to know the trainees. Team trainers will learn from each other, pick up strengths; the content guy will get to be a better facilitator by watching the gal who is so good at it, for example.

The ideal team make-up is a mix of age, race, and sex. I've visualized it as resembling the cast of that old Mod Squad television show—a young woman, a middle-aged male (for Father Figure duty), and a younger black male. That just about covers all constituencies.

TEAM SIZE

Several variables determine the size of a team. The number of trainees is usually the primary influence, especially if group work is involved. Cost is a determinant, and can be misapplied. It's a false economy to assume that a really good trainer can handle a big crowd of trainees. The fall-off comes in an almost total reliance on lecture and the lack of learning as a consequence.

Content has an influence on how many trainers are needed. If it's highly technical, or complex, then more specialists may be needed. How the content breaks out, how the training load is spread, frequently writes the prescription for team size. Trainers usually have preferences in content, and generally do better with what they prefer. But there is always some dirty work that nobody wants; each must do her share.

The length of time of the training event matters, too. In a protracted session, like two weeks or more of daily sessions, trainers can run out of gas. Time to bring in relief. Once in a great while, there's a problem of too many trainers, giving the participants the feeling that they are outnumbered and dominated. Too frequently, this condition is caused by too many nontraining hangers-on—monitors, observers, evaluators, the only curious who further disrupt the session's dynamic by dropping in and out. There ought to be a rule against that "parachuting" practice; one is to require visitors to stay from start to finish; another version is to make all visitors go through the training as participants.

TEAM STRUCTURE

How a team is managed is vital, a delicate blend of freedom and control. The team leader must be a boss, particularly on administrative matters and during delivery, when numerous instant decisions can't wait for team discussion. On strictly training questions, the team is the final authority, usually by consensus, except that on specific units assigned to each trainer, a kind of academic freedom obtains, limited only by ultimate accountability to the team.

But all that democracy can get out of hand and the temptation then is for the team leader to exercise too much control, provoking resistance. I ran into this as a team leader. The way out was to talk it out. I drew up a long list of tasks and responsibilities, covering every conceivable situation. We went to my place one afternoon, away from the office, and threshed out who would be responsible for what. Control was distributed among the team, the individual trainer, and me. I held out certain functions, such as personnel, as nonnegotiable. When it came down to cases, they were not nearly as covetous of power as even they expected. With our roles and duties thus clearly defined, we functioned smoothly and freely.

We used a deployment plan that assigned a lead trainer to every major curriculum block or time slot, with a back-up trainer for support. Within that block, to some degree during design and development but absolutely during delivery, the lead trainer was boss. She could instruct the rest of us on what she wanted us to do in small groups, alter the content, reallocate time; whatever she said went, in her subject.

QUALITY CONTROL

The assurance of quality in team training must be attended to throughout the development cycle—from needs assessment to delivery. Waiting for the evaluations is too late.

We had a serious problem, in a training organization with several teams, of inadequate and uneven performance; some teams doing fairly well, some very poorly. Our study backed up the problem to square one; the teams were messing up at the start—inadequate needs assessments, faulty goals and objectives, poor content development. Then they floundered through delivery, piling on trouble.

We set up a procedure that called for a team to be checked at four points during the preparation for a seminar. At each check, their work was reviewed by a quality-control group, which made a go or no-go decision about whether the team could go on to the next phase. If their work didn't pass muster, they had to do it over until it did.

The review group consisted of a member of a team not undergoing review, representatives of the evaluation and logistics departments, and the training director and myself. Paperwork produced by the team was distributed to us to read before the review meeting.

The first check was on goals and objectives, after a team had been assigned a seminar topic, and had collected needs data and evaluations of any past seminars on that topic. The second check was at the end of curriculum design, the third at the conclusion of materials development, and the final review was the week before delivery.

The teams hated it, at first. Being held so closely accountable was new, but those of us doing the monitoring were new to the process, too, and we contributed our share to long, stormy meetings that were at times counterproductive. After a round or two of the review process, cantankerousness on both sides subsided. Teams got to appreciate the system; so much that when we proposed some cutting back on it, to save time and sanity, they wouldn't hear of it. They had discovered that when they took to the field with a seminar, it was with a new confidence born of the backing of management, and the fact that they now had us on the responsibility hook with them.

The obvious, overall escalation in quality proved the worth of the system.

THE AGONY OF DESIGN

Let all who have never weathered the season of strife known as design meetings be warned. This is when egos clash, tempers flare, the weak flounder, and the strong mutter to themselves. I don't know why this is, but it is. I have seen trainers pound the wall, pace the room, leave in a huff, and spew out expletives in torrents. This is where decisions are made which touch the deepest and hardest-held convictions. Here the Process and Content adversaries go after each other. Here, the schedule mongers keep asking things like, "Well, what are we going to do on Day II?" The objectives freaks make everybody miserable and the group minded invent outrageous exercises.

But it is worthy warfare—creative conflict. Out of it comes, not just the design for training, but harmony. If the team members hang in there, they'll come out more together than ever, unlikely as that seems. The pay off may not come until they hit the training floor, but then they see that the parts fit better than expected, that the curriculum flows and makes sense and that they know how to help each other.

It is not easy, this agony of design. Personally, I have been tempted to chuck it many times, especially when I found myself with a new team saying, "Not again!" If you've never been through this, it can be a small shock, but if you have the stuff to be a team player, you'll make it.

I offer you a go-get-'em cheer and a few tools from my survivor's kit:

- Hold team design meetings in isolated places, away from interruptions, where you can mess up the room, paper the walls with charts, and your shoutings cannot be heard.
- Make candor the rule, within limits. This is the time for speaking up, not smoldering in resentment.
- Limit attendance to only those who have undeniable reason to be there and who will stay from beginning to end. Avoid outsiders if you can.

- Once you start, keep going as long as you can and don't change the cast of characters. New people stifle your progress.

- If things get too tense, stop and get away from each other for a while, maybe overnight. Let things cool. But then go back at it again because reconciliation can occur when the pressure is off.

- Fatigue can be an ally. You may wear each other out and give in when you are just being stubborn.

- Keep constantly before you the belief that good is going to come from this.

TEAM BUILDING

The through-conflict-to-harmony shakedown of design meetings is a form of team building. More intentional means are needed to forge the kind of unity that makes a team's work natural and re-enforcing. Retreats are invaluable—getting away somewhere for a few days to deal directly with each other. I found it a good idea to take along a third party facilitator who is free of internal involvement (and who takes the team leader out of the authority role).

Teams should have a lot of play time together—socializing, eating, drinking, recreating, with spouses and Significant Other Persons along occasionally. You grow close that way; a team can become almost a family.

Having fun together is not only for the sake of team building. Just enjoying what you do and the people you do it with is reason enough.

During training events, it's a good practice to have team meetings every night, to critique what went on that day, go over what is coming up tomorrow, and take up any special problems. Small tip: let trainers who did sessions during the day begin the critique of their own sessions. They know where they goofed and it is salvaging to the ego to admit it yourself, instead of hearing it from your teammates. By the time the self-critique is over, others who were going to criticize are coming on with it-wasn't-that-bad reassurances.

The together team grows in interdependency, a constructive need of each other that reaches the point where any one trainer's flop is the whole team's loss; if one triumphs, all others soar on her success. That cohesiveness is a track on which quality can ride. If a team decides that it intends to go first class, then any team member's effort that falls off becomes a matter of team concern. A team can be a stern taskmaster and a far more effective disciplinarian for wayward teammates than any single boss. You don't want "to let the team down."

SUPPORTING EACH OTHER

Team training is not the place to "do your own thing." Your thing depends too much on help from others. Trainers help each other in many ways, some noticeable, some not. During development, team members serve as sounding boards for each other, testing ideas, getting advice, and breaking each other loose when bog-down time comes. You don't realize how valuable this help is until you find yourself working entirely alone, with no one to bounce off of, no source of correction, no one to show off a good, exciting piece of work, no stimulating shoptalk.

In sessions, trainers love to help by giving those inaudible, television-type signals to the one up front. You know the kind, pantomined from the back of the room: five fingers held up means five minutes to go; rolling motions of the arm means hurry up; pulling both hands away from each other means stretch it out; and the cut-throat hand across the Adam's apple is the demand to cut it off, *right now*. It's hammy, but it helps.

Even the scut work can be shared. I worked for a team leader who insisted on cleanliness and cooperation as signs of a class act. Before every session, the entire team was on hand to help the lead trainer set up the room, arrange lighting, put up charts. At every break and after every class, we cleaned up the room—emptied ash trays, cleared away coffee cups and pop bottles, threw out waste paper. When it was time to tear down at the end of training, everybody pitched in and it was finished in a flash.

This expectation of sharing housekeeping chores became such second nature to us that if a team member wasn't on hand to help, he felt it necessary to apologize. The norm wasn't lost on participants, either. They saw us helping each other and got into helping each other. And they helped keep the training room from becoming the mess that training rooms can become.

Some trainers are too "professional" or elitist for such mundane dirty work. They don't make good team members.

There's an unwritten code of do's and don't's about trainer interaction. Never take the lead trainer's session away from her by making comments, however apt they might be. Any extra air time is reserved for participants. If you are in another trainer's class, stay in the back of the room and don't move around, except to break up extracurricular conversations and close the door when noise is coming in. Bring the lead trainer's attention to any unrecognized questioner. Go see why the coffee isn't there yet, things like that.

One of the best examples of teamwork is in the almost extrasensory communication between a lead trainer and back-up trainer, or two persons who have co-trained for a long time. They get so they know each other so well they sense when each other needs help. Maybe the stand-up trainer has drawn a mental block or gotten in too deep in a digression. The support trainer creates a diversion, asks a meaningless question or refers to something in the handbook. The momentary interruption gives the lead trainer time to get his bearings and get back on track.

Once in a while, a trainer will have to come down hard on a disruptive participant. It happens, despite the entreaties of group dynamics. When it does, the back-up trainer should move quickly to pick up the trainee that has been cut down. A word of encouragement, some recognition of the point that the offended participant was making, can begin the healing before the hurt festers.

One situation in team training remains an enigma: how to "rescue" a trainer in trouble with a trainee, or a group of trainees. Sooner or later, every trainer encounters the participant who, under cover of a rhetorical question, sets out on a long, haranguing speech. Or maybe several of them fiercely challenge the trainer. Standard practice calls for hearing out the complainers, or indulging the speechmaker. What if patience doesn't work? What if other tricks—walk right up to the speechmaker and hover over him in silence—are to no avail? And the other trainees are getting restless and disgusted?

I got my taste of this once when I was doing a piece on media relations with government. An otherwise pleasant participant got spooked by something I said about some leading newspapers. Suddenly, he was on his feet delivering a ringing indictment of the Eastern press, a political phillippic far beyond the discussion of the moment. He wouldn't quit and took the displeasure of the other participants as the need to convince them further. My attempts to settle him down were useless. He just went on and on.

At this point, one of my teammates who was to do the session following mine came rushing into the room. "You're into my time," he said for all to hear. It wasn't true; I still had 20 minutes to go. I knew he was trying to rescue me. And it worked, because he drew the attention of the audience away from the speechmaker.

But I was piqued, and later on told him so. I had intended to give the orator a little more time, to let the participants' chagrin build to where he felt it and I could be rescuing *him*. Then I would have taken over with some diverting remark like, "I'd like to talk to you some more about that later." And if that didn't work, I'm afraid I would have verbally clobbered him.

Well, what would you have done?

5

Learning Your Craft

The superintendent of an electric utility company which had just hired its first training director was asked by the new man how long it took to train line maintenance custodians—employees who operate those terminal transfer stations along power lines.

"Fourteen years," replied the superintendent.

"Why fourteen years?" asked the training director.

"Because it takes that long for all the emergency situations to occur." The superintendent explained that routine operation of the stations was no problem, but what a custodian had to know was how to deal with untimely crises—a break in the lines, lightning shorting the wires, kids shooting out conductors, "acts of God" like fire or flood or blizzard. The company had determined that all these emergencies would occur at least once in a fourteen-year period.

The training man was aghast. He showed the superintendent how each of the occurrences could be simulated, reconstructed from the experience of the past, and a custodian could be trained in what to do in every emergency—all in about two weeks time!

Here is an absurd example of the abject reliance on that old saw: "Experience is the best teacher." Training that depends entirely on experience is nontraining, yet it still passes for training in many places.

I relate this episode, told to me several years ago by that training director, to acknowledge my recognition of the limitations of learning by experience. This is a sly caveat, because my prejudice is *in favor* of experience as the best teacher, although not the only teacher. My prejudice is built in; that is the way I learned most of what I know about training. When I broke in, adult-ed curricula were still focused on teaching and train-the-trainer seminars were rare. Learning to train was essentially trial and error, imitation of others, and scrounging for guidance from a paltry literature.

The trouble with trial-and-error learning is that it takes too long, like the superintendent who thought it took fourteen years to learn to be a custodian. The scope of experiential learning is also too narrow. You get little or no theory to answer those "why?" questions that come up. And you can't reach beyond what happens in your own restricted experience.

People entering the training field today, or those who want to improve on their present capability, have numerous opportunities for formal training. Colleges are continuously expanding their offerings in human resources development, which covers training. Short-term train-the-trainer courses are plentiful, spread across the spectrum in length, depth, and quality. Most furnish a shorter route to more background in training than experience can provide. They have their drawbacks, however. I do not wish to fault formal education in the field of training. If I'd had the chance when I needed it most, I would have grabbed it. Inevitably, though, formal education suffers from being long on theory and short on practice.

My contention is that formal schooling can give the trainer the grounding needed, but the leap from theory to practice, and especially the achievement of mastery, comes through learning from experience.

Now, having made my obeisance to academe, I can hurry out into the "real world" where we genuflect to Practical Experience, our sacred cow.

EVEN EXPERIENCE NEEDS A PLAN

Merely absorbing raw experience, like osmosis, won't produce much mastery in training. An intentional, almost systematic effort is needed to extract learning from experience.

I propose to pass on some suggestions for learning the most from experience. First, a reminder: I am dealing only with doing training, not consulting or counseling or managing or developing. Second, a declaration: There is no mystique about the craft of training. Any apparent mysteries unravel astonishingly by the application of diligence and straight thinking.

The person who would aspire to be the consummate trainer might take a cue from the actress seeking stardom. She builds on talent first uncovered in high school or college productions. She goes to a drama or acting school, works with a voice teacher, a drama coach, a dancing instructor. She may travel with a road company, do night clubs or commercials. She practices her craft in every circumstance open to her, polishing her skills, seasoning. No one pays much attention to what school she is from or how long she was there. Her credits, the breadth of her practice of her craft, that is what counts.

That pro-active drive to gain experience and learn from it, rather than settling for what comes to you in the natural course of working, is the increment needed to attain excellence.

Here are some ways to use experience to learn the craft of training:

Try every task.   Many of the numerous activities of the training-development cycle will be assigned to you; some will not. If you've never done a needs assessment, for instance, or produced a slide show—volunteer. Let it be known that you want new and different experiences; it's a compelling argument. Trade tasks with a colleague. Try out different techniques on familiar tasks—giving exercise instructions, feedback, group work. Take on the unfamiliar. Try to be able to say: "I've done that," for every step in training. Don't deny yourself experience because you believe you wouldn't like doing some task. It's like your mother said about spinach: "How do you know you don't like it if you won't try it?" You'll not only gather awareness of your true preferences and strength, but you'll learn how the parts fit into the whole.

Seek practice in diverse settings.   Every job offers something new to learn, but repeating the same job is limiting. If you're in a large organization, maybe you can transfer into a different branch of training, such as switching from management to technical. Changing jobs is a move not to be taken lightly, especially in recession times, but there is also a time to move on, when you have stopped growing in the rut you are in.

There are also opportunities to practice your trade outside your job. Volunteer to do training for your church, your club, or one of the countless community organizations that need such services. Training, as such, may not be what is needed, but one of the skills that are part of training—writing, research, visual aids preparation, speaking. I piled up a lot of experience in public speaking with a newspaper speaker's bureau. Going out to address a cold audience, some dinner meeting or club group that knows nothing about you but what they read in a glowing publicity release, which makes it even tougher, can be a learning experience, for sure.

A friend of mine wanted to develop a slide show, but the company she worked for had people to do that, so she offered to do one for the humane society she was serving as a volunteer. She not only got advice from the company's A.V. staff, she borrowed their equipment.

In preparing, try a little overkill.   When you take on something unfamiliar, overprepare. Do your homework better than usual. Rehearse more. It takes some of the anxiety out of it to know that you are solidly prepared.

A young woman who was eager to enlarge her job as personnel clerk got an assignment to train employees of the firm in a new personnel appraisal procedure. She messed up badly her first time out and came to me, full of failure and tears, because I had done some of that training before. Instead of sympathy, I gave her more work. She went back over her material, studied it until it got boring; then studied it some more. We rehearsed and re-rehearsed her presentation. I threw her every question I could think of that might come up, which sent her back for more homework. By the time she did her second session, she was so ready she could hardly wait. And it turned out to be, as she said smugly: "A piece of cake." She was flying high with confidence. Overkill slays a lot of training's dragons.

Emulate the successful.   Most of us don't observe a lot of training done by others, let alone exemplary training. We're confined to what we see in our own organizations. Even if we wanted to take a look at some outstanding work outside our own shops, it is hard to find. Not that it isn't out there, but because the word doesn't get around. So ask around, and if you get even two or three people to agree on, say, a certain trainer who is supposed to be one of the best, invite yourself out to see her at work.

I imagine a lot of people enroll in workshops at national training conventions as much to observe the big names in action as to learn the subjects they are covering. Good idea. We get precious little chance to learn from the masters.

If you are early in your career, try to find work with an organization with high standards of performance in training. You may not have the luxury of such a choice, but if you should get lucky, attach yourself to a place with top-drawer trainers. Success breeds success.

Borrow only from the best.   Nearly every trainer has a shelf of books, training packages, and other materials that he rifles through for ideas when he's putting together a creation of his own. Often as not, the inclination is to dig out some of your own past work. You don't learn much that way.

Collect materials that you have reason to believe are effective, or have endured in the training market. If you know of some company that is reputed to be out ahead in some course, try to borrow or buy the training package. Not to use, but to learn from. I'm not talking about using for-sale materials without paying for them or other forms of copyright infringement; that's a no-no. But there's no exclusive ownership on most processes—using a certain methodology on certain subjects, time allotted to do this or that, how the content was treated, and so on.

Example: one of the first films to use the break-in-the-middle-for-discussion process is "Eye of the Beholder," a professional production staring Richard Conte. It was first used in mental health training, but is so effective that it is still in lively use in all kinds of personal relations training. It would be wrong to show the film without paying the fee, but there's nothing wrong with using the device of showing part of a film or tape, stopping for discussion, then showing the rest. A lot of processes, like ideas, are beyond copyright. Yet there is always some pretender to inventiveness who slaps a copyright on everything he puts out, even if he has borrowed freely from others.

Put yourself through your own training.   One of the scarlet sins of the designer is to develop an exercise or task without ever testing or timing it. When participants flounder on group work that doesn't make sense or runs overtime, you can be pretty sure the trainer never tried it out. Do, yourself, whatever you are going to ask others to do. You save yourself embarrassment and you gain a different perspective, putting yourself in the place of the trainee. Notice whether you have a tendency toward unrealistic expectations, like overloading groups or fishing around for concepts that the exercise never makes clear. Look out for irrelevant case studies and data collection instruments that ask questions for which there is no reasonable answer, or enough space to write it if there was one.

Ask for criticism.   Evaluation systems which go for learning "results" are not always helpful to the trainer. Even if the training was a huge success, what made it work? What part was effective and what part could be improved? You need more particulars, more attention to segments within a single session, a closer look at how the training was delivered. Stuff which is extraneous, which wastes time better used on something else, is often beyond the reach of evaluation.

Here is where knowledgeable criticism by a fellow trainer is invaluable. I'm partial to having a back-up trainer sitting in the session, taking notes, timing segments, observing response, and then giving a quickie critique afterward. One benefit is far better use of time. Most trainers have only a vague notion of how much time they spend on this or that point, and the actual time devoted doesn't usually follow the training script. A critique may reveal that you gave this or that point much more time than it was worth.

The assessment-center technique has been used by a few organizations to appraise and improve the practice of trainers—giving each trainer systematic feedback from a cross section of the staff who have observed the trainer's performance.

Peer-group review is a practice in some professions—such as the college teacher undergoing examination for tenure. When the review is by peers who have directly witnessed the work of the teacher—rather than relying on what they have heard about—it can be an accurate report on strengths and weaknesses.

It takes a tough hide to go looking for criticism, but it can turn up overlooked gaps—and unrecognized strong points—that would otherwise go undetected.

Practice, practice, practice.   I once watched a television special about Johnny Unitas, the incomparable Baltimore Colts quarterback of yesteryear. Before every game, he was out there, practicing his hand-offs, practicing his passes, practicing his pivots, even practicing the cadence of his calls. Here was a professional at the top of his trade; you'd think he didn't need much practice any more, just a warm-up. Yet there he was, going through the repertoire of his skills with the zeal of a college freshman.

Superb performers are like that. Think of the long hours of practice put in by the ice skater, the pianist, the dancer. I know a surgeon who would never undertake an unfamiliar procedure without practicing on a cadaver and who even does a stint of refresher practice when he returns from a vacation.

Did you ever hear of trainers practicing much before they go on, especially if it is something they have done before? I have, although not nearly as many as I'd expect. Interesting thing: It's the best ones who do, the ones who seem to need to practice the least. Maybe that's why they are so good.

Study tapes of yourself.   The first time you see yourself on television is a jolt; makes you want to crawl under the rug. Is that really *me?* Unfortunately it is; the hard reality of all your warts and affectations—the way you swallow your words, what you do with your hands, how you start every other sentence with "You know . . ." Video tape reveals all those mannerisms you were never aware of, that leave you saying, "Why didn't somebody tell me?"

Maybe that's why video tape playback is used a lot less by trainers for self-assessment than is advocated. It's a useful device; I'd almost say mandatory. At least once, you ought to see for yourself how you come across to others. You'll see good things, too, that you might not have been aware of.

Taping your practice presentations is fine, but most benefit is in having your actual training performances recorded. If not on video, then on audio tape. When you play back the tape, have a few friends with you. They won't be as critical as you are; after all, they've gotten to know and love the real you, and they will balance your tendency to be hard on yourself.

Don't be afraid to flop.   You have to be bad before you can be good. You can't be perfect the first time out (if you can, you don't need this book) and fear of that first failure can paralyze, make you scared to try. I like something that the late Buckminster Fuller, the famous futurist, said about mistakes:

> *We were deliberately designed to learn only by trial and error. We're brought up, unfortunately, to think that nobody should make any mistakes. Most children get de-geniused by the love and fear of their parents—that they might make a mistake. But all my advances were made by my mistakes. You uncover what is when you get rid of what isn't.*

The first piece of training I ever tried was a crashing wipe-out. I was trying to "be creative," to make my mark doing something different. It was different, all right; so bad that the trainees felt sorry for me and tried to help me out of the mess. From sheer humiliation I learned not to go off half-cocked until you know what you're doing. Stick with traditional techniques until you have them mastered and have earned the right to experiment.

Watch yourself when you learn.   We constantly learn, intentionally and unintentionally. When you are trying to learn—taking a course, reading, observing—examine your own learning process. Listen with the third ear, as it were. Do you instantly test new knowledge, ask: "How can I use this?" Do you react emotionally? Do you hook up new concepts to your own experience? Do you resist? How do you learn best?

Such self-observation puts you in the place of the learner, the one you are going to train. Getting the learner's perspective can guide you through a lot of thickets of design, cause you to throw out some dubious approach because you can't answer yes to the question: Could I learn it this way?

Profit from your experience.   Remember the old saw that it takes a fool to make a mistake but only a damned fool makes the same mistake twice? How often do those of us in training keep making the same mistake, again and again? We keep right on lecturing, even as the evidence piles up that learning retention from lectures is lousy. We stick with training designs that are flawed, if not failed, because we are comfortable with them.

The other side of that coin: we find something that really works, or discover a genuine strength in ourselves, but don't stick with it because it goes against the system or pushes us out there all by ourselves.

Profiting from experience is not precisely the same as learning from experience. If you can *use* what you have learned by experience, you can be your own best teacher.

————————PART ONE CHECKPOINT————————

To restate the purpose of these Checkpoints: This is where you react to what you have read—agree, disagree, make comparisons with your own experience, criticize.

The Process, once again, is Item, Judgment, Reasons. The Reasons are most important, because they are your own thinking.

1. *Item:* If you trace back over the schooling of your past, which teachers return to your consciousness?

   Judgment:

   Reasons:

2. *Item:* The hierarchical system within which the trainer works seems to downgrade the on-line trainer.

   Judgment:

Agree		Neutral		Disagree
1	2	3	4	5

   Reasons:

3. *Item:* Pride in performance is the most reliable motivation for success.

   Judgment:

Agree		Neutral		Disagree
1	2	3	4	5

Reasons:

4. *Item:* The consummate trainer has experience in virtually all tasks and techniques of training methodology, and can carry out these activities at an acceptable level of proficiency, but prefers and performs some of them exceptionally well.

   Judgment:

Agree		Neutral		Disagree
1	2	3	4	5

   Reasons:

5. *Item:* The consummate trainer generates excitement in training, through a sense of drama.

   Judgment:

Agree		Neutral		Disagree
1	2	3	4	5

   Reasons:

6. *Item:* Who is the best trainer you have known?

   Judgment:

   Reasons:

7. *Item:* The skills and knowledge that the field of training holds in highest regard are not all that different from what they have been for years, despite the great growth and change in the field.

Judgment:

	Agree		Neutral		Disagree	
	1	2	3	4	5	

Reasons:

8. *Item:* Not anybody can train, at least not effectively. Some have the qualifications and some don't.

Judgment:

	Agree		Neutral		Disagree	
	1	2	3	4	5	

Reasons:

9. *Item:* Even with the best set of trainer qualifications available, measurement is primarily by self-assessment, a grading that is always open to the vagaries of introspection.

Judgment:

	Agree		Neutral		Disagree	
	1	2	3	4	5	

Reasons:

10. *Item:* Reliance on the presumed connection between means and ends—trainer effectiveness judged by trainee performance—is questionable.

    Judgment:

Agree		Neutral		Disagree
1	2	3	4	5

    Reasons:

11. *Item:* The chapter on "Basic Qualifications" contained a checklist of trainer qualifications, arranged by factor clusters, and included instruments for self-assessment.

    Judgment: Rate the Checklist:

Useful		Neutral		Useless
1	2	3	4	5

    Reasons:

12. *Item:* Not every trainer has what it takes to train with a team.

    Judgment:

Agree		Neutral		Disagree
1	2	3	4	5

    Reasons:

13. *Item:* Training teams should take responsibility for the full cycle of design, development, and delivery.

    Judgment:

Agree		Neutral		Disagree
1	2	3	4	5

    Reasons:

14. *Item:* If curriculum and materials designed by others must be used, then the delivery trainers are justified in redesigning as much as necessary to make it their own and relevant to their trainees.

    Judgment:

Agree		Neutral		Disagree
1	2	3	4	5

    Reasons:

15. *Item:* All team members should share in the scut work of a training event, such as setting up the room, cleaning up, and tearing down at the end.

    Judgment:

Agree		Neutral		Disagree
1	2	3	4	5

    Reasons:

16. *Item:* In a discussion of how to "rescue" a fellow trainer in trouble, I related an incident in which a participant interrupted the session with a long, haranguing political speech and wouldn't quit. Finally, the trainer up next broke in twenty minutes early and started his session. I didn't like it and would have handled it myself.

Judgment: What would you have done?

Reasons:

17. *Item:* Experience is the best teacher, although not the only teacher.

Judgment:

Agree		Neutral		Disagree
1	2	3	4	5

Reasons:

18. *Item:* Put yourself through your own training. Do, yourself, what-ever you are going to ask others to do.

Judgment:

Agree		Neutral		Disagree
1	2	3	4	5

Reasons:

19. *Item:* Evaluation systems which report learning "results" are not always helpful to the trainer.

Judgment:

Agree		Neutral		Disagree
1	2	3	4	5

Reasons:

20. *Item:* Stick with the traditional techniques until you have mastered them and have earned the right to experiment.

Judgment:

Agree		Neutral		Disagree
1	2	3	4	5

Reasons:

Part
TWO

THE FIELD

6

The Trouble with Training

A certain scholar was attached to the White House during a recent Administration, ostensibly to advise the President. Unfortunately, this one was not aware that what many Presidents want from their brain trusters is not so much new ideas, but rather to have the imprimatur of science bestowed on the President's ideas—certifying that they are sound in theory, unique, brilliant, and good for the country.

This unwary gentleman so persisted in trying to foist his own insights upon the President that one day the order came down: "Get this guy out of my hair! Let him peddle his theories to somebody else."

Accordingly, a subsection of an agency of a department of the government was assigned to divert the scholar's wisdom to some other audience. It happened that his latest enthusiasm was corruption in government, a subject that can always stand attention. He had a theory that corruption evolved from policies and legislation that, although legitimate, inadvertently afforded the opportunity and temptation for ill-gotten gains. Submit the problem to scientific analysis, he postulated, and by discerning what forces stand to gain and what ones stand to lose, you can deduce who the perpetrators might be and who are most likely to be the natural enemies of corruption.

His antidote for corruption—the scholar's pride—was dazzling in its clarity: strengthen the forces opposing corruption and weaken the forces gaining from it.

In due time, the subsection of the agency of the department of the government scheduled a conference to bring in selected officials, about thirty in number, from throughout the land, expenses paid, to listen to the scholar for a few days. The tab was about thirty thousand dollars, but it was always possible that some benefit might come of it, besides getting the guy out of the President's hair.

While preparing for the conference, an obscure staff assistant at the subsection, who was as innocent as she was lacking in status, was going over some background material about the scholar's theory. She was puzzled about something and finally, hesitantly, asked the chief of the subsection: "Isn't this force field analysis?"

(Force field, as familiar as flip charts to trainers, being a problem solving technique advanced long ago by psychologist Kurt Lewin.)

The chief of the subsection ruminated for some time. Then, he asked how the preparations for the conference were coming.

Never again was the question put by the lowly staff assistant with the emperor's-new-clothes vision ever permitted to arise. The conference was held, enjoyed by one and all, and soon forgotten.

GROWING PAINS

Such docile acquiescence in anything that passes for scientific thought is not unknown in the field of training. Any field that has expanded as training has since World War II acquires a thirst for theory. Almost any theory can get a hearing, if dressed in scholarly robes. Not all theories deserve equal attention, of course, but if there is no innocent around to notice that the theory actually has no clothes on, the parade of sophistry marches on.

The field of training is emerging, fluxing, dynamic, suffering the pains of growth. It is broad, diverse, and uncertain—starting to be taken seriously, and confronting challenges and expectations it may not be quite ready to meet. Thus, training is inordinately vulnerable to any conjecture that will help explain itself, to add certainty and credibility.

The gap between theory and practice remains wide, because the theory is less sure than the practice. The latest models of new approaches to learning appear with regularity in books and journals of the field, evidence that we are still unsettled about how people learn. New technologies vie for adoption, yet practice clings to much that is traditional.

To read training's literature, one would fear that the field is moving so fast one can't keep up. But to look at general practice turns up more that is familiar than strange. Perhaps this is not atypical; it has been said that it takes twenty-five years for a new concept in education to work its way into common practice.

Theory can be oblivious to practice. Some years ago, I was designing a personnel system for a small organization, which included writing position descriptions keyed to the organization's objectives. I came across an article in a professional journal stressing the value of task statements in job descriptions with both quantitative and qualitative criteria for appraisals. Wonderful, I thought; this is just what I need. I located the author to find out where the concept had been tried. Well, he admitted at last, he had never actually *used* the concept. He put me onto a department of government that he said was creating a "task bank". My inquiries there disclosed that so far, the bank had collected task statements for only one job.

I ran down several organizations that were mentioned in the literature as having something to do with task statements. One of them had received hundreds of thousands of dollars in research grants and had published numerous periodicals. But none of them could point me to a place where such advanced task statements had been put to use.

Inadvertently, while reading a newsletter on law enforcement, I learned of a police department that had written task statements with criteria for positions in a special new unit, for instruction of newly assigned officers because the jobs were so different. When I contacted the department for more information, they were ignorant of any theory on the practice or anyone else who had tried it. They just thought it would be a good idea.

Another odd thing: In my literature search, I found a single example of a prototype task statement with criteria. As I continued to read other articles, I kept coming across that very same example, repeated again and again. Apparently, that was as close to practice as the theory could venture.

The malleability of training research puts a heavier-than-usual burden on the practicing trainer. In older, more established vocations with a more stable body of knowledge, the practitioner applies her theoretical groundwork, shakes it down, and moves toward improvement by combining theory and practice. In training, the theoretical base seems to be soft and shifting. The practitioner must make his own way to a much larger degree, using independent judgment and reality testing to find his own foundation.

This need for each trainer to chart her own course through the field requires some examination of it. Each individual gains impressions, limited by exposure and the reliability of reports from outside her own experience.

The field is so manifold that any one person's survey of it is bound to be flawed, if not foolhardy. Nevertheless, I shall attempt my own perception of what is happening in the craft of training, primarily to offer up observations to stimulate your own.

This will not be a state-of-the-art survey; that would be beyond my reach. My purview will be those dysfunctional conditions in the field that affect the performance of the trainer who wishes to excel.

TRAINING'S PUT-UP-OR-SHUT-UP CHALLENGE

The evolutionary changes in American society in this decade are fraught with both hope and dread for training. The move from an industrial to an informational society, vacillations in the economy, internationalization of commerce, high technology, shifts in population and influence, the fall in productivity, changing demographics of the work force, dislocated workers needing retraining, computer culture, emergence of the mobile, multi-career, uncommandable professional—these trends put new demands on training. Probably not since World War II has so much been asked of trainers. People must be trained not only to increase productivity in present jobs, but in countless new ones, besides.

If training can respond successfully to this challenge, its stature and permanence—and probably its professional status—can be earned. If not, training could fall back into that just-tolerated, unessential-luxury position it has long resented. It is put-up-or-shut-up time—an exciting time to be a trainer with a contribution to make.

TRAINING'S IDENTITY CRISIS

One of training's vexations is that many of its sponsors—the executives who call the shots and pay the bills—have an incomplete understanding of training as it is perceived by those who practice it. This comes through at budget time, especially during economic downturns, when training rediscovers how dispensable it can be. Every trainer knows that the first step in the development cycle is selling management on what can, and cannot, be done.

In many executive minds there is continuing confusion over the distinction between training and teaching. Isn't a solid, inspirational lecture by a pedigreed academic the best training? The anybody-can-train syndrome is operative here, too. The manager who wouldn't dream of seriously questioning the advice of an engineer or chemist doesn't hesitate to second guess the trainer because he believes there isn't anything very unusual about training.

True, there are managements that are conversant with adult learning theory—generally the big companies with a big investment in training. And there are some who care only for "results" and what's "below the line," hang the theory.

Training can be unfairly judged when hidden agendas are at work.

Some government agencies, for instance, look on training as a way to gain political points with their constituencies, so impressing becomes more important than instructing.

Some of management's uncertainty about training is due to training's uncertainty about itself. As training confronted the larger needs of its clients, and while it was muscling for more room in the corporate world, it expanded its self-identity to "people development." Thus came "training *and* development." When concern for solving the problems of entire organizations grew into a specialty, organizational development was added to the fold. Other specialties carved out of a piece of turf, bringing the need for a still larger umbrella term. So we have human resources development, which embraces just about anything, but isn't too serviceable for the practitioner who is asked, "What exactly do you do?"

Defining the field has become an exercise in updating, leading to confusion inside and outside.

THE PURSUIT OF PROFESSIONAL STATUS

In a world in which an automobile mechanic passes out business cards describing himself as a "car care consultant" and professional associations of janitors—maintenance custodians, that is—refer to those not of their group as laymen, trainers would be out of step if they didn't aspire to be known as professionals. The term is so loosely applied, it almost seems that somebody should just proclaim training to be a profession and be done with it. Of course, the standards of the classic profession are not in place—no accepted body of knowledge, certification, code of ethics, or element of public service.

The drive for professional rank appears to be relentless, and produces aberrations. One is the frantic search for theoretical foundation, and maybe some distinctive, exclusive concepts, turning on a gusher of theorems, models, matrixes, and constructs. Another is the hatching of polysyllabic jargon, as if to invent a secret language not understood by outsiders, the way lawyers and doctors used to hide their communications in Latin. Creating a mystique seems to be the mark of an emerging profession, for fear its practice will be taken as commonplace. Social workers went through this in the 1950s; their mysteries were hidden behind the confidentiality of case material.

When a field of labor is without significant standing, as training was not so many years ago, it is also relatively free of the maladies that growth brings. But now that training apparently has outgrown itself, and the push for professionalism intensifies, the field takes on a deadly seriousness. The most exaggerated and exotic experiments are not to be questioned; mild criticism might suggest disloyalty. Such defensiveness stifles the satirical comment that could restore a sense of balance. Only in very recent years have training periodicals admitted articles which poke fun at pretensions, as well as opening their pages to open-forum debate over issues.

FADS, FASHIONS, PANACEAS, AND ASSORTED NOSTRUMS

Training is trendy. New subjects, new methods are introduced, flourish in vogue for a time, then fade, replaced by new fashions. Yesterday, management by objectives and transactional analysis were in; today, it may be time management or quality circles; tomorrow . . . T-groups were the thing for a number of years, now they are mentioned only in retrospect. Teleconferencing was heralded as the answer to high travel costs; already there is sniping that teleconferencing is the same old stand-up training, without nonverbals. Will suggestology and neurolinguistic planning be with us long? Will we sit around one day recalling with nostalgia our fruitful sessions in the quality of work life? When will computer illiteracy become camp?

Training's trends do, indeed, reflect changes in needs and some can be justified as valid experimentation. Advances must not be discouraged. Still, one wonders whether the work that training prepares people to do has changed as much as the training has, or whether work ebbs and flows in trends. The fall-off of the "soft" topics—those centered on personal growth—is blamed on marketplace pressure for more "hard" topics that will increase productivity. Can topics of more currency like wellness training and stress management be considered "hard?"

Management training seems to withstand the worst storms of change. The steady perennials—skill development, sales, supervision, technical—are bread-and-butter topics that don't stir up bandwagon excitement.

Methodology changes some, too, but not as much as advertised. High technology is still more written about than utilized. I attended a satellite teleconference once on video disc, during which much anticipation was generated among several thousand educational technologists. The potential of that medium *is* rather mind boggling, but some of the thrill went out of it for me when the question was put to one of the panelists: "Are there any training modules using video disc available that we could view?" The man answered, sadly, "Unfortunately, no."

At times, training seems to be on a restless expedition to discover the dramatic, undeniable vehicle that will assure its future.

FRAGMENTATION

If it is American to organize, then training is all-American. The proliferation of special interest groups has come remarkably early in training's short history. Almost every specialty, every common cluster has its own organization, usually national in scope. The divisions of ASTD suggest some of the groupings—government, media, organizational development, international, career development, minority, women, technical, sales, and marketing. Then add the associations for audio-visual, programmed instruction, consultants, vendors, human relations, computer assisted instruction, and others.

Undoubtedly, these organizations serve the interests of their members well, provide exchange of information and support, gain recognition for the issues and problems of the specialists. It is encouraging to see in this branching the vast growth in the field. But such scattering also fragments the field and denies the holistic approach that training espouses.

Overorganization can create small fiefdoms, the perpetuation of which requires denial of the validity of others. In some cases, a certain specialty is held up as superior and all-inclusive—such as the straight-faced advocacy of teaching "faith" by computer, or interpersonal relations by audio cassette.

Will the time come when the audio visualists won't speak to the curriculum developers, or the computer crowd will have nothing to do with the group facilitators? When training goes up against the challenge to retrain the work force for the new society, can it speak to Congress, to industry, to its clients with one voice?

Will the specialists force out the general practice trainer?

VENDORISM

Most professions are supplied with goods and services by a satellite industry. Such an industry can become so profitable and powerful that it exerts inordinate influence, stepping over the line of supply to subtly direct the practices of its customers. Often, vendors are the primary source of updated knowledge in the field, such as the detail man who keeps the physician current on new drugs. The contribution of vendors can be valuable, but there is always the danger of vendors exploiting the field to create a market for their products.

Training is acutely vulnerable to this danger. Because so many vendors are former trainers or academics who have opened shop as consultants, the line between commerce and contribution is thin. The consultant/vendor usually makes the case that she remains in active practice, testing and validating the products she sells. The unwary trainer may blur the distinction between fellow practitioner and seller of services and allow the vendor to define what is needed and effective. The offering of a new training package can become the reason for using it.

If keeping current depends on reading advertisements or articles by leaders in the field who also happen to sell services or products or by visiting exhibitors' booths at meetings, seduction is possible. The latest developments in equipment have the pulling appeal of adult toys and the hype with which they are displayed calculates the notion that not having one is to be behind the times. Hardware usually precedes software by a long way and gullible buyers may find themselves with the latest equipment and little use for it.

Vendors are beguiling with their assistance. They offer products for virtually every need a trainer could run across, with the promise of unheard-of results. There's a package for every problem and a seminar for every subject—even a seminar on how to attend seminars. The savvy practitioner is not enticed by expansive claims, of course, and knows enough to determine the needs of his clients before shopping for training wares.

COMMUNICATIONS, CONVENTIONS, AND BAD CONNECTIONS

Nowhere is the burgeoning of the training field more visible than in its publications and conventions.

Magazines that only a few years ago were thin, gray-pale, and willing to publish almost anything sent in are now slick, fat, splashy with four color ads, and fussy about their editorial requirements. Some periodicals once given away to churn up circulation now charge for subscriptions. Even stodgy association newsletters and vendor promotional organs reflect a new prosperity.

The convention phenomenon is even more booming. Veterans can recall the teeth pulling promotion once necessary to turn out a crowd. Today, conventions draw thousands. Once a year in one place isn't enough to accommodate everybody, so training meetings are regional and frequent.

Half trade fair, half instant-learning institute, these meetings put attendees in the dilemma of splitting their time between the extravaganza of displays in the exhibit hall and the smorgasbord of workshops, demonstrations, speeches, and social gatherings in the meeting rooms.

For the busy trainer who seldom gets to leave his own shop, these meetings and magazines are the primary connection with the field. These sources are not always an accurate picture of what is going on.

By their nature, trade journals tend to focus on what is new and unique, the so-called new developments. This emphasis can leave the impression that the subject of the story is sweeping the field and if you want to keep up, you'd better get with it. When you check around, though, you may discover that your colleagues are just as far behind as you are.

Coverage of advances in the field is one of the functions of the trade press. But readers have the right to expect some measure of objectivity or skepticism, or even the obligation to ferret out the phony. Indiscriminate fluff gets published, with no more foundation than a few footnotes and references. The magazine protects itself from responsibility by an all-purpose disclaimer in the masthead.

One reader who wrote complaining that a training journal ought to serve more than the academics' need to publish or perish may have spoken for others in asking for more reports from the real world that might be of practical help.

Training journals have improved remarkably in recent years, in willingness to take on hard issues and admit differences of viewpoint, less ax grinding of their own promotions, not quite as much gee-whiz treatment of trends and fads, recognition of some leaders in the field besides the habitual gurus, some solid contributions of new information, more coverage of the working world, and better writing, better editing. The changes are reflected in letters columns, which suggest that readers are not as conforming and undiscriminating at may have been assumed.

My personal gripe with training periodicals is their unashamed commercialism; they have come to resemble mail-order catalogues of goods and services. This is not altogether surprising; in other media, where the revenue from advertisers in newspapers, magazines and broadcasting is five times more than received from readers, a certain amount of kowtowing to advertisers goes with the territory. Most media at least pay lip service to that thin ethical line between advertising and editorial content; in training publications it is blurred beyond recognition. Almost as much space is devoted to the "marketplace" in unpaid columns as in the ads, with all manner of merchandising aids for ad buyers. A subscription is guaranteed to fill your mail box daily with junk from the sale of subscription lists. One of the most unconscionable sell-outs to advertisers is one magazine's sponsorship of a contest for articles from the training field, with the eligibility requirement that each entry must deal with the use of some product sold by members of a vendors' association.

The training field could use more of the open forum kind of periodical that encourages healthy criticism, puts new developments to the test of debate, perceives sacred cows as sacred cows, and whose sine qua non is effectiveness in training.

TURF AND TERRITORY

Backhanded testimony to the new importance of training are the turf battles being fought in the field. One polite but mounting clash is between higher education and the private sector side of training. Academics tussle with practitioners to formulate new directions in the field. The universities invade the field with almost as many seminars and short courses as consulting firms offer, operating with some taxpayer support, which the vendors regard as unfair competition. All parties seek to stake a claim on any significant investment in training by government, with the predictable alarums over government interference.

Less in view are the territorial disputes between the company trainers and the outside consultants, the high-tech minded and the human relations advocates, technical and management trainers, and special interest groups competing for recognition.

Sometimes, the needs of trainees get lost in these shuffles. Training can be twisted to prove something rather than serve the learning of the clients.

A TOUCH OF IRONY

Training is not without its little ironies, some amusing. The vendor who rails against the evils of the lecture method, in a lecture on an audio cassette; the endorsements of management systems and training techniques by football players; the starring of celebrities in films on topics they learned about from the script; training conventions that violate every rule in the book on group size, room arrangement, and excessive use of lectures; the egalitarian posture trainers assume while straining to climb into the highest levels of management.

No matter. Every field of endeavor has its small anomalies. If taken with a touch of merriment, they can be enriching.

Candor is in rather short supply in training. Perhaps it is the compunction to sound all pronouncements in cant. Complexity gets confused with profundity and simplicity becomes a pearl of great price. An industrial psychologist, lauded for his contributions to academic research and solid accomplishments as a practitioner, was asked his secret. "The secret is," he said, "that there is no secret . . . We have gotten so carried away with complexity and theoretical contemplation that we forget important organizational problems often have simple solutions."

The trouble with training is that there aren't enough of his kind around.

——————————PART TWO CHECKPOINT——————————

1. *Item:* To read training's literature, one would fear that the field is moving so fast one can't keep up. But to look at general practice turns up more that is familiar than strange.

   Judgment:

Agree		Neutral		Disagree
1	2	3	4	5

   Reasons:

2. *Item:* In training, the theoretical base seems to be soft and shifting. The practitioner must make his own way to a large degree, using independent judgment and reality testing to find his own foundation.

   Judgment:

Agree		Neutral		Disagree
1	2	3	4	5

   Reasons:

3. *Item:* One of training's vexations is that many of its sponsors—the executives who call the shots and pay the bills—have an incomplete understanding of training as it is perceived by those who practice it.

Judgment:

	Agree	Neutral	Disagree	
1	2	3	4	5

Reasons:

4. *Item:* Now that training apparently has outgrown itself, and the push for professionalism intensifies, the field takes on a deadly seriousness.

Judgment:

	Agree	Neutral	Disagree	
1	2	3	4	5

Reasons:

5. *Item:* Has the work that training prepares people to do changed as much as training has?

Judgment:

Reasons:

6. *Item:* Special interest groups within training serve their members well, provide information and support, gain recognition for the issues and problems of the specialists. Such scattering also fragments the field and denies the holistic approach that training espouses.

Judgment:

Agree   Neutral   Disagree

1   2   3   4   5

Reasons:

7. *Item:* Will the specialists force out the general practice trainer?

Judgment:

Reasons:

8. *Item:* The contribution of vendors can be valuable, but there is always the danger of vendors exploiting the field to create a market for their products. Training is acutely vulnerable to this danger.

Judgment:

Agree   Neutral   Disagree

1   2   3   4   5

Reasons:

9. *Item:* For the busy trainer who seldom gets to leave her own shop, meetings and magazines are the primary connection with the field. These sources are not always an accurate picture of what is going on.

Judgment:

	Agree		Neutral		Disagree
	1	2	3	4	5

Reasons:

10. *Item:* High technology is still more written about than utilized.

    Judgment:

	Agree		Neutral		Disagree
	1	2	3	4	5

    Reasons:

11. *Item:* Training periodicals have come to resemble mail-order catalogues of goods and services.

    Judgment:

	Agree		Neutral		Disagree
	1	2	3	4	5

    Reasons:

12. *Item:* Candor is in rather short supply in training.

Judgment:

	Agree		Neutral		Disagree
	1	2	3	4	5

Reasons:

Part
THREE

THE APPROACH

7

Not All Grown-ups Are Grown Up

Once upon a time there was a trainee by the name of Adultnikov who was straggling down the road to Learning one brittle winter's day and came upon a trainer named Andragosky.

Andragosky, the trainer, greeted Adultnikov, the trainee, and inquired, "Where might you be headed, my good man?"

Said Adultnikov to Andragosky, "I am searching for Learning, but I don't know where it is."

"Ah," responded Andragosky, "so you are searching for Learning?"

"Indeed," answered Adultnikov, "that is what I said."

"And you don't know where it is?" said Andragosky.

"That's what I said," answered Adultnikov, pulling up the collar of his greatcoat against the quickening wind as the sun went behind a cloud. "Can you help me?"

"You want me to help you?" fed back Andragosky.

"Yes, if you know where Learning is," said Adultnikov.

"Bless me, my friend, of course I know where it is," responded Andragosky. "But you must find Learning by yourself."

"What?"

Andragosky stroked his beard for a time. "Consider, dear colleague," he said finally, "you are obviously a fine fellow with much of life's experience that can assist you now in your readiness to reach Learning. But you must solve this problem yourself, just as you have solved so many others."

"Pray tell me, why?"

"If I were to tell you where Learning is," spoke Andragosky, dipping his thumbs into his pockets, "you would not retain my directions. Even if you chanced upon Learning that way, you would not know it when you found it."

"Give me a chance," asked Adultnikov, his teeth chattering.

"I am not permitted to do that," responded Andragosky, "it is contrary to the rules of my guild. Telling you would not facilitate your achieving Learning."

Adultnikov turned, downcast, and plodded away.

"Be of good cheer, my man," Andragosky shouted after him, "You shall gain the prize."

The sun went down, the sky darkened, and snow began to sweep the road in blinding swirls. Adultnikov stumbled on into the night. He took to the woods to escape the biting wind and lost his way, groping endlessly in circles through the dark until he fell over a precipice and tumbled down into the black, freezing river below. With a great effort, he dragged himself out, up the bank to shelter behind a dead tree. There he dropped, chilled and exhausted. Weary sleep came upon him as the night turned bitter cold.

Meanwhile, Andragosky arrived at his guild lodge, where he warmed himself by the fire, drank hot tea, and mused about how well he had enabled Adultnikov to find his own way to Learning.

In the morning, a boatman plying the river found Adultnikov, frozen to death.

TRAINING'S APPROACH TO ADULTS

We are admonished, by the dogma of adult education, to treat adults as adults. They are different from children and our approach to them should be different.

What is different about adults? Of course you know this, if you are conversant with andragogy, a term that has gained an almost unassailable place in the patois of training as a "unifying theory" of how adults learn. Andragogy was introduced in the United States by the redoubtable Malcolm Knowles, our "father of adult education," who learned it from a Yugoslav who had picked it up from its German originators. The concept marks the difference between the education of adults and pedagogy, the teaching of children—a useful distinction.

Andragogy points out that adults are not dependent upon a trainer for learning in the way that children are dependent upon a teacher. Adults have a lifetime of experience against which they test, compare, and relate what they are offered for learning. They seek to learn not merely to earn a grade or degree, but for their self-development, to solve their problems.

Training adults takes different methodology. It has been said that in pedagogy, the teacher manages the content; in andragogy, the trainer manages the process. In pedagogy, the teacher is the one who *knows* transmitting that knowledge to those who don't know. To accommodate the knowledge and experience adults already possess, training must be more participatory, give adults opportunity to control and apply their own learning.

Before the advent of andragogy, Carl Rogers stressed the principle of each adult learner taking responsibility for her own learning and the creation of a climate that encourages self-learning. John Dewey advocated much the same approach in his emphasis on learning by doing.

Lately, andragogists have been suggesting the extension of this adult approach to the education of children, those dependent subjects who are not so full of life's experience, not so intent upon solving problems as growing up to have them, and not necessarily resentful about being treated as children.

An ironic turnaround to this is a suggestion that adults might learn better if they were more like children, set forth by that expansive thinker, Ashley Montagu, in his book *Growing Young*, (McGraw-Hill, 1981). Montagu advances the concept of neoteny, a term coined by a Swiss zoologist that describes the retention of juvenile traits into adulthood. He sets out twenty-six neotenous drives of the child that seem to diminish with age—such as playfulness, imagination, sense of humor, need to learn, honesty and trust, curiosity, sense of wonder, resiliency, open-mindedness, and explorativeness. Montagu likens some adults to the pupil of the human eye—the more light exposed to it, the narrower it grows.

The natural receptivity to learning of children has also been substantiated by the late Jean Piaget, the great Swiss biologist who devoted sixty years to pioneering studies in child development. He concluded that the structures of a child's mind lead to a spontaneous development through interaction with the environment. Teaching plays a limited role; the child is his own best teacher.

Could it be that the careful way we approach adults is not so much out of respect for their maturity, but in actuality a sad recognition that they have lost much of the capacity for learning that they had as children?

We trainers tread fearfully to avoid dependency between learner and trainer. Yet isn't any learner, adult or child, dependent upon something, someone, as the source for what she is to learn? Maybe depending upon a book, a film, a computer, or other adults is not as offensive as depending on a trainer. Less chance to be treated as a child. But that learner sitting before the user-friendly CAI screen being guided step by step and fed cheery re-enforcements—"Nice going, Joe Hardy!" "That's right, Julie!"—isn't he being treated like a child?

A TEST OF FREE LEARNING

The catch in adult learning theory is that it doesn't always fit in practice. What if adults don't behave as adults are supposed to? What if they prefer to learn by traditional means, the ones they are comfortable with—to be taught, to be told, to be lectured to, to be dealt with as a student?

In the time of my own childlike naiveté about training—when I didn't even know what I didn't know—I got a chance to see adult learning theory in action in pristine form. We were doing a series of management seminars for executive directors of community agencies—a preservice, inservice, and advanced, spaced six or eight months apart. Some of the Process zealots on our staff imbued with the concepts of Carl Rogers argued that the advanced seminar cried out for their approach. For once, those of us in the Content camp had to admit that maybe they had something. We acquiesced; more than that, we swallowed it whole.

We took the favorable climate part literally and booked sites in resort areas (we took some flak for furnishing free vacations, but we countered that going to resort hotels off-season actually cut expenses). The directors were allowed to bring their spouses for ten days of fun and sun and easy learning. Enrollment soared.

Our design scheduled sessions on only the first day and a half, devoted to training the participants in how to set their own learning objectives. The rest of the seminar, they were to be on their own to work on their objectives and recreate. A daring experiment in adults taking responsibility for their own learning.

We assembled and shipped a library of resources for every need we could conceive, enough to fill an entire room. We developed an interview questionnaire to inventory the resources to find out what each participant could contribute. We labored to pare down our own presentations to fit the foreshortened mold. And packed our golf clubs and sun lotion.

The seminar got off to a shaky start. We followed Mager faithfully in our instruction on objectives—pounding on specifics, measurability, and time. The participants didn't latch on. They tended to set vague and timeless goals like "learning more about personnel administration" or "getting more support from the community." Hardest of all was getting them to limit their objectives to what they could accomplish at the seminar.

We sensed more at work than failure to limit objectives, resistance to the very idea of learning on their own. We charged it off to natural reluctance to work in an atmosphere of play.

We did the resources inventories and collected the objectives—some never did submit acceptable objectives; one said, "My secretary takes care of things like that." Then we did matchups. In a long, drawn-out staff meeting, we clustered objectives that were similar, then searched for any participant (or trainer) who could be a resource to the cluster. We did the same for those whose objectives didn't cluster. We papered the walls with those matchups.

The next morning, we presented our work, suggesting—only *suggesting*—that for any cluster of five or more participants, we would set up training sessions, at their option. For the others, we suggested conferences with resource participants, at which they could decide for themselves how to proceed.

After that, we turned them loose. At their request, we arranged for meeting rooms, and they met or did not meet, worked or did not work, according to their own felt needs. Our only control was mere maintenance. Each trainer was assigned several participants to check with every few days and see how they were doing and what assistance we could offer. Otherwise, the trainers became equal participants.

It is tempting to report that the seminar was a resounding success. As far as rest and recreation, it was. Many of the directors did reach their learning objectives, and those who didn't finish said they learned. One omnivorous reader tried to consume the entire library at the rate of nine books a day, but his objective was hardly touched.

No doubt, our well-intended venture in unfettered learning could be faulted on many counts. The recreation may have been too much of a temptation, but rest from burn out was one of the implied goals. Perhaps there was too much freedom, which is also the freedom not to learn. Perhaps the insistence on objectives as a learning contract was too much structure.

In any case, the reluctance and resistance of the participants to learning on their own clearly indicated that they were not ready for it. It was too much of a departure. Adults apparently need preparation and practice to learn how to learn independently.

Our team, and others of our training staff, did several seminars of this model. The results were generally the same—some participants took quickly to learning on their own; others floundered.

The model also revealed some significant attitudes in trainers. One team regarded the advanced seminar as a free ride—a day and a half of work and then off to the beaches and bars. Others—my own, naturally— were conscientious but discovered there is nothing easy about training this way. To be of even minimal help, we had to prepare for almost anything. When confronted with unexpected requests for help, we found out how much we didn't know. And managing the process calls for skill and patience far more demanding than in more structured training. One of our trainers who had been a college professor said the Rogerian approach was the toughest he'd encountered. "Compared to this," he said, "lectures are a snap."

NAGGING QUESTIONS

Experiments like that one are fascinating, but rare. Despite a lot of trainer talk about how adults learn best, we seldom practice what we preach. How often do you give your trainees free rein over what and how they will learn? When was the last time you put your curriculum up for negotiation?

There is reason in our reluctance to go whole hog with adult learning theory. It seems to confuse training with education. We are told that half of the people around are pursuing learning of some kind, often to help them in some transition in their lives. Obviously, their need to know is acute at such times and motivation is high. This is self-development to be sure, lifelong learning. But what if, at that teachable moment, they want something other than what we are offering?

Most training has to do with preparation for work, the skills and knowledge required to do a job. The content is usually prescribed by analysis of the job. By its nature, that kind of training loses some of the keen motivation that drives a person intent upon solving some life problem. In training for work, we must rely inordinately on the learner's desire to do a better job and his willingness to accept the content that evolves from that job.

As much as trainers might hope to follow the research and theory of adult learning, they are constantly denied any one-size-fits-all principles. For every new hypothesis, there are bothersome exceptions to the rule.

Adults don't fit into neat categories. The research on brain theory is intriguing, but one keeps wondering how to use it—should we put the right brain thinkers on one side of the room and the left brainers on the other, like smoking and nonsmoking sections? How do you target training for people who fluctuate from one learning style to another? Maybe I'm weird, but I never seem to fit tightly into any single box when I submit to those style assessments. Sometimes I'm a 9.5 on the management grid; other times, I'm a fierce 1.9. I can be high assertive and low responsive on occasion, and after lunch, fall off into low assertive and low responsive. I don't even look out of the same Johari window all the time.

I do not mean to dismiss adult learning theory out of hand or to deny the contribution of the theorists. Far from it. I don't believe I'm alone in wishing the thinkers would get together and give us something we can use. Maybe ASTD could call a summit conference of the best minds, put them in a room, lock the door, and not let them out until they have reached agreement on a theory of learning for adults that will stand up in practice. Simplistic and unrealistic thinking, yes. Unreasonable need, no.

One of those offhand remarks that stick with you for years was made to me by a man I worked for and respected, Dr. John Ivey, Jr., then Dean of Education at Michigan State University. We were chatting with the Superintendent of Schools of Detroit about the use of television in the classroom and I asked about its effectiveness. It couldn't be very well nailed down, he said, because "We don't really know how people learn."

What Seems to Work

Theories about adult learning are helpful but still too wavering, contested, and incomplete to accept on blind faith. Ultimately, trainers must rely on their own eclectic judgment about what works best in training adults.

The trainer is, without question, the expert on *execution*, the forgotten factor in much research. Especially is the trainer the foremost authority on her own circumstances, trainees, and subject matter. Over years at the craft, a trainer can acquire a strong sense for what works and what doesn't work, how adults will respond, that will stand up as a dependable guide.

Acquiring that sense takes time and some trial-and-error testing. In his own practical laboratory, the trainer can experiment with new methods, new approaches—particularly where there is evident need for improvement. He can quickly—and quietly—chuck the variation if it doesn't work, and learn from his mistakes in the process.

Of course, adults are not guinea pigs and should not be used capriciously as experimental subjects. An opening admission that "I want to try something new" usually brings their cooperation, and even helpful advice.

By now, you have unquestionably formed some conclusions about what works for you in the training of adults, as I have. Naturally, we stand ready to alter our conclusions if they blow up in our faces. Until then, here are some of mine.

THE WHY'S AND WHAT FOR'S

Kids ask the darndest questions and the darndest of all is "Why?" Adults don't outgrow that question, but it takes a different form—"Why should I learn this? What good will it do me?"

That's the pervasive question in the minds of adults at the outset of training. What sometimes comes across to us as resistance born of discomfort in a strange setting—and that we handle by making them more comfortable—may be hard skepticism about the very purpose of being there at all.

We trainers are quite thorough about putting forth the "what" of training in all those goals and objectives, but we are not always as forthcoming with answers to the "why should I learn this?" question. Adults need a rationale for learning, to be sold on what it can do for them; more than "At the conclusion of training, you'll be able to . . . " or "This will make you a better manager."

Sometimes, a strong problem statement that includes the solutions that training will offer provides some rationale. This assumes, however, that those in the room really want to solve the problem, which is not always so. Convincing reasons why they should *want* to solve the problem, even the personal payoff, may be needed.

You know how frequently adults are practically ordered to "take training" or do so for frivolous reasons—to get out of the office, because it will look good on a resume, or as a lark. That kind of motivation will tell as training goes along. They need to be given legitimate reasons for their presence.

Trainers have to sell their programs to management. They also need to sell participants on the value of training. When adults fully grasp what learning can do for them, they become proactive about it and turn up ways to learn that go beyond what we offer.

"SEEING" THE OUTCOME OF LEARNING

Adults seem to take to training better when they have a clear, complete picture of its goal—the skill they can learn, the way a procedure works, what a program will look like in operation. For all of our attention to goals and objectives and overviews, we can still fall short of a vivid perception of the end product. When trainees can't quite see the outcome, they spend inordinate time trying to capture that picture for themselves.

Perhaps it is because *we* know what we are shooting for, and assume that they do. Or we may be so engrossed in the parts of training that we lose sight of the whole. Stating the goal isn't enough, we need to show them what we mean.

If the intended outcome can be visually depicted or demonstrated— a skilled operator using the word processor, the successful closing of a sale, how someone handles a stressful situation—a film or slide show or live exhibition will help. The testimony of someone who has effectively applied the learning or a case study of what happens when the desired attitude is put in practice can give adults a fuller grasp of the goal. These goal illustrations should come at the beginning of training, at the same time we would normally describe the goal.

THE TWO EDGES OF EXPERIENCE

Adults come to class bringing their years of experience, but that contribution can cut two ways. It can enrich learning; it can also get in the way.

Past experience with training, good or bad, carries into the future. Someone who "always hated school" or got burned in some earlier workshop may be on edge about this one. People with a positive background in learning can't wait to get started.

How adults are accustomed to learn also creates a mind set. Once, when I was designing a session for judges, I was cautioned by a bureaucrat to "stick with lectures, none of that Mickey Mouse stuff." At a later planning conference with judges, one of them told me, "Whatever you do, don't give us a lot of lectures. Judges hate them. But they eat up case studies and role play." And why not? Their legal training is loaded with case readings and mock trials.

The depth of an adult's background in the topic makes a difference. Those with plenty of knowledge can be a help, or a pain. A "we-they" situation can evolve—your knowledge versus theirs. Sometimes you wish they knew little or nothing, were all blank slates.

The touchiest past experience to deal with is the emotional. I suppose every veteran trainer knows the shattering effect of a trainee who breaks down in training; bursts into tears or unwarranted hostility or some bizarre behavior. Short of psychoanalyzing every participant, there's no way to prevent or predict how some will react to the mild stress of training. Everyone brings some emotional freight into training and our design and methodology is intended to unblock resistance. It is not uncaring, though, to suggest that a trainer is not a psychiatrist and should not try to fix every psychological problem she encounters. Help if you can, but only if you can; good intentions sometimes make matters worse.

The perplexity of adult experience is that it can come in as many varieties as there are adults sitting in the room. How to use that experience to advantage, that's the test. Finding out as much as possible about each trainee ahead of time is a beginning. Needs assessment can give some information, but usually it is in some combined form that misses what you need to know about each individual. Personal interviews with trainees are invaluable, if time permits. Not only does this take people out of the faceless trainee image, but it often turns up case study material, candidates for panel discussions, and a much more precise aim at the comprehension level of the group.

Using a training group's experience is sometimes best done on the spot. Some trainers are marvelous at this. They are good listeners to begin with, able to draw out incomparable illustrative material and then fit it adroitly into the content so that everybody understands how it applies. Twenty minutes of "Q and A" at the end of a lecture seldom gets this done; it takes active reconnaissance.

Adults constantly exert their experience on each other and invariably report in participant evaluations that the best part of the event was what they learned from their peers. There's a touch of trainer put down in this, but there's no doubt that they pick up a lot from others. A challenge for the trainer is to move that learning out of the corridor and happy hour conversations and blend it into the training.

When the trainer can make the past experience of adults work for learning and not against it, then everybody benefits.

THE EGO BARRIER

Years of close and careful observation have brought me to the deduction that the single most obstructive barrier to learning is Ego—mine, yours, and theirs. Ego is always there, getting in the way. It prevents people from listening. It uses up time demanding to be soothed and stroked. It fouls things up defending itself.

Forgive me for being so blunt and unscholarly. Surely there is a nice, tidy scientific postulation about Ego and its manifestations that I am ignoring, but I know this much for sure about Ego—everybody has one and brings it to training.

What's more, adults have bigger ones than children.

The Ego tripper that is present at all events is only the most obvious. Consider the executive big shot who detests the idea of being a mere participant, or the quick learner who loves to show off her smarts, the constant maverick who is always in a minority of one, the trainer's little helper who endlessly volunteers evidence to support whatever the trainer says for the benefit of all those others who don't understand. You've seen Big Ego in action; add your own list.

Let's be fair about it: trainers are not immune to seizures of runaway Ego. Not you and me, of course, but there are some—prima donnas who use training as a stage for self expression, for example. Most trainer Egos are more subtle—insisting on his way as the only way, taking offense at any objections from the audience, relentlessly pounding her own agenda, taking a paternalistic posture toward trainees, jumping in with unnecessary interventions, never knowing when to shut up. Surely you have witnessed this *in others*.

The most outrageous example of a runaway Ego by a trainer that I can recall was a consultant who insisted on a clause in his contract providing that his name appear first among the authors listed on the title page of the participant handbook. And he contributed nary a whit to the book.

Truly, Ego goes with the territory in training. What can be done about it? Not much, except to work around it. One way is for the trainer to keep his foot on the neck of his own Ego and try to set a norm that takes attention away from personal aggrandizement. Another is to ignore it, in a proactive manner. Trainers who are big on positive re-enforcement can make problems for themselves by indiscriminately feeding Big Egos. Selective re-enforcement is a better practice, meeting obvious displays of excessive Ego with meaningful silence.

Ego is a positive force in accomplishment, maybe even an indispensable one. In training, though, it needs to be set aside to let learning in.

LEARNING CLIMATE FOR ADULTS

As far as physical facilities are concerned, I doubt that anything special is essential for adults. Learning can occur in a dirty classroom off the shop floor or the poshest of mountain retreats. Equipment may be more necessary, whether it be a projector or a chain saw.

Don't you think it odd that we have come to assume comfort and convenience are the crucial inducements to learning—coffee breaks on time, four star restaurants nearby, easy transportation, comfortable chairs, no evening sessions? Heaven forbid if the air conditioning breaks down!

It's not that I have anything against creature comforts. I worked for years in a luxurious training center, where a lot of learning took place. But I have also seen some of the most productive training occur under almost adverse conditions. I have trained, literally, in a barn, where the rude surroundings brought out the best in folks. One of my favorite sites was Hilltop House, a ramshackle inn at Harpers Ferry, Maryland, which had no telephones, no television, no locks on room doors, wake-up calls by the manager walking down the hall slapping two boards together, meals served so punctually that if you weren't there on time you didn't eat. The training room was small and odd shaped and the chairs were hard and the only recreation provided was a snooker table. But we did some exciting work there.

It's the emotional/psychological/learning climate that matters most, as you know, and here the trainer's influence is vital. She sets the tone that can be sustained by the others.

Adults want to be taken seriously—not soberly or grimly, but with respect for their individual worth. That attitude is acted out in many

seemingly minor efforts. Taking the trouble to use the terms and nomenclature of the trainees or, failing that, simple English instead of polysyllabic jargon; looking out for the "sleepers" who never make much noise
but sop up learning and have much to offer; guarding against picking fa-
vorites; not forgetting to extend common courtesy to all, and listening, listening, listening.

Adults frown on the phony, and size him up quickly—the gushy,
oversolicitous glad hander who wants to make everybody happy; the un-
prepared presenter who tries to wing it; the one who can't say "I don't
know." They also know "busy-work" when they see it, when an irrelevant
case is being pushed on them, and when they are being manipulated.

Climate setting has a lot to do with expectations, sending signals that
the content is valuable, that you respect their endeavor to learn it, and that
this is the time and place to open up to something new.

MAKING DEMANDS ON ADULTS

Somehow, a vague presumption has crept into training that adults should
not be required to work hard, that not too much should be demanded of
them. Sessions that don't fit the nine-to-five work day are verboten; the
fifty minute metabolism must be faithfully protected in class duration.
Homework is almost as abhorrent for adults as it is for teen-agers. Presentations must be spiked with humor and at all times entertaining. If participants don't show up on time or wander in and out: well, you just have
to expect that.

Hogwash. This notion that learning must be palatable is more in the
minds of trainers than adult learners. When we make no demands on
them, expect no labor from them, then we really are treating them like
children.

I have not encountered genuine resistance from adults to pitching in
and working hard. Oh, there is some grousing—more facetious than
real—but they almost always do what they are asked. Rarely does a
trainee flatly refuse to do what is expected. More often, adults seem to
welcome increased demands; it can increase the value of their learning.

Asking—not ordering—is the key to extraordinary work; that and
giving learners sound reasons for doing it and what they can expect to
gain. Even homework can be made more interesting with a little thought.
Instead of "Please read Chapter Six tonight," or "Would you go over the
material for tomorrow," how about some teaser questions or a little exercise that spices the reading with mystery or controversy. Make the homework integral, not supplementary.

That goes for pretraining preparation, as well. Riding on an airplane one time I noticed my seat partner pouring over abstracts of speeches to be given at a meeting he was going to attend. Some months after that, I was facing one of those meetings where there is far more to get done than you have training time for, so I developed an "airplane kit." We had scheduled a retreat in Albuquerque for members of a board of directors of a troubled agency in El Paso. The flight from El Paso to Albuquerque took an hour and a half. From a needs assessment my team had done on a prior visit, we listed fourteen major problems besetting the organization. We put these in the kit as a prioritizing exercise. They were asked to add any problems they had observed and to rank order the list as to severity. We time tested the exercise to be sure the board members could cover the material in the flight time.

You could say they landed running, because when they arrived in Albuquerque, they were chomping to get to work, full of ideas about the problems they had predigested in their plane work. We got into the substantive issues immediately; they demanded it.

RE-ENFORCEMENT, POSITIVE AND/OR NEGATIVE

We don't pass out grades or degrees in training, but adults sure do love those certificates. If you think not, take note that nobody ever refuses one and if you overlook anybody or misspell someone's name, you will hear about it. And if you ever visit any of training's alumni afterward at their work, you can bet your jacuzzi the framed certificate will be hanging on the wall.

Adults may feel that they ought to be above all such kids' stuff, but they practically purr when they get those strokings known in the trade as positive re-enforcement. At one point in my apprenticeship, I almost became a zealot for stressing the positive. People don't need to be told they are wrong, I reasoned; they already know that. Besides, focusing on wrongness is a way of re-enforcing error.

There's plenty of empirical evidence to back up the contention. A trainer wrote an article describing what he had learned about positive and negative re-enforcement while teaching a class on writing. At first, he followed the age old practice of having students exchange papers and criticize each other's writing, marking the mistakes. He noticed that while the student's writing improved somewhat, the skills they were learning most were how to edit and how to rewrite. Worse, they were gradually coming to the conclusion that they couldn't write well. He made a simple change; in the exchange of writing exercises, students doing the editing were instructed to look for and mark out only what they regarded as strong, significant writing. The result was an almost magical shift in learning. That supportive feedback revitalized the students, gave them confidence that they *could* write.

Negative criticism has been blamed for a child's inability to read well. If a teacher stops and corrects a pupil every time she makes a mistake in her faltering first attempts at reading, what the child learns is that she makes mistakes, that reading is difficult, that she can't read very well.

Positive re-enforcement remains, for me, the predominant way to go, but it doesn't work in all cases. There's the concept of unlearning, the need to give up old learning before it can be replaced with new. This is tough for adults to do; all that past experience has to be defended. Change is threatening and must be resisted.

Judicious application of negativism now becomes almost inevitable. The old must be shown to be wrong, or no longer true, or to be wasteful, inefficient, or inappropriate. There is probably no really nice way to do this, and sugar coating negative criticism is a sham, like the so-called "evaluation sandwich"—a thick filling of negatives covered by thin layers of positives.

Sometimes, pride can be preserved by showing, without personal application, how wrong, how outmoded, how unworkable the old knowledge is now. If the wrong way can be presented objectively, the learner has opportunity to ponder and adjust to his wrongness, without appearing to give up what he has long held to be true. Acceptance of the new knowledge may not come until long after the training event is over, when defenses can drop. Gradually, the learner admits some part of the new knowledge into awareness and lets go the old. Then more, so that when learning is fully embraced, she may not quite recall where she got it.

A friend of mine used to characterize training as "giving them time bombs, set to go off when they get back home."

When adroit means of unlearning fail, confrontation may be in order. This is when the trainer flatly and firmly tells the trainee, "You are wrong," and tells him why, chapter and verse. No place for ridicule or sarcasm here, but forthrightness is preferred.

Unfortunately, confrontation is usually a last resort for most trainers, which means the case has become aggravated, and frayed nerves can be expected on both sides. This is when the trainer really earns her pay.

When confrontation is indicated, I favor the one-two approach—one knocks them down and another picks them up. If one trainer must administer the unlearning tonic, another is standing by to give comfort and support.

This approach was standard practice for two seminary professors who conducted a clinic on chaplaincy training. Their student chaplains worked in pairs in hospitals, ministering to patients. Each gave daily reports on their activities, including the performance of their partner. A persistent problem among the chaplain internes was the overly evangelistic ones who saw in the patients' vulnerable condition the chance to save souls. One thought he was especially gifted at working with children because he could bring them to tears when he convinced them of their state of sin. In cases like this that had to be corrected, one of the professors verbally clobbered the offending trainee for using patients to meet his own needs. Then the other professor came along behind, lifted up the chastised chaplain with steadfast support, but left the message of the confrontation stand. The approach was notably successful.

9

Learning from Learning

How did you learn to drive a car?

Did you take driver education in school? Or private lessons from a commercial driving school instructor? Maybe you learned from someone in your family or a friend.

Now *there* is a learning experience. Remember how you sweat out your driving test? Did you pass it the first time or have to go back and try again? I knew a woman who flunked the driving test fourteen times—the examiners almost ran when they saw her coming. Then there's the story of the man who taught his wife to drive, and as soon as she got her license, she divorced him.

How would you rate your instructor as a trainer, on a scale of one to five?

In your driving since you first learned, have you noticed any flaws that could be traced back to your training, like trouble with parallel parking or still backing out of alleys?

Now let's go back further—did you ever play hopscotch?

Maybe the kids in your neighborhood didn't go in for hopscotch. Then how about Stone School? Or Duck-on-the-Rock? King of the Mountain? Red Light, Green Light? Maybe you called them something different. How about your basic Hide and Seek? Here's one—Spin the Bottle. You must have played that; it's a kissing game.

Question: Where did you learn those games?

From the other kids, wasn't it? Certainly not from any book or in a class. Did it ever occur to you how remarkable it is that the knowledge and skill to play kid games is passed on from child to child, generation after generation, without the aid of any adult instruction?

Kid games can get pretty complicated, too. I found this out many years ago when I was called upon to arbitrate the seventeenth argument of the day between my two daughters. My then seven-year-old was complaining, "She swings too high on Blue Bells and makes me miss." The five-year-old merely demurred.

I was tempted to cop out with some parental dodge like, "Go play," because settling the dispute meant I had to find out what they were talking about, i.e. what is Blue Bells? My dumb questions caused the fuss to evaporate, because it put the girls in that position that kids dearly love—explaining something they know to an ignorant adult.

They educated me, and showed me how uninformed I really was. Blue Bells is a rope-jumping game, what the kids call "skip rope." So is High Waters, Down in the Valley, Windmill, Hot Pepper, Donald Duck, Louder and Powder, Charlie Chaplain, Cold and Salt, and Mother, I Am Ill.

Who would have believed there were so many variations, each with its own unique jump and swing of the rope, and rhythmic ditty. The intricacies fascinated me, so much that I did some exploring into kids' games, using the neighborhood kids as my primary sources, and wrote a magazine article about them.

One thing I found intriguing is that the games were the same that I played as a kid, and as far as I know, they go back for generations, almost traditions that are perpetuated solely by children. And they are not simple, but rather, quite complex. Take hopscotch. Did you know there are dozens of variations, like Chinese hopscotch, Hollywood hopscotch, and Snail? Some have different grids that you draw on the sidewalk— one is round. You throw your stone and hop a slightly different way in each.

LEARNING OR TRAINING

Learning and training are not the same. There can be learning without training, and training without learning. The mission of the trainer is to put the two together, so that learning comes from training.

A trap that we trainers can fall into is to become so concentrated on training that we lose sensitivity for learning. Training is what *we* do; learning is what *they* do, and in that role separation our acuity for the feeling, the ferment, the exertion, and the pace of learning may erode.

To unite training and learning, we need to capture and sustain the perspective of the learner. We must revive our own awareness of learning.

To help with this, I'd like to suggest a little memory exercise. This is no test or measurement, merely a device to stimulate recall of your own learning history. It will take some mind stretching to reach back and revive the consciousness of how it was to learn some skill or acquire new knowledge. The idea is to examine those experiences, to see what they might add to your know-how about the learning process.

Here's the procedure: For three different periods in life—childhood, youth, and adulthood—I'll offer some skills or knowledge that you might have learned in those periods. Let's call them "learnings" (although, as a language purist, I normally abhor the pluralizing of compound nouns, like "behaviors," "knowledges"). Read the list of "learnings" and mark those that you can recall. Try to whet your memory, to call up as vivid a picture of what happened as you can.

After you have regenerated several of these "learnings," I will offer some questions about them for you to ponder. The questions are merely thought stimulators. This is one of those consciousness-raising exercises that make you feel a bit foolish at first, but can be kind of fun after you get into it. When I did this, it sent me off on a nostalgia trip.

"LEARNINGS" AS A CHILD

A little scene setting first. Where did you live as a child, say from birth to ten years old? Remember your house, the neighborhood, your school? Think about the people in your life—your family, playmates, teachers, relatives. Have any pets? Anything happen to you out of the ordinary, like sickness or an accident? Think about the photographs taken of you at that age.

Got the picture? Now, here is the list of "learnings." Don't hurry; try to remember:

How did you learn:

—To tie your shoes?
—To tell time by the clock?
—To brush your teeth?
—To make your bed?
—Bible verses, poems?
—To swim?
—To play the piano or some other instrument?
—About the birds and the bees?
—To make change?
—To ride a bike?
—To sing "The Star Spangled Banner"?
—To make model airplanes or cookies?
—To whistle?
—To read a map or a menu?
—To take care of your dog, or cat, or parakeet?
—To read a thermometer?
—The rules of a game, like softball?
—The names of the streets in your neighborhood?

Questions: Take one of the "learnings" at a time and mull it over. Did the "learning" come easy or hard? What made the difference? Did you have any special incentive to learn? Did you practice a lot? Anything special about who you learned from? How did you feel about learning what you did? If you were teaching any of these things to someone else, would you do it the way you were taught?

"LEARNINGS" AS A YOUTH

This is the period from eleven to nineteen years old, probably your most fruitful period.

How did you learn:

—To dance?
—To reconcile a bank statement?
—To dress properly?
—First aid?
—To do your laundry?
—To tie a tie?
—To take an airplane trip—reservations, airports?
—To grow flowers or plants?
—Who to vote for?
—To cook?
—To manage money?
—To study?
—Crafts, like ceramics, weaving, needlepoint?
—Sports like bowling, skiing, sailing, golf, tennis?
—To repair a car or appliance?
—To shop?
—To make a speech?
—To sew?
—What to do in case of fire?

Questions: These "learnings" are more involved, take more time. Think about your motivation to learn and what effect it had. How about those you just picked up on your own, compared with those for which you sought instruction; any difference? Anything you found particularly helpful when you were trying to learn? What about your thought process, any pattern to it? Did embarrassment have an influence? How did you move from just learning how to performing well? Any generalizations emerge from all these about your mode of learning?

"LEARNINGS" AS AN ADULT

How did you learn:

—To play bridge or poker?
—To speak a foreign language?
—To take and develop your own photographs?
—To remember telephone numbers?
—To read stock quotations?
—To safely shoot a gun?
—To read music?
—To fly a plane?
—To lose weight?
—To break a bad habit?
—The words to songs?
—To operate a machine?
—To identify the stars?
—To get a job?
—To use a computer?
—To mix drinks?
—To manage your time?
—To diaper a baby?
—To understand abstract art?
—To train your pet?
—To ride a horse?
—To care for a child?
—To prepare a budget?
—To write a news release?
—To plan a meeting?

Questions: This time, make up your own questions, or just think a while about these "learnings" to examine your experience as a learner.

WHAT'S HAPPENING HERE?

Now, let's take a look at this exercise. As I went through it, I had trouble reaching what I knew to be its objective. The suggested "learnings" did take me back and get me thinking about how I had learned, but there was too much, and it came too fast. The questions piled on top of each other and made it difficult for me to answer for each "learning."

Did you have the same problem?

There's a built-in limitation here, the one-way communication of the printed word and the space restrictions that place items in such close juxtaposition. No pauses, no thinking time, no stimulation of sharing the "learnings" of others.

You might very well comment: "Look, Buster, if you knew the exercise had bugs in it, why did you put me through it?"

And I would answer, sheepishly, "Well, all I wanted to do was raise your awareness about your own 'learning.'" But this minor critique may do that as well as the exercise, because raising these shortcomings grows out of some awareness of how the mind works, the thought process of learning, i.e., that one needs time to think, that the mind can't jump back and forth from item to item and question to question without soon giving it up. And that is the kind of purview that is needed to gain the learner's perspective—putting yourself in her place, putting yourself through the thought process and examining it minutely, to find out if the method you are employing allows the learning process to flow, or clutters its path with obstacles.

A good way to acquire this perspective is to observe yourself, your own processing, when you are learning. We ought to take some training for ourselves once in a while, just to put ourselves on the receiving end and watch ourselves learning.

Robert Mager does this all the time, even on such unorthodox skills as learning to ride a unicycle, so there must be something to it. Even minor "learnings" that you seek without thinking about them can be opportunities to examine learning. Throughout many years of living alone, I have never found out how to fold a fitted sheet. Don't laugh, unless you know how. Finally, I asked my sister to show me how. She did, and I was amazed. The trick is to fold the sheet inside itself. She told me, she showed me, but she didn't let me try it myself. I still can't fold a fitted sheet.

The next time you put together some training for adult learners, visualize what it would be like if someone came along and told you that you were going to have to change roles and be a participant in your own training.

The Content Finders
Keepers Process

One of training's internecine feuds is the recurrent debate over which is more important, Process or Content. You can hardly escape getting drawn into it. My encounter with it got pretty sticky and in working my way out, I came across an approach to training adults that not only resolved the dilemma for me, but worked wonders in practice. There's nothing revolutionary about it, but it was new to me and maybe you can find something usable in it.

The arguments in the Process-Content quarrel are familiar enough. Some people contend that Content—the *what* of training—is paramount, so important that it diminishes everything else. Content will carry the day by its own weight; just don't get in its way. Those who dispute for Process—the *how* of training (more properly called method)—admit grudgingly that Content is important, but hold that Process is at least equally important. Without the *how*, they say, nobody will ever learn the *what*. "Ha!" sniffs the Content crowd, "without the *what* there wouldn't be any place for the *how*, so Content is supreme."

It's a winless argument, about like a parent being asked by the children: "Which one of us do you love the most?" If ever there was a case that is not either/or, but both/and, this is it.

Nevertheless, the debate goes on, heatedly at times. It can split a training staff into warring camps.

You can get caught on one side or the other of this hassle simply by representing your background, if you don't see it coming and think through your position. I joined a training organization after several years as a practitioner in the field we were training for. I knew the Content, but I knew nothing about Process. Automatically, I became an exponent of Content. The organization had wisely tried to mix practitioners from the field with specialists from adult education. It was, however, an uneasy marriage, with the practitioners pushing Content, because that was what they knew, and the training specialists pushing Process, because that was what they knew. Soon we were polarized. Our design meetings became battles in the Process-Content war, with the adversaries frequently backing themselves into extreme positions they had never intended to take.

Those extreme positions, in either Process or Content, are what perpetuate the conflict. The defenders of Content supreme, who usually lack familiarity with the methods of modern training, fall back on the more traditional modes of education. They take the academic posture that knowledge is power and thus is to be sought, to be dug out by arduous study in the classical pursuit of knowledge. Whether the student learns is mostly up to him. Content is offered—in books, lectures, laboratory experiments, and an occasional film—and the student is expected to grasp it, no matter how difficult. Indeed, some extremists believe that the more difficult the pursuit, the more valuable the knowledge. Hence, the accolades for the "tough teacher" (of *Paper Chase* fame), and the attendant assumption that to make learning too easy would be a disservice to the learner.

The Process camp followers usually are grounded in the more recently evolved technology of training. Training is of shorter duration, takes on less learning at a time, and reaches beyond the acquisition of cognitive knowledge to include the learning of skills and attitudes. Because time to learn is limited, training looks for the quickest, most efficient methods—the so-called laboratory techniques. Training doesn't mind making learning easy and pays more attention to the learner as a person, to those factors in human make-up that assist learning.

THE EXCESSES OF PROCESS

Although the extremists of Content look askance at efforts to make learning easy, the extremists of Process sometimes try so hard to assist the learner that they move beyond motivation to manipulation. Especially in the overweening stress on personal behavior does Process tread heavily.

My entanglement with the Process-Content confrontation came at the time when sensitivity training was in vogue. Out of the ken of interpersonal relations, Process trainers drew some valid concepts—the learner should have a supportive environment, be freed of personal resistance, and open to learning—but some went too far.

When Process is in excess, Content is all but forgotten and training sessions can degenerate into orgies of feeling. The facilitator is forever asking the all-purpose question: "How do you *feel?*" In the spirit of sharing, she volunteers how she feels, especially if it is a "negative" emotion, like anger. Participants are encouraged, even badgered, to open their psyches and pour out their most intimate concerns, in the name of openness and authenticity. After such pseudopsychiatric ventilation, the trainees are deemed to be divested of their emotional blockages and ready to learn.

There's an assumption that this sort of Process, with its emphasis on full participation and personal attention, is somehow more *democratic*, and therefore is superior to the autocratic domination of the Content traditionalist. Not necessarily so. Some Process tactics can be severely intimidating and freedom limiting. I've been in those head-feeling sessions where the facilitator sits stony and superior through endless silence while the pressure builds for somebody to break. The sensible folks say, "To hell with this," and walk out. The rest of us learn more than we care to know about the intricate pattern on the carpet we have been staring at so long. I didn't feel free until I got out of there.

Where the improvement of interpersonal relations is the primary objective of training, I can countenance the use of special methods, even the touchy-feely kind. It is when the subject is not interpersonal relations and Process trainers kept trying to make it that, jumping in with interventions like, "What is happening here, right now?" that I part company. What bothered me in my unwary observation was that there was much opening people up—at times revealing painful stress—but very little putting them back together again. I became suspicious of the motives of some of my colleagues, who seemed to be meeting a dark need of their own to see others exposed and vulnerable. The blind leading the blind.

All training is manipulative to some extent, but this only increases the responsibility of the trainer to protect the autonomy of persons in training. No rationale of personal growth is sufficient to justify emotional damage to people. Furthermore, training that is threatening to people fails to achieve its own purpose; trainees are closed up rather than opened up, prevented from learning.

It was this interference with learning that turned me against the extremes of Process. In the agency that I had managed, I had observed the same dysfunction. We had selected a number of indigenous neighborhood people to become community workers. I brought in an outside consultant for their training who convinced me that it should include ten hours a week of "self-awareness" discussions. At the end of their three month training period when we put them out into the field where they were supposed to help others, they flopped. They had become so introspective, so fixed in their self-awareness that they couldn't get unstuck enough to do much for others. In the next class of community workers we trained, we eliminated the self-awareness sessions and concentrated on the work to be done. That class performed admirably in the field.

A fellow trainer recounted a similar experience. He had been with an organization that provided continuous opportunities for the staff to unburden themselves. "It was great," he said. "We were so happy. We never got any work done, but we sure did feel good."

I suppose every trainer can relate a horror story about the abuse of sensitivity training. It is not my intent to indict that kind of training because I believe it has its place, and under the guidance of skilled and responsible leaders, it can be useful. It is also possible, even probable, that the Process training I experienced was an aberration, a misapplication of the method.

SEARCH FOR SYNTHESIS

Some good did come of the Process-Content conflict in which I participated. The confrontations knocked the abrasive edges off our hardened positions and we began to learn from each other. I was astonished to discover the egregious inefficiency of the lecture method. One of the stars in our Content crowd was an absolutely magnificent lecturer. His performances captivated his audiences, but afterward they would ask, "Do you happen to have a copy of that?" They were so enthralled with him they could hardly remember what he said, and posttests proved it.

Interestingly, I found it was easier for those of us on the Content side to acquire Process skills than it was for the Process trainers to get knowledgeable in Content. Later on in my training work, when I moved into assignments where I was unfamiliar with the Content, I found myself regarded as a Process specialist. I had to dig for the Content and learned the value of a mix of Content and Process specialists.

Every trainer, it seems to me, needs to resolve the Process-Content dichotomy in a way that takes her out of that disabling clamp of subordination to one or the other so that she can blend both. My endeavor to find that equilibrium led me on an odyssey of experimentation.

"Form follows content" became the watchword of my experiments. Content is essential. It is not only the beginning, it is the raison d'etre of training. Enabling the learner to gain the content *is* training. So finding the form that most advantageously transmits the content is obligatory, even if it is easier said than done. What I had heard from my Process adversaries about the need for a favorable climate for learning, the unfreezing of those cold blocks of resistance, and above all, making it possible for the learner to respond as a whole person, not just intellectually but physically and emotionally as well—made a lot of sense.

CASE METHOD

First, I tried case method. Our content was management, so I read the Harvard literature, the approach by the Wharton School, and the British business school approach of the "case within the case." In my best eclectic style, I tried it in practice.

I wrote a case for a curriculum unit on grantsmanship, "While You Are Up, Get Me A Grant." It was fictitious; I made up two agency directors, in similar circumstances, who were each going after a grant for identical purposes. One followed the eight rules of grantsmanship I had offered when I lectured on the subject. The other didn't. One did it the "right" way and the other the "wrong" way, although I fuzzed the different tactics to avoid being obvious.

In class, I gave each trainee a copy of the case with instructions to work on it individually. The case came to no conclusion but on the last page asked: "Which one do you believe got a grant? Why? Write down some reasons for your answer."

The first time I used the case, I wrote the eight rules on a flip chart that I kept covered while I processed the answers from the group. Those I wrote on a separate chart. When I uncovered mine and compared the two, to our mutual delight, they had hit every one of the points.

I used that case many times, with various procedures. Sometimes, I put the participants in dyads or triads to share their conclusions after their private work. Sometimes, I wrote their responses on a chalkboard and then put my phrasing of the same points underneath. Once, I waited until I got out all of their answers and then gave them a handout of my points, and let them tell me how right they were. Usually, I augmented what they told me with comments on each point. Discussion brought up other points and illustrations from their experience. The outcome was the same, no matter what variation I tried; they discovered the concepts I had written into the case for them to find.

From that case I learned several things:

- The trainees learned what I had for them to learn, without me "giving" it to them in a lecture.

- There was no resistance to the content or to me. The concepts of the case became their points, not mine.

- Every discussion was lively, with full participation.

- They added applications of the concepts that went beyond what I could have given them.

- Delivery of training that way is ridiculously easy; you just start it and let it roll.

- The clincher came from our evaluators. Pretests and posttests showed that this use of case method had recorded the highest standard deviation of any unit in our entire curriculum.

SIMULATION

Case method is just a step away from simulation, my next venture. For a unit on personnel administration, I pulled out all the stops—used case data, role play, group competition, and video tape. The case of *Harriet Singletary* v. *John Rider* involved a neighborhood center director, Singletary, who had been fired by Rider, a new broom executive who was sweeping his agency clean. She appeals her dismissal to the agency's personnel committee. The case question is whether the committee will sustain the dismissal or reinstate her.

Built into the case materials and narrative were fourteen errors in personnel administration—failure to give proper notice, insufficient cause, lack of documentation—the sort of blunders that could be grounds for Singletary's appeal. How much of this maladministration was detected would come out in the simulation's climax, a hearing before the personnel committee at which both Singletary and Rider, represented by attorneys, would make their cases for the committee to decide.

I carefully selected—cast is more like it—the trainees for the principal roles, and then coached them at length to get them "into" their characters. All participants who did not have a major part were assigned to be supporters of either Singletary or Rider, to assist in preparing for the hearing. I intentionally built conflict into the case. The simulation came in the second week of a two week seminar; by that time the breakout groups had established some identity, so I pitted them against each other behind the principals.

The case was introduced on a video taped newscast (taped the night before) in which Singletary and Rider were interviewed about the upcoming hearing. We distributed a file of materials to each trainee—agency bylaws, personnel policies, correspondence, Singletary's personnel file, and a case narrative. Later, I eliminated the narrative when I was satisfied that the video tape gave sufficient background.

While the two sides and the personnel committee were in their breakout rooms preparing for the hearing, we sent a reporter (a trainer) around to gather material for a later newscast, shown during a lunch break. We also video taped the entire committee hearing, which turned into something like a Perry Mason trial. I marked the tape, recording counter numbers at places where errors of the case were touched on, or missed. In the debriefing of the case, I could replay segments to let them literally *see* the teaching points.

A couple of runnings of the simulation showed me two important requirements. Ground rules had to stress that all participants, and the training staff, must stay in their roles for the duration of the case, to serve the illusion of reality. If a procedural question came up, a trainee could come to me, go "out of role" a bit like King's X in a game of tag and get the question answered, then go back "into role." And, in the very brief introduction before the case began, it was vital to let the trainees know that the outcome of the case was entirely up to them, that I had no idea how it would end.

The intense involvement and impact of Singletary-Rider was nothing less than amazing. At first, we ran it in morning long sessions on three consecutive days, but the folks got so immersed in their roles that the trainers holding afternoon sessions couldn't get them to concentrate on other topics. So we ran it continuously, beginning to end, for a day and a half. At that, I had to hold a three-hour decompression period afterward to bring the participants down from the exciting high they were on.

That simulation went a long way toward resolving the Process-Content hassle for me. It showed:

- People can be completely absorbed in learning if they are put on their own and the subject matter is realistic and interesting.
- Their behavior in simulations is holistic—emotional and physical as well as intellectual—when they can respond naturally to the content and are protected from direct revelations of their intimate selves.
- They learn far more than a trainer could manage from the shadings and insight evoked.
- The learning can be real—that is, practical. Several trainees contacted me after experiencing Singletary-Rider to say that the very situation, or something close to it, had occurred when they returned to their jobs. They felt as if they had been there before and knew what to do—which is, after all, what training is supposed to provide.
- Training can be fun; and simulation can pick up a slowly grinding seminar and get it zinging again.

A TOUCH OF REALITY

By now, I was getting warmed up to variations on the case method theme. I took a shot at the Wharton School executive participation technique. In this one, students are given an actual management problem in a real company. They get all the necessary data, study it, then devise a solution that they put into a short letter to the firm's chief executive. The executive later comes to the school and reacts to the student recommendations.

In my modification, I chose an agency beset with problems and visited the place to interview the executive, staff, and board members. "The Ironton Case" became a study in priority setting and problem solving. From data distributed to trainees, they were to identify the agency's problems, propose solutions, and put their corrective actions in priority order. They reduced this to writing and I mailed their conclusions to the executive. Before the end of the seminar, he showed up to respond to them personally.

There were some snags. The material was sufficient, but different people interpret data differently and management style makes a difference. There was usually agreement on the problems, but not on what to do about them or what to do first. With so many courses of action recommended, the visiting executive couldn't contribute more than his own hunches about results.

I let that case cool for a year, then visited the agency again, this time with a video crew. We set up interviews and simulated scenes for a before-and-after depiction of the case. As edited for training, the first half of the tape re-enacted the problem situation in the organization a year before. The second half showed the situation a year after, when the executive director had taken numerous actions to cure the agency's maladies.

In class, trainees viewed the problem presentation half of the tape, then did their analyses and wrote their prioritized solutions. After they finished their work, I showed them the other half of the tape, so they could compare their proposed actions with what the executive had actually done. Where their recommendations coincided with what the director had done, they could learn the consequences. Coming at the case this way made far better use of its reality than the earlier version.

The Ironton Case showed me:

- When learning is left for trainees to uncover, the concepts must be exact or empirically accepted—the so-called school solution. If one answer is as good as another, or the concepts are open to widely varying interpretation, training must take a tack that admits the absence of certitude.

- Television, film, video tape, or most any other audio-visual medium are not very efficient for transmitting sizable amounts of detailed data that must be retained for later use, especially if trainees get only one viewing. When facts and figures are needed, there is no substitute for written documents.

- There is incremental value in the "real" case, as opposed to the hypothetical, fictional one. Awareness that this "really happened" gives a case credibility.

BIRTH OF A MODEL

Did you ever notice when you are doing a presentation that the more you put into the preparation, the more rigid you are in giving it? You've got an investment to protect and you can get a tad impatient about questions that take you off track until you get all that heavily wrought, finely polished material put out for others to admire. That's the self-mesmerizing effect of the lecture method.

In my experiments, I discovered that the less ownership I had to claim for the content—especially in presenting it—the more I could get out of the way and leave the stuff some place where the trainees could find it—and the more anxious they were to go after it, almost take it away from me.

Wrapping the content around some unresolved problem or unfinished task that the learner can work out by acquiring the content provides strong motivation to investigate. When the trainee's solution is as defendable as the trainer's, the challenge is increased. The appeal of case method is that it has a detective story suspense that makes you read the book to solve the mystery.

The trainer cannot turn loose all control over the content. One time, I tried a form of team teaching by trainees. For a piece on personnel actions, I assigned subtopics—hiring, firing, organizing, motivating, and so on—to participant teams, gave them starter material and content outlines and told them to take some time to prepare and then to train the rest of the group any way they chose. I reserved the right to jump in with comments if they strayed too far. The resulting minisessions were animated, participative, and enjoyable. Participant evaluations of that unit were sky high. But I had my doubts. Most of the content that got covered was a recycling of their pet personnel practices. Fresh learning came only from a few participants who had new insights; the rest mostly rehashed the status quo. From that I concluded that handing over a training session to the trainees may be a noble expression of democracy, but it can also be an abdication of the trainer's responsibility. Enabling people to learn something they didn't know before is what a trainer is supposed to do. Some control over the content is mandatory, even if the control is indirect.

As I searched around for an escape route from the either-or prison of Process-Content, I became more and more impressed with the effectiveness of my reversal of trainer tell-and-show time, which I thought of as the "discovery" approach. I wasn't sophisticated enough about training then to realize that no model can pretend to legitimacy without a capitalized title and an acronym. So I have since dignified it as the Content Finders Keepers Process (CFKP).

CFKP is not entirely facetious. Over the years since its imaginative conception, its legitimacy has been verified. Not long ago, I used it in a piece called "Government and Media: Estranged Bedfellows" in a series of workshops for public officials. I had some solid content to offer from my fifteen years as a newspaperman. I found out quickly, however, that most public officials have been burned badly by the media at some time or other. They turned all my good stuff back on me in what became bitch sessions. Fine. I played it that way, reaching into my trusty CFKP bag. By giving them my media background at the beginning, I offered myself up as a target. Then I showed them a short video taped interview I'd done with an ombudsman for a major newspaper who talked about relations with government from the newspaper viewpoint. That's all it took for the fury to fly. As soon as I invited comment, they came out smoking. I stirred the caldron more by doing a walk around number, instead of hiding behind the podium.

Rather than them reacting to me, I reacted to them. For every gripe or rhetorical question, I had a response that came right out of my lecture material. We went at it, back and forth, for an hour and a half. By the end of the period, I had covered virtually every point in my material. For the most part, my contributions were direct responses to their complaints and permitted me to enlarge on each point. The sequence of the content was not orderly, but what I forsook in neat chronology, I gained in intensity.

Being put on the spot didn't bother me much. An adversary exchange between trainer and trainees can be singularly effective. It can also be a bomb, that produces more heat than light. In this case, I have reason to believe it worked, from feedback afterward and invitations to come out and do the piece for their back home crowd.

IMPLEMENTING THE MODEL

The Content Finders Keepers Process is not unique; it is just an approach that worked for me and I put a fanciful name on it. You have probably used the same approach, or some variation.

If you haven't tried it, here is a rough procedure:

- After you've done your beforehand chores—needs assessment, objectives, content review—reduce the content to the hard core concepts. Throw out all that nice-to-know stuff. The concepts have to be fairly concrete for "Finders Keepers" to work. If your subject matter is mushy or moot, try some other method.

- Find some carrier for your content—a case, simulation, exercise, programmed instruction, whatever. Make it as interesting and as close to the learner's world as possible. Bury your concepts in your training vehicle, but not so deep or disguised that they can't be recognized.

- Contrive a motivator, such as a problem to be solved, decision to be made, priorities to be set, competition to be won—something that requires trainees to find your buried concepts to fulfill the task. Nothing hokey; make it serious enough to earn their effort.

- When you start your session, dissociate yourself from the whole process as quickly and completely as you can. Lengthy task instruction just perpetuates your identity with the outcome. Handouts are good, because they have a neutral look, if not cluttered up with by-lines and organizational credits.

- Allow plenty of time for the trainees to work.

- When discussion time comes, use your best process skills to draw out their conclusions. Expect phrasing not like your own. After they have described what they have learned, add any points you think are necessary, but put down the temptation to let them know that you knew all the time how they would come out. Let them be the smug ones.

- If you get that "I already knew that" retort, live with it. You've heard it before; the pride of some participants requires it, even if it is all entirely new to them. In using CFKP, trainees can take such ownership of the content that they act as if they invented it.

- Most Finders Keepers sessions are hard to shut off. Allow for a rush of participation, then use your best closure tactic.

- Resist the urge to restore yourself as the expert at the end. Watch out for those closing remarks or summaries that are sneaky reminders that you know a lot more that didn't get covered. Let them have their triumph.

- Be advised, CFKP doesn't work for every topic. It's just one tool you can carry in your training kit.

To illustrate what I mean by the Finders-Keepers approach, I've included an example on the following pages. It's a case on the delegation of authority that I designed for a management seminar for community development directors from Micronesia, held in Hawaii. Later, I used it with other groups.

TYPHOON

The sky over Hawaii International Airport was beginning to darken and the wind was rising when Trans Pacific Flight 608 took off from Sidney, Australia, and United Flight 302 left Los Angeles, both bound for Hawaii. Weather reports from the islands told of local disturbances with rain and gusting winds, the usual situation for Pacific air travel.

The United flight was twenty-two minutes late in departing because the pilot, Captain Isaac Nelson, was a stickler for detail and insisted on doing the preflight checks himself, both cockpit and fuselage. "Never can be too careful," he told Second Officer Terry Hagan, the copilot. "An airplane like this, with over four hundred passengers, is a big responsibility. You can always make up the time en route if you get a break on the winds aloft."

The big 747 had a full passenger manifest, the routine collection of tourists, businessmen, Navy personnel, government officials, and a rock group called the Screamin' Meamies that was booked to play in a Honolulu hotel. The passengers were always restive at first, looking out over that endless expanse of ocean. If Diane Kosko, the head stewardess, didn't handle the FAA-required safety announcements right, some people would get all stirred up when she covered the part about ditching procedure. Captain Nelson sometimes made the announcement himself, because his voice had that reassuring tone.

He knew the passengers wouldn't really settle down until he did his walk-through of the cabin. So he concentrated on climbing to flight altitude before turning the controls over to Hagan. This always miffed the copilot, because climbing on course was no more complicated than straight and level flight, but it didn't bug Terry nearly as much as the fact that the captain would never let him make a landing. He'd been flying with Nelson over eight months now and had yet to log a landing, even those times when they were only carrying cargo.

"Take it, Terry," commanded Nelson after he had leveled off, in that authoritative voice that irritated the copilot. The captain stopped to check with Isamo Powell, the engineer, on his way to the passenger cabin. "Everything smooth, Sam?" The engineer pointed to a pressure gauge. "Running close to limits, sir," he said. "Well, keep your eye on it," said Nelson.

The captain's walk-through of the passenger cabin was an experience he enjoyed, and it seemed to do the passengers so much good. Diane and Kitti would accompany him through the first-class section, introducing him to almost everyone, especially any V.I.P.'s who happened to be on board. Then, Joyce and Natale would take him through the tourist cabin, pointing out special people or those who might be a little nervous. There were too many to speak to all of them, but he made his presence felt.

One lady rocked a baby who was obviously fitful. "Mrs. Newman would like to have the baby's bottle warmed. I told her we'd do that just as soon as you came back and we were on course," Natale explained. "Yes, by all means, go right ahead," the captain instructed.

The man in Seat 24 wanted to know what the movie was going to be and a boy asked how fast the plane was flying. Nelson had the answers. It was answering little things like that which gave passengers the feeling that he knew what he was doing and everything was fine.

When he got back up front to the flight deck, Sam was obviously worried. "That pressure has been over limits for eight minutes now. I'd like your permission to transfer tanks."

"Do it," said the captain.

The copilot seemed put out when the captain resumed his seat at the controls. "We're 10 minutes overdue on the radio check with Pacific Control," he said, "and the spanner is reporting turbulence this side of the islands."

Nelson grumbled and put on his head set. "Pacific Control, this is United 302. Do you read?"

The warning to rig for storm had gone out to vessels in the harbors throughout Hawaii and people in the cities scurried from place to place in that time-worn ritual of getting ready for a big blow. The sky was ominous and ugly now and the palm trees were bending noticeably in the wind. Ship to shore radios crackled with static.

Vince Caponiti, second officer of the Trans Pacific flight two hours out of Sidney, shifted the earphone forward on his head and said to Bruce Page, the captain, "Looks like we might be in for a bit of a blow. Port Moresby is reporting storm centers with gale-force winds closing on Hawaii."

"You don't say," answered Page. "See if you can get anything down route."

The copilot turned the dials on the radio console. "I think I can raise Wake or Saipan on the emergency frequency."

Page turned toward Noah Hart, the engineer navigator. Before the captain could say anything, Hart had anticipated him. "An hour and twenty minutes to point of no return. That is, for all the way back to Sid. Plenty of fuel if you want to find some nice cozy little island and sit out the blow."

"Thanks, Noah," said Page.

He rang the stewardess' signal bell and very soon Lori Arbogast, the chief stewardess, stuck her blonde head into the door of the cockpit. "What's up, captain?" she asked.

"Weather ahead," he told her. "May be bad. Better go into your calming routine."

"Will do," she nodded. "I have only two problems so far. A Mr. Clark from Toledo is air sick and has a heart condition. But we have a doctor on board and I've got him watching the heart and administering the Dramamine. And there's a sweet little old lady with her grandson who is scared because she's on her first flight, but she doesn't want the boy to know it. Sue and Doris are giving tender loving care."

"Good," said the captain. "No need to excite anybody with any alarming announcements from me. It's too early to tell how this is going to develop."

After Lori had left to go back to her passengers, Noah spoke up. "No problem with passengers with Lori and her gals in charge. She could hold a singing session through a typhoon."

"Yes," agreed Captain Page. "She's a lot better with the passengers than I am. And never rattles in an emergency."

The copilot tapped the captain's arm, "Get on Six Point Five," he said. "I've got Hawaii Control. This is what you need; I'll take the wheel."

Page listened intently for several minutes, then depressed his microphone and spoke crisply, "Hawaii Control. Hawaii Control. This is Trans Pacific 608 three hours west of your station. What is your weather situation? Over."

He listened as the radio control station responded, then thought a minute, lifted his hand to signal the copilot and engineer, and stated: "Looks serious. We'll go on Plan B Alert. Noah, monitor that fuel close and get me consumption on winds at 35 knots. There's some slack at 15,000 and I've got clearance to descend."

"Vince, call Lori and tell her the plan. Tell her to put away the booze but to go ahead with the movie. Hope it's a good one."

Wet black shadows now covered the island of Hawaii, howling winds whipping the shores and churning dark waves to white caps. Rain dashed hard on the land in sheets that swept like curtains coming down.

Traffic had thinned as people made for cover. Boats bounced in their moorings and a tug hurried for port.

The warning had gone out: Typhoon.

*   *   *

Which pilot would you rather be flying with, Captain Nelson or Captain Page? Why? What does he do or not do that is different from the other pilot? Write down your answers.

HOW THE "TYPHOON" CASE WAS HANDLED

No deep mystery here. If you don't want to get lost in the storm, you'll go with the delegator, Captain Page, despite any macho appeal of the lonely commander, Captain Nelson.

The overwhelming majority of trainees decide for Captain Page, although there are always a handful who prefer Captain Nelson, usually because they perceive some steadiness or maturity in him. He loses favor rather rapidly, though, when they hear the reasons why other trainees picked Captain Page.

These reasons translate into the training concepts built into the case, some common reasons for delegating or not delegating.

Reasons for Delegating

- More work gets done. An entire staff can do more than one executive.
- People learn how to do work. The boss doesn't have to do it again and again.
- Delegation permits the manager to manage. She can do what the executive gets paid to do—manage the work of others, provide leadership.
- Work gets done on time. More hands can do more in a shorter time than one person trying to do it all.
- Shared responsibility is generated.
- Work gets done when the boss is absent. The one person show is over when the only actor can't appear.

Excuses for Not Delegating

- Standards will drop if the executive doesn't do it. "The only way to get it done right is to do it yourself."
- The manager enjoys *doing* the work, rather than managing the work done by others.

- The manager has had a past failure in delegating.
- The leader wants to do things within his area of expertise, to remain comfortable and secure.
- The executive doesn't know *how* to delegate.

—————————PART THREE CHECKPOINT—————————

1. *Item:* Could it be that the careful way we approach adults in training is not so much out of respect for their maturity, but rather a recognition that they have lost much of the capacity for learning that they had as children?

   Judgment:

   Reasons:

2. *Item:* The catch in adult learning theory is that it doesn't always fit in practice.

   Judgment:

Agree		Neutral		Disagree
1	2	3	4	5

   Reasons:

3. *Item:* Despite a lot of trainer talk about how adults learn best, we seldom practice what we preach. How often do you give your trainees free rein over what and how they will learn? When was the last time you put your curriculum up for negotiation?

Judgment:

Reasons:

4. *Item:* "We don't really know how people learn."

   Judgment:

Agree		Neutral		Disagree
1	2	3	4	5

   Reasons:

5. *Item:* The trainer is, without question, the expert on *execution*, the forgotten factor in much research.

   Judgment:

Agree		Neutral		Disagree
1	2	3	4	5

   Reasons:

6. *Item:* We trainers are quite thorough about putting forth the "what" of training in all those goals and objectives, but we are not always forthcoming with answers to the "why should I learn this?" question.

Judgment:

      Agree   Neutral   Disagree

      1   2   3   4   5

Reasons:

7. *Item:* Adults come to class bringing their years of experience, but that contribution can cut two ways. It can enrich learning; it can also get in the way.

Judgment:

      Agree   Neutral   Disagree

      1   2   3   4   5

Reasons:

8. *Item:* It is not uncaring to suggest that a trainer is not a psychiatrist and should not try to fix every psychological problem she encounters.

Judgment:

      Agree   Neutral   Disagree

      1   2   3   4   5

Reasons:

9. *Item:* Don't you think it is odd that we have come to assume comfort and convenience are the crucial inducements to learning?

Judgment:

Reasons:

10. *Item:* Somehow, a vague presumption has crept into training that adults should not be required to work hard, that not too much should be demanded of them.

Judgment:

Agree		Neutral		Disagree
1	2	3	4	5

Reasons:

11. *Item:* When adroit means of unlearning fail, confrontation may be in order. This is when the trainer flatly and firmly tells the trainee, "You are wrong," and tells why, chapter and verse.

Judgment:

Agree		Neutral		Disagree
1	2	3	4	5

Reasons:

12. *Item:* When confrontation is indicated, I favor the one-two approach—one trainer knocks them down and another picks them up. One administers the unlearning tonic and the other is standing by to give comfort and support.

   Judgment: What do you think of this approach?

   Reasons:

13. *Item:* A trap that we trainers can fall into is to become so concentrated on training—what *we* do—that we lose sensitivity for learning—what *they* do.

   Judgment:

Agree		Neutral		Disagree
1	2	3	4	5

   Reasons:

14. *Item:* The chapter on Learning from Learning contained an exercise that asked you to recall "learnings" from your childhood, youth, and adulthood and reflect on them to gain awareness of the learner's perspective.

   Judgment: How would you rate the exercise?

Useful		Neutral		Useless
1	2	3	4	5

   Reasons:

15. *Item:* Every trainer needs to resolve the Process Content dichotomy in a way that takes her out of that disabling clamp of subordination to one or the other so that she can blend both.

    Judgment: How have you resolved the Process Content problem?

    Reasons:

16. *Item:* Did you ever notice when you are doing a presentation that the more you put into the preparation, the more rigid you are in giving it?

    Judgment:

    Reasons:

17. *Item:* "Typhoon" was a case exercise in the delegation of authority using the Content Finders Keepers Process.

    Judgment: How would you rate the "Typhoon" case?

Useful		Neutral		Useless
1	2	3	4	5

    Reasons:

Part
FOUR

THE PRODUCT

11

The 4-D Plan of Production

Plans for the production of training range from simple to complex. At one end of the continuum is the bare Assess-Design-Implement-Evaluate scheme. At the other is the baroque flow chart with boxes for every activity and yes-no decision trees with arrows marking the circuitous routes of action until the end loops back to the start.

Almost any generic planning technique can be applied to training production—PERT, Critical Path, six-step, seven-step, ten-step, etc. Most experienced trainers follow some sort of plan, often an amalgam of several others.

Plans are useful to put first things first and assuage the fear that everything is out of control. A plan also marks off stopping places for reporting and review.

The trouble with most plans is that they are not completely applicable. The budget step may get pulled out of its place in line and put up front because the organization is short on money and the first step is deciding whether you can afford to do any of the other steps. When several people are working on different steps, their tasks may get delayed beyond the meshing point. Some activities overlap or depend on other activities that have to be put off. Time crunches squeeze out some activities—many a curriculum gets well into design before the needs assessment analyses are finished. Plans are neat and orderly; production is not.

It could be, however, that a plan is necessary to know when you have departed from the plan. A production plan serves as an early warning system that tells you something is missing or late.

The 4-D Plan of Production I am going to follow here is one I have used in developing training, as much for its simplicity as anything else. Simple as it is, there's a good deal of overlapping. How can you carry out design without knowing something about the delivery conditions, for instance? I have found it more realistic to lump production into *phases*, when the steps or activities are primarily of one phase, but may include partial results or work from other phases.

The 4-D Plan, alliterated for easy remembering, is Define, Design, Develop, and Deliver.

Define. This phase is the equivalent of what is euphemistically called front end analysis—needs assessment, job analyses, competency studies, content review, and so on. The primary purpose of this phase is to define what you are going to produce.

Design. The Design phase is primarily a time of decision making. Data collected in the Define phase leads to selection of content, goals and objectives, participant selection, choices of methodology, arrangements for facilities, and other Design judgments. The end result is in outline form.

Develop. This is the hard work phase, developing the design. A time of heavy production, when outlines and intentions are turned into detailed, finished products, ready for delivery.

Deliver. Put-up-or-shut-up time, when all that has been defined, designed, and developed is delivered to a live group of trainees. The pay off.

12

THINGS TO DO...
1. FEED DOG
2. WATER PLANTS
3. CALL MOTHER
4. FILE TAXES
5. CLEAN FRIDGE
6. WASH SOX
7. POLISH SILVER
8. MAKE SHORTER LIST
9. DEFINE TRAINING PARAMETERS

Define

Getting started is an ambivalent transaction. When your project is no more than an unformed intention, it is both inviting and uninviting. There is so much to be done, such potential for new achievement, and so many places to goof.

If you just can't wait to get started, you may dive in anywhere, just to relieve the anxiety. If you're a master of procrastination like me, you activate your warm-up mechanism—water your plants, reconcile your bank statement, see that the light bulbs are working, consult your horoscope, count the clouds. When stalling reaches overpowering guilt, you, too, plunge in somewhere.

Once you get going, apprehension gives way to murk. Everything is so undone, so undecided. Whatever you begin depends upon knowing the results of something else that isn't begun yet. You know that starting off right prevents problems down the way, and it doesn't help a bit to know that.

It does help to have some end product in mind that can give some structure to the Define phase, or whatever you call your preplanning. The training strategy paper is such a tool.

You may have some other term for the strategy paper. It's the synopsis of all you have undertaken to firmly define the training product. The information you have gathered is summarized; the information that is missing and needed is mentioned. Major questions to be resolved and problems that will be confronted are listed. The general strategy you propose to reach the training goal is outlined. Although the strategy paper is a tentative analysis, it covers matters in sufficient detail to be understandable—mine usually run from twenty-five to forty pages.

The strategy paper serves two purposes. It gives discipline and a format to the work you do in the Define Phase and it becomes a planning paper that can be submitted to those who must give approval or those who will contribute to the training product. After it is revised from comments and corrections by others, it becomes a forecast of the work ahead of you.

But even before you get into the strategy paper, there are some preliminary questions to be considered:

Where did the proposal for training originate? If the idea that training should be done comes out of determined need—by organizational analysis, personnel appraisals, attitude surveys, job analysis, introduction of a new product or procedure—that tells the trainer a lot about how he can expect to proceed. On the other hand, if the idea comes down from higher authority as an unadorned order, or is decreed by someone with a vague conviction that "they need training," or is suggested because a good package is available, or others are doing it, that says something quite different to the trainer.

A training program decreed by the top brass may turn data collection into a pro forma exercise in substantiating what has been foreordained, or put the trainer in the position of carrying out orders even if the data don't support a genuine need. It is not unknown for training programs to be initiated for reasons other than need—to impress clients, to sell some organizational philosophy, or to satisfy some other hidden agenda.

Unfortunately, the people to be trained are not often the ones who originate the idea of training. Looking back over the training I have done, I was struck by how rarely the trainees had anything to do with its initiation.

There may not be much the trainer can do if the training project is a given, but giving some thought to where the idea came from helps her adjust her expectations and know what has to be overcome.

Is training the answer? This is a fairly standard question that must be asked, because if training is not the answer, the trainer is courting failure. The problem may be better addressed by other means—changes in procedure or personnel, restructuring or reorganization of work, or improved communications.

Is it worth it? Even if need is evident, will the investment of time and money to produce training make enough difference to be justified? Maybe this training is of low priority or will not be readily accepted. Not infrequently, training is aimed at a problem so severe that, though it will help, much more than training will be required. Tackling the impossible should be avoided.

If the project survives the preliminary questions, then other substantive questions must be answered in the defining period. A simple format that can start to shape a conglomerate of considerations is the journalistic five Ws and H—Who? What? Where? Why? and How? They can translate into headings for the strategy paper—Participants (Who), Content (What), Site (Where), Schedule (When), Rationale (Why), and Methodology (How).

Here are some questions to be addressed in the Define phase:

Why is this training necessary?   A rationale states the problem that training is to address—the big "Why?" Because it is a justification, documentation is advisable. Any studies, surveys, job analyses, preplanning meetings, product introductions, inquiries, or other research that has been done give substance to a clear statement of the problem.

If you are training to an organizational problem or program, more delineation will be needed than training for a job, where the need statement can be a fairly straightforward description of the skill or knowledge level expected.

That simplest of all planning models can help to outline the problem statement: What is the situation now? What should it be? What will it take to get there?

Some history of the problem is helpful, together with past measures for improvement. The rationale is also the place to put any hard questions that cannot be resolved by training, so expectations are kept reasonable.

What is to be learned?   Not just a bare description of the subject, which can be broad, but what part, what specific content is to be learned.

Content is not always self-evident; analysis may show that the subject is not what it appears. In planning for a workshop on the application of forensic science to police work, the subject appeared to be how to use forensic science. As we dug deeper, however, we uncovered dysfunctional disputes among the parties. The forensic scientists tended to look down on the police who were supposed to use their findings, the police didn't trust the scientists, and the scientists didn't talk to each other. The content had to switch from a transfer of research findings to a workshop on communications.

Occasionally it is necessary to set down a description of what is *not* to be learned, to delimit the subject matter.

How is the learning to be used?   The context or conditions under which the learning will be put into practice certainly influences training. Can training replicate the situation in the workplace or are there factors that will throw the training out of whack? What reception can the trainee expect from supervisors, colleagues, and clients?

A common problem I encountered in government training is the decision maker myth—the assumption that changes or new practices can be spread across the land by pulling in the chief authority persons for training, who will then go back home and implement the change, by fiat. Not only do many local structures deny such authority but even when it is present, the evidence is clear that change isn't that simple. The context in which learning is to be implemented is an integral part of training.

Who is to be trained?   For some training, the answer to this question is obvious—new employees, people who will carry out some new system, those whom the topic naturally selects. In other cases, participant selection can be endlessly debated. This is particularly true when training to a problem or program. I encountered it on the problem of unwanted teenage pregnancy. Who do you invite, the pregnant teen-agers, the fathers, their parents, all teen-agers, the youth serving agencies, teachers, counselors, media, clergy—who? All have a part in solving the problem.

In undertakings like that, someone will come up with the simplistic suggestion that the press and politicians are needed. Which politicians? Which members of the press? Publicity can help, but seldom solves a problem. Politicians usually act after some base of public support is built.

The same confusion can occur in implementing a new company policy or initiating a broad scale program. Choosing the right trainees may require some study of who is involved and that may produce some surprises. How often do you hear some trainee remark, "My boss ought to have this training." It's a valid comment and reflects the desirability of clustering participants—the boss *and* workers, whole departments, work units.

What is the goal of training?   At this point, it is probably too early to deal with objectives, but a definitive statement of the desired outcome should be written, so that it can be threshed out and agreed to by all concerned. Of course, the goal should be as specific as possible and address the training problem.

How is the training to be done?   This is the methodology question, which will be dealt with in detail in the Design phase, but some attention to methodology now is needed if only for cost predictions. If you'll need equipment demonstrations or special facilities or field trips, it helps to know now. If experts are to be brought in, that's both an expense and a scheduling matter. If prepackaged training is to be purchased or in-house capability to deliver is a factor, that needs to be stated early on.

The how-to question should be kept as open as possible so you don't get locked into a commitment to some technology, only to find later on that it is inappropriate.

Who will do the training?　An obvious question, but the answer can go to the matters of availability, time assignments, cost, and the search for special expertise.

Where is the training to be conducted?　Even if the answer here is obvious, declaring the need of the facility at this point helps with scheduling. If training is to be off-site, the business of logistics and bookings can be aided by as much advance notice as possible.

When will the training be done?　This is more than picking a date. Hard thought ought to go into how long it will take to produce an effective training result—two days, three days, a week; one session, a long session with a short follow-up, continuous classes? When duration has been settled, you can get out your calendar.

How will the training be evaluated?　At this point, formative evaluation may be all that can be considered, but whether evaluation is to be done in-house or by an external evaluator are cost and time factors.

What will the training cost?　This is the place to attach an estimated budget, the so-called ballpark configuration that nobody ever plays in. If your operation does not require cost breakdowns for each training event, it is still wise to mention any unusual expenses that can be anticipated.

Are there any special problems?　Occasionally there are, the kind that break out of the orthodox pattern and take special attention.

One I have encountered: will the invited participants come to the training? A similar one: will the season or the workload or some other involvement of the potential trainees interfere?

If this project is new or experimental, that should be acknowledged.

Next steps.　Assuming approval of the training strategy, what is the schedule for production? How long and who will be involved in design and development? A Gantt chart or other person loading display may be needed.

From reading your own strategy paper, you can draw up a work plan for the next phases of training production. The information that is lacking in the paper is disclosed as a data collection task.

Before, during, or after the time the strategy paper is written, you may hold planning conferences. If possible, include some candidates for training, to avoid a roomful of nonparticipants deciding how "they" ought to be trained.

A pilot test before a live audience or an in-house walk through should be part of your planning.

SUBMISSION FOR APPROVAL

Tentative as it may be, the value of the strategy paper is that it puts down your best judgment of how the training ought to go and raises up the sticky questions that have to be resolved. It can be submitted to management or sponsors for their advice, comment, and approval. It also serves as a planning document for all colleagues that will be involved and starts toward the consensus from them you need. Their reactions may be as important as the go-ahead from the boss.

When your strategy paper comes back down from on high, don't fuss over the comments. If they are weighty, you must deal with them. If not, it is easier to let the brass have their say now and get it over with.

If you get back a paper replete with corrections of typographical errors or mistakes in grammar, and little else, that is tacit approval. If the paper is heavily edited and the margins are full of terse observations for the first several pages, and hardly any after that, your reviewer ran out of gas or got in over his head with concerns that had never occurred to him before. In which case, you have done well.

13

Design

The consummate trainer savors the Design Phase because it offers the opportunity to use those powers of imagination and originality so often held in check. Design is the most creative part of training.

Two cautions should be made about trainer creativity. One is that it should be controlled and understated. Innovation in service to learning is a worthy contribution; sprayed around in indulgent display it is counterproductive. The caution is probably needless, because training has built-in restraints aplenty—the inertia of past practice, fear of violating some theory, pressure for results, limits of time and money, and conservative managements.

The other caution is against the opposite extreme—trainers should not be afraid to be creative, to try something new, even if it does sometimes go against tradition. That takes guts, because nothing is more disconcerting than a new idea. Innovators apt to risk criticism might take comfort from the words of Rod Serling, the superlative television writer of *Twilight Zone* fame who once delivered the penultimate put down to his critics by asking, "Where were you when the page was blank?"

The Design Phase is not a blank canvas. Two limiting concerns should govern:

Keep the goal before you.
Keep the learners always in mind.

The operative skill required now is to be able to juggle. All manner of options and alternatives are before you while new information is coming in that can change things around. You have to stay loose; this is no time to latch on to the first idea that comes along. Consider all possibilities and variations on possibilities. You can't tell now whether an alternative that seems remote might one day become just what you need. If your design doesn't work in its first try out and you have to redesign, the option you threw away earlier may be right. If your training population changes and you have to adjust, a new variation on an old theme that crossed your mind before may be the perfect fit for the new group.

The ideal design is one that, besides achieving the goal, is almost trainer-proof and has structure that is unnoticeable. If your design is so effective that even a lousy trainer can't louse it up, you will help him to shine, convinced it is his own brilliance. If your structure is so unobtrusive that trainees begin to wonder what, if anything, you had to do with the training, you may smile knowingly.

That's the trouble with design. Your very best work is apt to go unnoticed.

In this phase, shun the temptation to be a schedule monger. So many designers, those with a nervous need for order when things are uncertain, rush to put up charts of the training days and times and find no peace until every hour of every day is filled in with something, anything. Training is not filling time slots. The schedule should fit the training, not the training fit the schedule. If you can, it's a good idea even to ignore the number of training days until you know how long it takes to learn what must be learned. Then fight like crazy for the time needed.

In this treatment of the Design Phase, I'm going to take up some of the activities that occur during that time of creative confusion. This will not be a primer on design but rather some eyewitness observations that might increase your options. As you know, the tasks of design don't happen in tidy order; neither does my treatment of them.

DESIGN TEAM

Design is not always done by a team, of course, although the link between a curriculum developer and a delivery trainer is a form of teamwork. When the two don't know each other, such as the case of a training package purchased from a vendor, some redesign may be needed to make the package applicable. It ought to be exposed to the same questions and weighed against the same data as a design done from scratch.

When design is done by more than one person, some ground rules are in order. Some were covered in the chapter on The Trainer as Team Player. Here are some others:

- The design team needs a honcho, somebody in charge. Even in the most collegial organization, an acknowledged leader is needed to schedule and chair meetings, handle housekeeping, break deadlocks, and otherwise keep things going. If a leader is not administratively obvious, the team ought to agree on one.

- If at all possible, the team should include someone who represents the trainees. Letting the participants speak for themselves can do so much to keep the design relevant. It's tough to find someone for that role—even a single trainee can't represent all the others fully, but it's worth trying.

- If you've done a strategy paper, or some other first cut at design, the team should absorb it and shake it down in their first meetings. They should come to consensus on the goal, content, participant selection, and other essentials before going on to objectives and methods. All data collected so far should be shared; the team has to move from a common information base.

- When the known information plays out and more needs to be gathered, assignments can be made for individual work to be reported at the next meeting. The question to be decided is: Who does what by when? Some teams like to plow through the entire design process together, but I question this. Fatigue and group-think take over and crowd out better ideas that can come from individual reflection. A repeating cycle of separate work by team members shared and threshed out in team meetings is more productive.

- Periodic review points should be scheduled for quality control. These can be progress reports to the overseeing authority or merely checkpoints for the team to stop and take stock.

- When the time comes to pass out assignments of different pieces for members to outline, a natural selection process occurs that deserves to be questioned. The one with the most background or who has done that sort of thing in the past usually gets chosen. But familiarity with the content isn't quite enough; that trainer may be weak on methodology. Pairing trainers on a topic is a way to close this gap; one strong on Content, working with one strong on Process.

NEEDS ASSESSMENT

Few investigations offer us more guidance in design than needs assessments and yet none do we seem to neglect more. Certainly it is not for lack of techniques or sources. Perhaps it is because there are too many—job monitoring, performance surveys, competency models, assessment centers, observation, records and files, time and motion studies, critical incident analysis, visitations, questionnaires, key person consultations, evaluation, and so on.

Help from the literature is ample, too. Two good examples are *Human Resources Development: The Theory and Practice of Need Assessment*, by

Francis L. Ulschak (Reston, 1983); and *Figuring Things Out*, by Tom Kramlinger and Ron Zemke (Addison-Wesley, 1982).

By my reckoning, needs analysis has three critical elements—the person to be trained, the performance to be learned, and the place in which the performance is to be carried out. What appears to happen is that stress is made to collect information on one or two of the elements and the third is all but ignored. I cringe when I think of the programs I have been involved in that gave exhaustive attention to what was to be learned to achieve the desired performance—but only cursory attention to the persons to be trained, and none at all to the places they came from.

We may overspecialize on our favorite device for data collection, too, presuming that all techniques produce the same information. The questionnaire is an example. I once had the benefit of a direct comparison of information collected by questionnaire and by interviews. We circulated questionnaires for needs information for a possible seminar on personnel administration. We got them back, analyzed them, and then—to make sure our information was valid—made site visits to a selected number of the same clients we had surveyed by mail. The difference in responses was astounding. From reading some of the completed questionnaires, you'd have thought that the candidates for training were blooming experts on the topic. In our interviews—supported by a look at some of their personnel procedures—we found they had claimed knowledge and skill they simply didn't have. The Hawthorne effect in those questionnaires was steep and I refuse to charge it off to improper instrumentation.

My preference is a kind of case study approach, because it can combine several techniques—on site observation and in-person interviews, study of germane documents and work samples, with some critical incidents thrown in. While I agree that data collection should be somewhat standardized, such as structured interviews, that can be overemphasized. A certain amount of fishing around can turn up important information that would be missed by properly confined instruments.

Objectivity can sometimes be a straitjacket. Haven't you ever come across some factor or condition during an analysis that was not anticipated because you were not looking for it? The temptation is to dismiss it, but it could be critical. Trainer judgment, particularly that of the consummate trainer, is more trustworthy than our systems will admit. Even the most scientifically acquired data needs the application of human judgment for analysis and I am ready to assign the trainer more responsibility for examining the needs situation through the perception of her own insight. Supported by study, the trainer is the ultimate judge of the content to be supplied, what the trainee needs to learn. And why not? If the trainer is not the final word on training, what is he for?

In structuring my judgment, I have come to rely on that simplest of all definitions of learning as Knowledge (Cognitive), Skill (Motoric), and Attitude (Affective). I shorthand it to: what does the learner need *to know*, *to do*, and *to be*? When probing for the present resources of the trainee, the questions become: what does she *know* now, what can she *do* now, what can she *be* now?

Accurate needs assessments depend upon asking the right questions, and asking them in the right places.

GOALS AND OBJECTIVES

A caveat is necessary here; I do not follow the conventional wisdom on the value and necessity of goals and objectives. You may want to keep my oddball attitude in mind in reading this.

My quarrel is not with goals, those statements of overall purpose— but with *specific* objectives—whether they be called behavioral, terminal, or performance—and the use of them. To begin with, the very writing of objectives is arbitrary and inexact. It is the quantification that makes them so ludicrous. Who is to say that if the participants list six of the causes of inflation or identify nine ways to skin a cat that they have learned? The demand to "show results," undeniable as that may be, pressures us to forget everything else we know about learning.

If we believe what we say about individual patterns of learning, that it is not always linear or precise, why do we insist upon a one-and-only route to learning? Is it not possible for a learner to arrive at the goal without completing the exact numbers we put in the objectives? Or to achieve all of them and more and yet not reach the goal?

The irony of it is how seldom measurable objectives get measured.

My primary peeve is the practice of announcing objectives at the outset of training. It seems almost arrogant if not foolhardy to inform trainees that they will learn this or that. How do we know they will?

At best, the completion of specific objectives can be only an *indication* of learning. That much, and only that much, can be helpful. Moreover, my reading of the research on the effect of objectives on learning does not support an unqualified faith in them; in fact, it comes down slightly against them.

Isn't the underlying purpose of objectives to give intention and direction to training? Used this way, they can be of inestimable value to the trainer. Without them, the trainer is flying blind. So in my book, objectives are fundamentally for the trainer, not the trainee.

Some trainers feel that announcing the objectives at the beginning is simply a way of stating their intentions, or hopes, for the session. That's honest enough. But sometimes, objectives cannot be shared with trainees. I once wrote, as a *trainer's* objective, "to disabuse participants of the notion that their jurisdictions are protected against corruption simply because there are some laws on the books." That was my intention—hidden agenda if you prefer—and to reveal it might have made it impossible to achieve.

I still play the numbers game, when the rules are laid down by others. And I have had some success in separating goals from objectives—giving goals to the participants and keeping objectives for the guidance of the trainer. Even objectives-crazy sponsors of training go along with this, because they never had much thought of measuring the objectives, anyhow. At the end of this chapter, I have appended some formats for face sheets describing curriculum units which show this separation of goals and objectives.

PARTICIPANTS

If the "right" participants—those who should be trained to solve the training problem you are addressing—have been selected in the earlier Define Phase and your needs assessments have turned up sufficient data, it is possible to compile a general description of your training population. From the same data, you may also draw a profile of a prototype trainee. This person is nonexistent, of course, but keeping the "typical" trainee in mind sharpens your focus in design.

You may follow the practice of compiling a dossier on each trainee. This information should be shared with trainers who lead breakout groups.

The clustering of participants is a design decision. There are many arrays—geographic mix or separation, urban-rural or urban only or rural only, by organizational unit, by work assignment or position, cross sectional, special need or interest, random, or for a special training purpose.

Some trainers have favorite clusters that they repeat time after time for no good reason. The rationale for some clusterings is problematical— is it better to keep likes together for their comfort, or to mix them with unlikes for stimulation and exchange of viewpoints?

Some rules of thumb:

- Grouping of participants should be an intentional decision to serve a training purpose.

- People who should share the same learning to use it effectively in practice should be grouped together.

That last one can be a little delicate. Putting bosses and workers together can rattle the chain of command. If it is done, it should be a fairly even split of authority types and working stiffs; it's not fair to outnumber one or the other.

It goes without saying that the welfare of participants should be paramount in designing training. For instance, special arrangements should be made for handicapped persons, who now make up about ten per cent of our population. Occasionally, a quandary will come up in design that requires a decision for which there is no ready reason to move one way or the other. That's one to decide on the basis of whatever is best for the learners.

CONTENT ANALYSIS

Remember the little girl who wrote in her book report, "This book told me more than I cared to know about elephants." That's the way it is when you're reviewing content. But more is better than less.

Research is re-searching, looking further to find more and better resources, from both print and persons. There is almost never enough if you are after the context of content, those major and minor details that lend authenticity to design.

When you get that mass of material, the problem is narrowing it down, winnowing. It has been said that writing is actually *selecting*, deciding what to put in and what to leave out. Content analysis is that way. You have to keep your goal and needs analysis at hand as criteria for what to keep and what to pass up. You have to be brutal about separating the essential from the nonessential. You have to shake out "hard" content from "soft" content—and in deselecting, not take all the zing out of the content so what you have left is lifeless and boring.

Not easy.

At some point, an outline becomes necessary. I don't find the standard academic outline—with its alphabetical and numerical format—to be very useful because it forces a rank ordering by significance or chronology. Writers sometimes use a "spoke outline"—a diagram with the main concept (goal) in a small circle in the center of a page and connecting concepts listed on spokes emanating from the center. It's a gestalt, a way of seeing the whole thing on one page.

Content analysis during design is the meeting place of Content and Process. The limitations of methodology become an influence on the way content is organized. If you are lecturing, maybe you can start out with definitions of terms, historical background, state of the art, and then a chronological unfolding of the rest. But if you are designing for a case study or simulation, you may have to hold back some of content so the trainees can find it for themselves. Your outline will look quite different in that case.

Trainers with an academic bent like to lay a paradigm or matrix over content as a way of seeing the "whole picture." Difficulty is, it takes some straining and squeezing to fit everything into the mold. The result may bring intellectual happiness but have little to do with reality. Learners are less picky about the neatness of content, in my view. If it works into a pleasing paradigm, fine; if not, chuck it.

When content is viewed as *functional*, it becomes easier to organize for learning. How can this be used leads to how can it be learned? Learnable pieces are seldom discrete, because function flows from unit to unit, overlapping and repeating. Some concepts bear repeating, in different form. It's a mistake to assume that material covered once has been learned.

METHODOLOGY

Choosing the best methods for the most learning ought to be one of the quintessential skills of the trainer. The literature gives goodly advice on selection of appropriate methodology. And yet, all too often, designers fall back on the familiar, predominately a lecture with overhead transparencies and some time for questions.

Methods get picked for the wrong reasons—because we've done it that way before and it worked; because it's the quickest way to cover the material, that is, lecture; maybe we happen to have a package or the equipment available, or we have a hotshot speaker.

Methods selection should be a careful decision, with the goal of training paramount, the trainees in mind, and awareness of what use is to be made of the learning. Whatever method comes closest to ultimate use is preferable.

It's not a question of choosing the right method, but the right methods, in combination with others used in the same unit and other units. There are models that are worth following. Technical training's classic pattern of tell-show-do-review is simple; it works, and implies methods for each stage.

Unfortunately, poor methods selection can be blamed on not exploring enough options. That results, later, in the sad comment, "It never occurred to me." To prevent that ever happening to you, at the end of this chapter I have appended a list called Ninety-Two Ways to Train, an everything-but-the-kitchen-sink collection of every conceivable method I could lay my hands on.

PACE, FLOW, AND LINKAGE

My nomination for the worst advice ever given to trainers is that hoary platitude: "Tell 'em what you're gonna tell 'em, tell 'em, and then tell 'em what you told 'em."

Actually, the phrase has been dragged into training from homiletics. Preachers were advised to sermonize that way, the quotation attributed to some "good, old, country preacher." It's not even good advice for preachers. Those who follow it can only help tired members of their congregation catch up on their sleep.

What's wrong with this manner of presentation is that it is too pat, too predigested, too contained. It closes out the receiver; there is nothing for her to do, all has been done by the presenter. The presentation may be easy to remember, but it is also easy to forget. The listener has had no part in it, no questions to resolve, no applications to be made, no internalization.

Training that is too neat risks the same dismissability. When new ideas, new behavior are being tried out, things can get messy; it's the struggle of learning. Unresolved problems and unmet needs can actually stimulate interest; it used to be called learning dissatisfaction. The suspense in drama that keeps us paying attention is what we don't know yet, the same condition that compels learners to keep working on case problems.

I've known trainers to get upset at the end of the first day of a several day seminar because we hadn't reached "closure," when all loose ends are tied up. Closure is the trainer's need. Trainees that knew little or nothing to start with are not particularly disturbed that all is not revealed immediately.

Pace in training means change of pace, avoiding the deadly predictable sameness that shortens attention spans. Methods should be varied from session to session. Trainers should be alternated. Room arrangements should be changed periodically. Just working off a different wall—putting the podium and charts in a different place—freshens the perspective.

There's some good unwritten rules about flow. Never give a lecture after lunch; that's the time for something active. Allow time for digestion of heavy content; build in mental rest periods. After units that require intense concentration, follow with a frothy, brief interlude that demands no mental exertion. Count on the trail off of interest at the end of the day or the end of several days and don't put any imperative subjects there.

Overall flow can be structured in design. One progression is from the familiar to the unfamiliar. Another is from directive to nondirective.

More standard flows are from theory to practice or from problem to solution.

It has never bothered me to break flow, although some of my colleagues throw conniptions at this. I inserted a unit once that the building block approach would have saved for later, merely because it was a winner that the trainees could succeed on easily, and I felt an early success was needed. Occasionally, an out-of-sync piece can shake up a nodding off participant group.

Linkage is a harped on matter that we usually observe by transitions—brief little add on speeches about what is to come next and start off comments about what has gone before. The irony escapes us that it is always the trainers making the linkages. If they are as important as we tend to believe, why not look to the learners to make the link-ups, spontaneously or through some feedback mechanism?

TIME ALLOCATIONS

In other places, I have harangued on accurately timing the duration of curriculum units, especially those involving work by participants. I have also put stress on letting the training dictate the time allotted. (How is that for linkage?) Training time is precious and inexorably real. We tend to pack it, ignoring allowances for inevitable interruptions and even discussion. When the bind strikes, it's the trainees' time that gets cut, not ours. A rather obvious resolution: don't bite off so much. This may not be true with you, but the longer I train, the less I try to cover. Better that they really learn a few essentials than get swarmed over with a smattering of ignorance.

In allocating time for training, we have to consider variations in events. The range is wide—single day, two days, two and a half days, three days, a week, two weeks, and so on. One or two hour sessions once a week for an extended time. Split sessions are worth considering. I designed a Navy training event that called for two and a half day meetings with a six week interval between during which the trainees gathered on-the-job case material they had been directed to in the first session and which they worked on in the second. Another split is the elementary, middle, and advanced level spaced several months apart.

Contact with trainees between split sessions is rare but an interesting idea. Talks by telephone, giving them cassettes to hear at home or in the car, and follow-on correspondence are ways to continue learning and keep the interest level high.

The question that always occurs to me—and makes me wonder why it occurs to nobody else—is why we trainers put all our faith in one shot training? One conference, one workshop, one seminar seems to be all we ever devote to one subject, however complex. Surely we realize that no one can learn all there is to know about some subjects in a day or two, but we continue to take on complex content, knowing the best we can do is give them hardly enough to get by. And wonder why training is not always effective.

One more matter: contract time. If you have used this tactic, you know how effective it is. You make a contract with the trainees at the outset. Your part is to begin each session on time and to end on time, no matter what. The only way you will run overtime is with their permission. Their part is to be in their seats, ready to go, at starting time. It works so well you never have to worry about running over; they start calling "contract time" on you. It also gets them there on time.

MATERIALS

During design, concern about materials is largely what will be needed. Standard materials for most training are participant manuals, handouts, agendas, and the like. Your design tells you what others you'll need, as well as what equipment will be necessary.

Toward the end of the Design Phase, you may move to outlines of curriculum units, perhaps by the trainers who will develop and deliver them. Those outlines can be modified for inclusion in the handbook and serve as a format for complete development.

LOGISTICS

Also evolving from design are logistical requirements—space, travel and housing accommodations, dates, letters of invitation, and so on.

Picking dates is an exasperating tradeoff between what you want and what you can get. Availability of facilities is often a determinant and as much advance notice as possible is advisable.

Among dates to avoid: major holidays, big sporting events like the World Series and Super Bowl, heavy work periods such as the end of the fiscal year or budget making time, and in some parts of the country, the advent of bad weather. The dates we avoid for conventional reasons are not always bad. Summer is shunned because of vacations, but I have found summer to be no deterrent, except for August, the heaviest vacation month. Conventions are sometimes dodged as drawing off attendance, but it is also possible to hook a training conference before or after a convention.

When training people in-house, the problem is taking them off the job or away during heavy work periods. Splitting time for training between the employees and employer works for some—half an hour before work and half an hour on company time, or the same split after work.

THE FISHERMAN'S DAY

A Job Analysis

The standard techniques for analyzing a job—observation, time and motion study, job description, interview—are thorough, but time consuming. A quicker technique for obtaining job information is simply to ask the worker to describe his day, step by step. From this response, task statements can be written and training needs determined.

No day is entirely typical, so questions should be asked about variations. This list breaks down the workday of a fisherman from the Marshall Islands into its sequential parts. The information was obtained in a one-hour interview.

- Got information on when fish are biting.
- Checked out boat engine, fuel, and water supply.
- Rigged gear—lures, hooks, lines.
- Drove boat to fuel dock, filled fuel tank.
- Drove boat out channel to open sea.
- Watched for birds, followed them.
- Observed birds taking bait fish.
- Circled bird flock, put out trawling lines.
- Trawled, pulled in fish that were caught.
- When fish stopped biting, watched for birds moving to another school of fish.
- Followed birds to school of fish.
- Checked time to assure fuel supply would be adequate for return to dock.

- Circled flock of birds, caught more fish.
- Checked time to make sure return trip could be made before fish market closed at 8:00 P.M.
- Drifted and made entries on expenses, fuel consumption, catch, and fish sales in log book. Recorded time of oil change and fuel pump replacement.
- Called station on CB radio for weather report.
- Started boat trip back to dock.
- Stopped engine, drifted, and cleaned fish.
- Drove boat back to dock.
- Unloaded fish, carried them to fish market, and sold them.
- Returned to dock, drove boat to buoy in harbor.
- Tied boat to buoy, rowed dinghy to dock.
- Stowed gear.
- Returned home.

NINETY-TWO WAYS TO TRAIN

This is a raw list of methods, techniques, processes, devices, and assorted other ways to conduct training. They appear in no set order, although they are roughly clustered as methods for groups, for individuals, for trainers, and audio-visual aids. The definitions are loose, not all combinations are covered, and some methods are repeated. The purpose of the list is to describe as many options as possible.

Group clusters.   Dyads, triads, small groups, plenary; splits by occupation, community, region, cross section, need, or special interest; elective choice or alternating splits; buzz groups, cracker barrel. Identified by colors, letters, titles, or function.

Getting acquainted exercises.   Icebreakers, warm-ups, climate setting, familiarization; methods to help people get to know each other and get comfortable.

Structured learning experiences.   A variety of activities for a variety of objectives, as epitomized in *A Handbook of Structured Experiences for Human Relations Training*, by J. William Pfeiffer and John E. Jones (University Associates, San Diego), from which process can be lifted and used to achieve other objectives or content altered to fit.

Exercises. Sundry tasks for groups or individuals, usually intended to apply or internalize content, generally instructed by trainer and performed as group work. Designed or patterned to specific content.

Dyadic encounter. A one-on-one exchange between trainees who follow a programmed format by finishing incomplete statements that are provided, ranging from "My name and home town are . . . " to "My most frequent day dreams are about . . . " Can be used for opening up or skill building and can be controlled as to depth of probing.

Nominal group technique. Information or opinion gathering process that permits an individual to record responses to inquiries before sharing with group, thus reducing group pressure to conform.

Role play. Exercise in which participants improvise behavior of assigned, fictitious roles, interacting spontaneously with others to demonstrate or experience some condition or objective. Can be used for single purpose or in sequence to cover several situations.

Role reversal. Role play in which participants are intentionally assigned roles different or opposite from those they normally fill, to understand the viewpoint of other role.

Fish bowl. Role play in which players are observed by others, who may take over role of any player to make a contribution, but must continue in that role until replaced.

Case method. Case problems, hypotheticals, critical incidents; use of data from life or work situations, real or fictitious, to discuss, act on, or solve problems. Can be presented by paper materials, by audio-visual devices, or in role play.

Simulations. Similar to case method in that performance resembles actual situations or skills, with outcome dependent upon performance of trainees. Used for skill practice, sometimes with sophisticated equipment such as Link trainer, mockups of machinery, or programmed computer. Can be acted out as role play.

Games. Played by groups usually in competition, such as management games pitting one team against another, or to experience group interaction, such as the NASA game, Who Shall Survive? or the Kidney Machine, in which crisis decisions must be made. Games can be linked to computers that instantly report scores or outcomes. Grid games, of the

Monopoly or Parcheesi format, can be designed for decision making or values testing. Games can be as simple as Treasure Hunt and as involved as days-long community-planning exercises.

Puzzles, toys, artifacts. Generally employed as miniature tasks to illustrate a larger function, such as building model cars, making sculptures with Tinker Toys, or assembling an object to experience teamwork. Whistles, funny hats, noisemakers, masks, costumes, and other zany items can be used to give emphasis or fun.

Behavior modeling. Or role model, a live illustration of the desired performance, such as a properly conducted interview or personnel appraisal, or a demonstration of a master performer at work. Sometimes reduced to written description of model behavior.

Brainstorming. A search for new ideas by freewheeling sharing of imagining from group, with a rule against negative judgments, sometimes prevented by blowing a whistle or horn. More limited variation is laundry listing, the processing of contributions on a topic and listing on chart or chalkboard.

Microteaching. Singling out a discrete part of a larger function for attention, scaled to reduce complexities, with feedback at the conclusion of each episode.

Delphi. A systematic process for collecting opinions, often in long-range forecasting, from a number of persons, by submitting a question or scenario to each for separate response, compiling the responses, and resubmitting the results to the participants, who may alter their original responses. Several rounds of resubmissions can bring consensus not possible with other methods. Can be adapted to other uses.

Trips, tours, client visits. Field trips to see a program or performance in action, or visits to several sites involved in the content of training. Where training is for work with a specific client, such as disturbed child or purchasing agent, visits are arranged for live interaction.

Retreats. Session held way from work place, removed from usual setting for more freedom or intensive concentration. Also any intended change of environment for training purpose.

Report out, feedback. Participant reports on conclusions or progress at the end of group work, with or without reaction.

Debriefing, critiques.   Discussions of training experience for reflection, summarizing, and evaluation. Can be used as participant evaluation of training. Often used by trainers to evaluate their performance.

Trainerless laboratory.   Method of presenting training without trainers, sometimes facetiously suggested, in which participants are left entirely on their own. Can be employed at points in session when trainees are not informed that trainer will be absent.

Trainee teaching.   Presentation of content by trainees, with minimal guidance. Can disclose level of current knowledge or practice.

Rumor clinic.   Exercise in distortion or misinformation by exposing selected participants to verbal story or to picture, which they describe to others who have not been exposed. Repeated retelling usually brings distortion or exaggeration.

Recreation, social hours.   Leisure time activities, such as sports or games, or informal group gatherings like the happy hour, useful in team building and the sharing of learning.

Advance assignments.   Pretraining preparation distributed to participants, such as readings, cases, exercises, and overviews.

Manuals.   Also known as handbooks or workbooks, distributed to participants as text and reference. Trainer's manuals are more detailed and process oriented.

Handouts.   Diverse paper materials, usually not part of manual, given to trainees at various times, usually pertaining to a curriculum unit.

References.   Books, articles, and other background information cited in bibliographies or made available for information or optional use.

Question sheets, questionnaires, self-tests.   Form of handouts requiring action other than reading.

Checklists.   A prompting or guidance form of handout.

Kits.   An assembly of materials, often for a single subject or purpose, for study or action by participants.

Job aids, work samples, prototypes.   Work products, actual or models, that illustrate how work should be done and how end product will appear. Includes manufactured or processed objects.

Library. Collection of reference or background materials made available in designated place for use by learners.

Bibliographies, glossaries. Generally included in manuals but sometimes distributed separately.

Book reviews. Presented orally during training or provided as an expanded bibliography.

Practice. Opportunities to repeat learned skills as part of training or available in free time.

Drill. Similar to practice but usually structured as part of curriculum.

Study. Assigned or open time for trainees to read or prepare, alone or with other participants.

Electives. Offerings of supplementary or additional topics; can be requested by trainees, sometimes on noncurriculum time. Can be for selection by trainee from several simultaneous offerings.

Coaching, tutoring. Individual attention for trainees, informal or structured. May be on the job or part of training.

Observations. Opportunities for learners to observe behavior or skill practiced by master performer, or to see program or procedure in operation. Sometimes with preparatory instruction and report back.

Programmed instruction. Technique that permits trainee to study content and respond to questions, with answers given that instruct him to proceed if correct or return to earlier question if incorrect or divergent from general answer. Self-paced and immediately re-enforcing. Can show probable consequences of selected courses of action.

Computer assisted instruction. Generally regarded as programmed instruction using a computer, but continuously expanding in other uses, such as simulation, case studies, and dialogue programs. Data base can provide mathematical computations, comparisons, graphics, flow charts, decision consequences, and self-generated learning.

Mental imagery. Technique that asks participants to construct pictures in the mind to create a mental experience of some act or situation. Skill rehearsals allow mental practice of goal directed performance.

In basket exercises.   Simulation of a workday through progressive submission to trainee of items commonly found in desk in-basket, such as letters, memos, telephone messages, reports requiring action, delegation, and problem solving. Accumulation and increased intensity of items can cause stressful demands. Includes critique or group discussion after exercise. Can be presented by film.

Action maze.   Similar to programmed instruction; incident is presented with alternatives for action with consequences depicted on subsequent pages, with additional information and new set of alternatives that can lead back to start or to dead end.

Latent image.   Case problems or questions given on specially treated paper with place for marking answer by rubbing with chemical marker that reveals correct answer.

Predictions.   Participants given hypothetical condition or problem are asked to predict outcomes of forms of corrective action, generating discussion.

Note taking.   Common practice of recording content in listener's own words and form, sometimes illustrated with doodles. Effect on learner depends upon individual.

Action plans.   Participants declare what they plan to do with what they have learned, usually written at conclusion of training.

Participant presentations.   Units assigned and presented by one or more participants who may have special knowledge or experience. May include skill demonstrations.

Introductions.   Acquainting participants with each other and with trainers or special speakers. Can be done by advance mail.

Pretraining interviews.   Trainer conversation with trainees, individually or in groups, to elicit background information and gain familiarity. Can serve as last minute needs assessment or evoke case study material.

Task instructions.   Process and goal of exercise explained prior to group or individual work, usually crucial to successful execution.

Drama.   Content presentations or climate building through skits, satire, parodies, fantasies, or analogies.

Demonstrations.   Showing of skills by master performer or use of equipment, can be reversed to demonstrate wrong procedures.

Debate.   Discussion of opposite sides of issue, among participants or trainers, to delineate differences.

Panel discussions.   Different viewpoints and experience presented by small group of participants or trainers, sometimes with audience participation.

Interview with expert.   Trainer or participant conducts dialogue with content specialist to increase informality and address relevant questions.

Mock proceedings.   Improvised staging of event, such as trial, budget hearing, or staff meeting. Can be performed by trainers if specific points are to be stressed, or as role play by participants.

Questions and answers.   Opportunities for learners to question presenter and receive answers to inquiries. Can occur periodically or be reserved for special time.

Guided discussion.   Euphemistic term for greater trainer control over group discussion, but can describe stopping at frequent points during presentation to permit questions and comments.

Lectures.   Verbal presentation of content, usually with visual aids. Sometimes described as lecturette by trainers sensitive about too much lecturing.

Feedback.   Used interchangeably to describe reaction by trainer to trainee or by trainee to trainer, negative or positive. Can be gauge of trainee progress and comprehension.

Jokes, anecdotes, stories.   Levity that is often retained when all else is forgotten. Can be useful as vivid illustration of content.

Success stories, status builders.   Positive examples of performance or use of content, can serve as climate setting or upbuilding for trainees with negative self-esteem.

Audio-visual production.   Trainer role in designing and developing any audio-visual medium for specific content, such as films, video tapes, slides, transparencies, charts, recordings, and delivery mechanisms such as teleconferences and computer assisted instruction.

Films, video tapes. Media produced by others to provide overview, background, or aspect of topic, presented dramatically, or to immerse viewers quickly. Sometimes with prefilm preparation and postfilm discussions. Requires previewing and selection.

Stop film. A technique of showing part of a film or tape, stopping for discussion or work, and then showing remainder.

Video tape. Because of reasonable expense, portability, and ease of operation, provides endless variety of uses—such as playback and critique of role plays, interviews, simulations, behavior modeling, pretaping of content segments showing action or of practitioners unavailable for appearance. Overview tape of entire curriculum can be shown in full, then used in parts as appropriate. Dyad interaction can be taped with two cameras to disclose unnoticed behavior. Also used for trainer rehearsals.

Sound film strips. Short film or slides with audio, often displayed on automatic projector, convenient for individual or small-group viewing.

Slides. Reasonably easy to produce and can be inexpensive, for numerous uses; especially effective to show step-by-step progression. Built-in sound track can be cued to slides or slides can be advanced at will by trainer during narration. Can present case material or offer visual depiction of content similar to film or video tape.

Overhead transparencies. Popular mode for presenting graphic or brief form data during lecture or discussion. Can be altered or marked during viewing. Overlays permit evolving presentations.

Audio recordings. Cassette tapes of sound only, frequently part of vendor produced packages for self-study. Can be way of presenting busy expert by pretaping. Of limited effectiveness for long lectures or complex topics; valuable for recording live training or evaluation discussions.

Instructional television. Generally means series of television programs making up a course or delivered from remote place, such as a weekly television course. Outstanding feature is better production and use of first-rate performers. Often accompanied by print manuals.

Interactive television. Loosely applied term, sometimes referring to any mode in which viewer interacts with television screen, including computer projections, and other times describes two-way teleconference. Improvement on passive viewing, but requires significant outlay for equipment and production.

Picturephone. A two-way, audio-video medium developed by Bell System for teleconferencing that links participants in distant places with remarkable intimacy. Easy operation without technical help. Cameras can be operated automatically or by participants. Can transmit slides, graphics, and telefax or reproduce transmitted materials at receiving site. Restricted by necessity for participants to go to equipped site.

Teleconference. Mechanism for linking groups in remote sites. Two kinds: audio only, resembling an expanded conference call; and audio-video, with transmission of video signal by satellite and audio by long-distance telephone lines. Audio component limited by need to move callers to phone, unless speaker phone or hand held microphone is used. Can transmit training from central studio or include trainer input from remote sites, providing transmitting equipment is available.

Video disc. Tremendous but unrealized potential for training as "intelligent video disc," that is, linked with a computer. Can be programmed with textual matter, slides, video tape or film, and audio. Can be searched forward or reverse to find frames in seconds and operated on several tracks for branching, to permit self-paced instruction or programming at different levels of comprehension or in different languages. Capacity for thousands of frames allows storage and retrieval of enormous amount of data. Software is expensive to produce and extremely limited.

Gestalts, paradigms, matrixes. Graphic representation of entire curriculum or process on one or more charts to give overview.

Chalkboard. The ubiquitous teaching tool, no longer black or squeaky, but still as serviceable.

Magnetic board. Holds stick-and-stay magnetized words, letters, and pre-produced names and figures, but limited by inventory.

Flannelgraph. A favorite in Sunday schools, uses flannel figures and words that adhere and cling to flannel backboard. Used to illustrate lectures and in story telling.

Electronic blackboard. Trainer at home base writes on sensitized board and exact simultaneous images appear on television monitors at distant sites. Has been used in audio only teleconferences in which lecturer is not seen, but can be additional medium for audio-video teleconferencing.

Charts, posters, photos. Besides the trusty flip chart, any visual depiction of content, permanent or changing. Can also cover ugly wallpaper and brighten dismal rooms.

Art. Any fine art reproduction of paintings, prints, sculpture, or hanging related to theme of training. Sometimes interpreted for meaning in human relations training.

Music. Underexploited medium for training; can set moods, relieve boredom, and inspire. Appropriately chosen tunes may carry motif of training in unforgettable style.

Literature. Poetry, fiction, or classics of nonfiction used as moving or entertaining support of training theme. Can show historical context or evolution of content.

Displays, exhibits. Sometimes extravagant presentations of training theme, organizational promotion, or process progression by posters, charts, photos, models, mockups, and automatically projected films or slides.

Multimedia. Another confusing term, because any mix of one or more methods could be called multimedia. Often applied to training packages of print and audio-visuals. Mix of audio-visual devices, such as television and computer, is also multimedia. Some blockbuster multimedia shows include multi-image slides, films, charts, stirring music, and popcorn.

FORMAT FOR SESSION DESCRIPTION
For Participants' Handbook

Day:
On which session is scheduled.

Session Number:

Title of Session:

Time:
When session begins and ends.

Rationale:
A paragraph explaining why this session is included in the curriculum. Some statement of the background which makes this session needed.

Goal(s) of the Session:

A general statement of what the participant can expect to learn from this session. Can include content, method or outcomes of the session. If goals are separate and distinct, they can be stated as separate goals.

FORMAT FOR SESSION DESCRIPTION
For Trainers' Handbook

Day:
On which session is scheduled.

Session Number:

Title of Session:

Time:
When session begins and ends.

Goal(s) for Participants:
As stated in Session Description in Participant's Handbook.

Performance Objectives:
Objectives stated from the Trainer's perspective which describe:

- What do you want the participants to do?
- Under what conditions?
- By what measurement?

Personnae:
Who is to be involved in conducting this session and how? If any small group work or exercises are to be carried out by other trainers, instructions for tasks and expected outcomes should be outlined.

Materials Needed:
A check list of all materials—charts, handouts, cases, lists, etc., that will be needed in this session.

Equipment Needed:
Audiovisual equipment, such as projector and screen and other equipment, like easels for flip charts, in number needed and location.

Room Arrangement:
How training room is to be arranged and reason for arrangement, with consideration of any change required from room arrangement for prior session or session to follow.

Training Script

Process	*Content*
Describes what trainer or participants are to do, keyed to point in content description when action is to be done.	The content or subject matter of the session, stated in outline form, in sufficient detail to serve the trainer as a working script for presentation of the session.
Includes timing of segments of the session, notations on the use of materials (such as pass out handouts) and self instructions to trainer who conducts the session.	

14

Develop

Did it ever bother you, when you see some outline of the training-development process, that a lot of tasks will be listed that have to do with determining training needs and setting up objectives and choosing methods and then a lot more about delivering the training and evaluating it—and stuck in there almost as an afterthought will be a simple little phrase like "Develop Curriculum." That's all, just "Develop Curriculum." What an understatement. Developing the curriculum is the hard part, where all the work comes in. That's when you apply the seat of your pants to the seat of the chair for endless hours and turn all those plans into production. Nothing very complicated about it, just labor.

Planning is always more fun, because you don't have to *do* anything, just plan for it. You can be inventive or expansive and get away with it, until it comes time to produce what you plan. That is the Develop Phase, the time when you may find out that it doesn't come out as planned, and you have to back up and start all over.

A good end product and format for work in the Develop Phase is the training script or agenda. It can be as simple as sheets of paper with Content outlined on one side and Process on the other or as detailed as cue cards for every concept or course unit.

This chapter discusses the work of development for different training methods.

METHODS FOR GROUPS

Getting Acquainted. Time spent in exercises to break the ice is well spent. A few trainers demur from such exercises as childish and awkward. That's just the point. It's an awkward time, when almost everyone in the room is wary and a little uncomfortable. Doing something nonsensical or out of the ordinary breaks that protective reserve.

Don't think your participants are too stuffy for that sort of thing. In workshops for judges, we opted out of any familiarization exercise figuring that would be beneath their dignity. We noticed that they were slow getting started, in group work especially. In later workshops, we put in a simple warm-up. They took to it with relish, talked about what fun it was. Judges, it seems, get tired of the pomp that goes with their positions—as do the executive class—and like to let go. Doing so stimulated their work together.

Every trainer has her favorite warm-up. There are many. There's the familiar "Who Am I?" exercise, in which each trainee writes down a number of answers to the question, maybe pins them on his chest, and circulates and compares answers with others. In another, verbal version each in turn tells a little about herself, and a bit more in succeeding rounds. The trainer can deepen and control the level of revelation by the number of rounds and modeling the kind of personal information to be disclosed. Another approach is the introduce-each-other exercise, pairing participants for a few minutes together to learn enough to introduce each other to the group.

My favorite opener, because it is so simple and yet really works, is a variation on "Who Am I?" that I call "What's In A Name?" In introducing myself to a small group, I talk about my name—how peculiar it is, where it came from, what it means, the misadventures I've had with it. Then I ask each of them to take a turn telling the rest of us about his name. You'd be surprised how much people have to say. A name is something people live with all their lives, but seldom get asked much about except what it is. If you break through the early embarrassment by getting personal immediately, they follow your lead and the session can get quite lively. It gives everybody air time, gets them talking, and gets them acquainted.

That exercise does something else for me. I have trouble remembering names, so while they talk—conveniently repeating their names several times—I make a seating chart, with a few identifying descriptors. Next session, I can call them by name, providing they sit in the same place. And they do. They always do.

Getting acquainted ought to try for more than just finding out who is present. An exercise should aim for three objectives: getting acquainted, setting the climate, and getting into the content. Letting people contribute more than their identities sets the climate of participation. Getting into the content simply means using some of it as part of the exercise. This is sometimes done by asking participants "Why are you here?" or "What do you expect to get out of this training?" For my part, those questions are too hard and come too early. However, asking them to relate some experience or observation connected with the training topic is nonthreatening. And can be tough to shut off.

Exercises.   This term is so generic that almost anything trainees are asked to do could be called an exercise. The traditional format is a presentment of content, often by lecture, followed by a breakup into small groups in which participants work through an exercise, intended to internalize or apply the content. The reverse—an exercise first followed by the content presentation—is rare, but worth considering. Letting trainees experiment, even fumble around, with unfamiliar content can whet appetites for the proper exposition.

Exercises can be developed for individuals, and individual exercises can become group exercises. There are also sequential exercises that build by degrees to an intended outcome.

An exercise should add significantly to learning, not merely provide a time for the trainees to talk over what they have heard in the plenary session. This takes careful design and correct development. The exercise that seemed just right may fall apart as you develop it, when you perceive that the major learning is not what you intended. It may sound exciting in design and work beautifully in practice—except that the results are not what is expected. You must ask: if they do exactly what I want them to do, will they learn what I want them to learn?

An exercise must have focus. The worst I have observed, including some of mine, bite off more than anyone can chew—ask learners to do in-depth analyses or come up with solutions to complicated problems. Or worse, superimpose the trainer's favorite model and expect the trainees to respond in prescribed terms—words like resources, constraints, consequences, and benefits come to mind. These are glorified fishing expeditions hoping to catch an objective.

Naturally, the trainee should feel that the goal of the exercise can be achieved and that it will be of benefit to her.

A well-designed, well-developed, well-executed exercise is a joy to behold. Perhaps the best I ever turned out postulated some ethical dilemmas for resolution by public officials in seminars dealing with corruption in government. It was simple to use, always worked, on every audience, no matter who the trainer was. I've reproduced it at the end of this chapter so you can decide for yourself if I'm just bragging.

Allotting time for individual or group work is crucial, and often estimates are wrong. If so, adjust the time; don't try to hurry people around or keep pushing for them to finish. Shorten the lecture.

Task instructions, of course, must be clear and understood. It's a good idea to write them out as a guide to giving them verbally. And be sure they get distributed to group facilitators, who have a bad habit of forgetting what they are supposed to be facilitating.

Structured Learning Experiences. These are also exercises, but in common practice are more process than content oriented. Structured experiences tend to seek learning by acting out and then analyzing the experience.

Experiential learning is most effective in tasks and topics where intellectualization won't make it, such as interpersonal relations. No amount of reading or listening to lectures or talking about a skill like communications can approach the *finding out* of trying to communicate.

Structured experiences can get very personal and caution is advised. They can dredge up far more stuff than can be handled, let alone learned. An in basket structured experience I read called for a "short summation" afterward of tax write-offs, adverse publicity, political pressure, morals, collecting bad debts, minority groups, and rehabilitating ex-convicts as "management principles" covered in one session. Despite the label of structured "experiences," many of them rely more on talk than experience.

A structured experience ought to be short on structure and long on learning. I attended a sixteen hour church workshop of this kind that was so rewarding, afterward I commented to the workshop director that what had impressed me was the freedom from structure. She laughed and said, "You have no idea just how structured you were."

Developing such experiences requires more care than developing an exercise. Humans are unpredictable and may not "experience" what you want. Trial runs are in order.

Case Method.   The appeal of case studies is that they can bring a manageable body of reality into the classroom to dissect like a laboratory frog. It is not theory that they teach, but action—or the thinking that leads to action. They close the distance between trainer and learner because cases seldom have a schoolbook solution. The trainee's resolution may be as defendable as the trainer's.

Case method is varied and versatile. You can select prepared cases or write your own. They can be actual or fictional, positive or negative treatment of the situation, raise questions or merely describe performance. Case method can be used with role play, video tape, slides, simulation, and other techniques; can be presented standing alone or in sequence; can be analyzed as critical incidents or the case within the case.

Cases are undeniably engaging and that can be their weakness. Trainees may be absorbed, but not learn much, or dismiss the case as interesting but not applicable to them or not real. Some people do not learn well from case training and even those who do require some practice to get the hang of it.

The trainer must be a skilled, nondirective facilitator, one who is undeterred by confusion and slow progress and who recognizes that every problem has at least two solutions.

Selecting a case.   If you go into the marketplace for a case, the offerings are numerous. Besides the usual vendors, several university business schools publish cases. The hitch is to select one that meets your learning objectives and suits your group. You may have to read a lot of cases to find the right one, and be frustrated to discover one that fits your objectives, but not the circumstances of your trainees. Alterations to fit are sometimes possible, with permission.

Cases developed by others have the advantage that they are often based on actual situations and generally have been shaken down in practice. Their disadvantage is that no matter how reality based or tested they may be, your people may still write them off as inapplicable.

The right case that you might find on the market is one that is so universal in application, so lifelike, and done in such intriguing style that its irrelevancies are irrelevant.

Writing a case.   Writing your own case is the sure way to get one that suits. Developing your own material gives you control over it, to change and adjust, to concentrate on concepts you want to stress. Writing your own case is a reportorial job, calling for leg work, research, analyzing and selecting, as much as writing. The starting point is your objectives. If your content just doesn't strike fire by talking about it—you want them to "see" it—a case may do it. Case method follows the rule of show, don't tell.

Objectives will tell you what concepts you want to show in a case, and can point you to sources of material. The documentation for the training problem you're tackling is fruitful data. Gather up all that is pertinent. Go to the sources, interview people about the case situation or observe the performance. Get on the scene if possible to pick up environmental factors, descriptive details, and ambiance.

You may need to get permission to use the material. Disguising a case by changing names and places doesn't obviate the advisability of obtaining permission.

As you would in writing a lecture, review and analyze the information. Sift and sort for what is essential. Pare down to concepts you want dealt with, but keep background to lend authenticity.

The issue or decision your case addresses may be self-stating—a problem to be solved, a skill to be learned. What needs to be "worked" is evident in the case. If not, you may invent a case situation. This involves conditions, behavior, or changes that stand in the way of desired performance. The newly promoted supervisor doesn't know how to deal with her friends among her former coworkers. Detectives resent a study that shows beat patrolmen are the most important source of case solving information and are resisting a new procedure in criminal investigations. Customers are ticked off by the impersonality of computer billings and form letter responses to complaints.

The case must permit action to be taken by the trainees and the action should be realistically possible.

A descriptive case may show the "right" way to deal with the problem, or it can show the "wrong" way, leaving it up to participants to diagnose what's wrong and come up with the correct solution. Or, you can mix the "right" and "wrong" in the same case, to emphasize the difference, and hope they see it.

Your characters should be the likely actors in the situation. Some business school cases leave out characters, letting the student assume the role of protagonist with authority to act. The case question, "What should be done?" assumes that the learner can do what he advocates. If you introduce a protagonist, a sort of case hero that trainees can identify with, his authority needs to be defined or implied. Give your hero traits similar to those of the trainees; don't endow her with larger-than-life qualities. If the protagonist confronts others in the situation, don't portray them as villains. Let your characters speak in the case, include some dialogue. Believability is what you're after.

If your writing skill is a little short of Shakespeare, don't sweat. There's little evidence that literary style makes cases more workable. And there's no format that supersedes others; a trusty chronology will do. What matters is the pertinent data, all the facts. Don't let key information stick out from the rest, or in any other way point your people toward the solution.

Actual or fictional? "Real cases" that actually occurred have a certain veracity that may increase their value, especially for MBA candidates that professors are forcing to face the hard, cruel facts of the business world. Whether or not they have the same value in short-term training is uncertain. Actual cases may be too narrowly particularized for trainees who work with only a few, unlike the business school student who handles hundreds. Real cases are more difficult to research and prepare and gain permission to use. If a trainer uses his own organization for case material on an ongoing problem, he risks contaminating efforts to solve it.

Despite their reality, actual cases can suffer the same lack of believability as fictional ones if they don't "sound real." To my mind, what's important is the *illusion* of reality that is grounded in the experience of the learners. A fictional case can project that illusion.

A made-up case doesn't have to sound unreal. My flesh creeps when I read those cases with cutesy names and flamboyant characters and situations that are patently exaggerated. The fictional case can approach reality by writing it in the same way that an actual case would be written. Select plausible names, places, and titles—use the telephone book. Describe situations accurately. Keep behavior "in character." Above all, get the nomenclature correct. Don't invent artificial settings or action that couldn't happen. A fictional case can be made to sound more real than reality by striking that universal chord that makes readers remark: "That sounds just like my place."

Processing the case.   Trainers adept in the fine art of facilitating should have no problem handling cases. One rule of thumb: Don't go outside the case. Trainees may try to drag in new facts, new conditions, new characters even, to alter the case to meet their conclusions. If the case is intended as a take-off on a free-flowing discussion of many alternatives in different settings, no problem. More often than not, though, the participant is resisting new learning by trying to cling to past experience. Keep asking, "But what about *this* case?" Once in a while, there may be a loophole in the case that needs closing, to prevent digressions.

Discussion should include considering the consequences of actions recommended to solve the case, so trainees can't get away with flip or far-out measures.

Cases can be drawn from the experience of participants, but it is best to sound out the possibilities ahead of time to make sure they are relevant. If your training lasts over a period of time during which trainees return to their jobs between sessions, with a little case finding guidance they can uncover real work case material to work on in future classes.

Suppose you have a solid case that works well with paper materials, but seems to lack any pizzazz; try converting it to an audio-visual format. Cases gain vitality when they get away from paper.

ROLE PLAY

Almost everybody likes role play—it brings out the ham in us.

Yes, there are curmudgeons around who think role play is kids' stuff or play acting. One astute writer on management education titled a chapter, "Never Call It Role Playing," and then endorsed the method enthusiastically.

We are a people nurtured on movies and television, fascinated with show biz. We have an idea of what acting is, even if we have never done any. In training tapes I've produced, I've been repeatedly and delightfully amazed at how well ordinary people can perform. All they need is the chance and a little push. Some are reluctant at first, but if you start with volunteers, soon everybody wants to get into the act.

Role play is participation personified. It's the opportunity to try out a new role, to *feel* what it is like to act out new behavior, a skill, a different attitude. I once cast an activist Chicano, who had been growling and griping about everything, in a role as an establishment type, the antithesis of his self-view. He was to be chairman of a committee conducting a hearing, and since he was free to make up an occupation for himself, he decided to be a California grower, his archenemy and a nice touch of irony. He did a magnificent job, conducted the hearing with impartiality and cleverly conveyed his perception of a ranch owner. Later, he confided, "You know, I actually *felt* like a grower."

The potential to let people put on new clothes is also a limitation. They become engrossed in their own acting and sometimes miss the point that a role play is making, like the percussion player in the orchestra who hears a great symphony as only a series of booms and drum rolls. The trainer may expect too much in the discussion at the end; players may profoundly feel what they learned, but at that moment they cannot always articulate this for the benefit of others.

Role play can turn on the "A Ha!" light of insight while other methods are still groping for the switch. However, it can also sweep participants into such involvement that they go away feeling they learned, although they are not sure what. We are not running a school for actors, though, and role play has to be used as a means of learning, not an end.

Structured role play. Developing a structured role play—as opposed to a spontaneous one—is beforehand preparation, because in execution the trainer's part is only facilitation. Again, work starts with objectives, and follows a process similar to developing a case.

The kinds of role play are almost unlimited and can vary from a few minutes duration to several days. They can cover small segments of a subject, whenever a concept can be grasped better by acting it out. There is role reversal or rotation, fish bowl, alter ego, mirroring behavior, listening and repeating, paraphrasing, interviewing, hidden agenda, one-on-one confrontations, and so on.

A standard practice is to give written role descriptions to the chosen players, and some kind of situational narrative. Written roles are preferred to verbal assignments; people can forget who they are supposed to be. Role descriptions ought to be thorough, enough to fill out the character with clues on what kind of person they are supposed to portray. Those one paragraph descriptions, handed out a few minutes ahead of time, are unfair. Actors need a little time to think, to get into the part.

The scenario should let the actors know what they are doing in the play—where they are, what is going on. You also need to set the stage with any special room arrangements, and explain the scene to all, if it is significant to the action.

Some warm-up is helpful. One way is to put more than one role play in your curriculum; start with an innocuous one that serves primarily as practice. One tip: if you use video tape with a role play, set aside some time in advance for people to see themselves on the screen, at least the principal actors, to get over the excitement and settle down.

If your role play is to be of some duration—close to a simulation—I advocate careful casting and coaching. Observe the participants for a while to find the best matches for the roles you have in mind. Approach them in advance, and if they accept the parts, take them aside and give them some coaching. Address them by the characters' names; talk to them as if they *are* those characters.

During enactment of a role play, the trainer shouldn't hover, like a stage mother. Get far enough away to be an unnoticeable but alert observer. Take notes to mark meaningful turns in the action for processing later.

When the role play ends, the trainer ought not jump in and play schoolteacher, presuming to tell the participants what they learned. Interpretation should start with the principal actors, each describing her own reaction. Then any observers that have been appointed can give their conclusions. After that, participants in the audience have their chance. Maybe there will be nothing left for the trainer to add. What *they* say is the learning, even if it doesn't come out as planned. Legitimate interventions by the trainer, besides process questions, are to prevent excessive criticism or wallowing in embarrassment.

Spontaneous role play. To some, spontaneous role play is that in which the roles are loosely constructed and the players have almost unlimited freedom, letting results fall where they may. This approach is useful in needs assessment, problem identification, and behavior modification. Only skeletal preparation is required, but trainer interventions are more frequent. Psychodrama or sociodrama are examples.

Another form is what I term impromptu role play. It is a spur-of-the-moment move you make when you can't seem to get across any other way. One time I was dealing with an agency director in a small group session who complained that he couldn't get community people to respond to his program, to do what he wanted them to do. He was a prisoner of his own agenda, devoid of any empathy. Telling him this—either by me or more bluntly by his peers—got nowhere. Suddenly, I motioned to another trainee whom I had sensed could handle it and said, "You be a neighborhood resident and I'll be the director." We launched into an improvised visit, with me beginning, "Say, where did you get those hounds I saw out front? They're hunters, aren't they?" My partner, a born actor, picked up the role of the resident immediately, even to mannerisms and dialect. We went on for several minutes, talking about this and that of interest to the resident. Slowly, indirectly, I lead into some mention of his needs and how the program might be of help to him.

The agency director had been sitting silently beside me, taking it all in. Abruptly, he grabbed my arm. "Oh!" he said. "Oh, I see." His eyes were bright open. "I see what you mean." And later conversation bore out that he did.

That may be what some call the "teaching moment." If it can be seized by a spontaneous role play, it can bring learning.

GAMES AND SIMULATIONS

Who hasn't used the NASA Game to good effect? And how much more timely it is today, what with the actual chance of people wrecking their space vehicle on the moon and needing to get back to the mother ship, having to decide what items of the wreckage to take for their trip to safety.

Have you had a go at the game of "Who Should Survive?" What intensity, as a group struggles to decide which seven people among fifteen in a bomb shelter—the only humans alive after a nuclear attack—shall be allowed to live. There's only enough food and supplies to sustain seven of them for the two weeks it will take the radiation level outside to drop to a safe level. The people are young and old, of different races, religions, occupations, health conditions, and life styles.

Both are games, because their ostensible purpose is to resolve some barely real but demanding perplexity by using certain skills—priority setting, problem solving, group interaction, leadership. Those two games have been used in a variety of ways. The NASA game is fine as a study in teamwork or group interaction. "Who Should Survive?" can focus on values or on racial and religious prejudice.

Games are training activities in which reality is suspended, rules are contrived, there may be an element of chance, people compete against themselves, each other, or the environment, and the outcome is up to them. Games have two agendas—the obvious one of winning the game and the hidden one of learning the skills it takes to win. They are a sly but enjoyable way for people to get involved in learning, almost inadvertently. Tasks with Tinker Toys.

Or Erector Sets. Or model airplanes, play money, crayons, Lincoln logs, nuts and bolts, jigsaw puzzles, yarn, string, and other unadult paraphernalia. The kidlike nature of gaming materials, or the very idea of anything so frivolous as playing games, sends shudders of disgust through some participants (who might think nothing of spending hours at the tables at Las Vegas). One consultant advises against ever calling them games; refer to them as "learning instruments." Yet the reluctant ones may need an infusion of whimsy the most.

Games can get pretty complicated, too. I've had that trouble in playing them of not knowing what was going on, and wondering why everybody else did. They can provoke emotion, too, and trainers should watch out for the ugly competitor, the one who can't handle stress, the nonparticipant who hides in silence, the sore loser.

Most people think games are fun—which training can always use—and they are memorable, although sometimes the play is more memorable than the reason for it. They can be played with large groups or as few as two. The any-two-can-play kind are usually board games, of the Monopoly or Parcheesi type. Moves may be earned by responses to statements or concepts, sometimes after discussion with a partner. Others follow the flash card format (2 plus 2 equals ?), with decks full of problems with the correct answer on the back. That flash card format, incidentally, is essentially the mode of computer assisted instruction—a question appears on the screen, you punch up your answer, and the kindly computer tells you if you are correct, with a digital pat on the back if you are.

Simulations are games, as well, and the terms are interchangeable. Simulations differ, however, in their attempt to simulate reality. Time is compressed—some management games pack five years worth of decisions and consequences into one playing—but the endeavor of simulation is to equate performance conditions. Simulations can pit players against each other, but usually the competition is against the environment—such as making a profit under changing business conditions.

The more sophisticated simulations require intricate and expensive equipment—mockups like the Link trainer, movies of road obstacles used in driver training, data-heavy computer banks that supply instant computations for various scenarios. One household moving firm has a mockup house to teach van drivers and helpers how to handle furniture. The most fantastic simulator I ever saw was an Air Force navigation trainer that looked like a corn silo but could reproduce all the conditions of flight, a landscape moving underneath the pretend plane, stars overhead for celestial fixes, built-in wind drift and storms, even enemy attack.

The military services are old hands at dreaming up simulations. Their war games and maneuvers are simulations of the real thing. That is another feature of simulations—they attempt to be repetitions of the whole, not parts of it. Most of the skills, many of the conditions and consequences of the entire enterprise are there.

That's the drawback of some simulations; they can be so complicated that just learning how to play takes up time. A community planning simulation I participated in required the entire first day of a four day game just to learn how it worked.

Simulations seem to be more learning-worthy than games because they come closer to the skills and knowledge you are trying to impart. Debriefings are essential to games; the learning is more obscure and some trainees may fix on the fun and miss the message. In simulations, the learning is more self-evident.

Gaming should be balanced with instruction. A game *before* a presentation of curriculum can stimulate interest in the content. In training a messed-up organization on how to cope with its problems, I once used the double whammy of games followed by real work. A game about problem identification or priority setting would be played before a work session identifying problems of the organization and setting priorities for dealing with them.

Games and simulations offer something beyond learning. They can lift the dull-and-dread syndrome some people carry, so that in the future, training is more welcome.

Many games and simulations are available on the market or in training's public domain. There's nothing to stop you from developing your own; all it requires is some creativity and a lot of labor. The variations are so plentiful it is hard to lay down a process, but it's mostly a matter of matching up some learning tasks or concepts with a gaming format. A good approach is to look at some existing games, examine the mechanics involved, and then adapt your content to one that comes closest to meeting your objectives.

METHODS FOR INDIVIDUALS

Assignments. The strongest admonition I can offer about giving assignments to trainees before, during, and after training is: Don't be afraid to do it. Many a time I've heard trainees lament that they weren't sent some materials to look over ahead of time. And whenever I have given advance assignments, only a few failed to comply and there were no gripes.

Advance assignments—readings, exercises, pretests, inventories—give a leg up on a heavy load to be covered in too short a time. In sending them out, explain delicately but firmly that completing the assignment is *expected* and if not done, learning will suffer.

It is common practice during training to give reading assignments to be done on the learner's time. Trouble is, the assignments are given with faint hope, maybe brushed off with a facetious remark like, "We will have a pop quiz on what you have read." Then some trainee will ask why no quiz was given. Participants take the work more seriously than we do sometimes.

Ever notice how people gather around a reading materials table and go over almost everything there? Every training program ought to have a library of some sort—with supplementary books, reports, articles, references, even cassettes with equipment to play them on. Some trainees will give the place a once over and leave; others will browse. Some will come back on their own and want to borrow a book. Lend it; you'll get ripped off some, but that's as legitimate a consumables expense as the cocktail party.

Post-training assignments can also be given without hesitation, particularly when they have something to do with applying what participants have learned to their daily work. We occasionally make reference to our bibliographies and recommend further reading. Why not a structured exercise for back-home work handed out with the certificates? I did this twice, and got to wondering if I had wasted my time, so I made a telephone check with ten of the "graduates." After three weeks had passed, six of them had done the assignment, one was working on it, and the others all promised faithfully that they intended to do it. Even if those didn't, seven out of ten isn't bad.

Manuals. Aren't you ever touched in your trainer's heart by the vision of a learner walking about, clutching a manual like a prayerbook, fearful that losing it might mean the loss of all wisdom?

Whatever you call them—manuals, handbooks, workbooks, guides— they are worth all the effort you put into them. Not only during training but afterward, when they are kept on a shelf nearby for ready reference.

Participant manuals ought to be put together with the participant in mind. How learner oriented is all that front matter—the credits, logos, commercial messages from the sponsors, acknowledgements to everybody that needs to be paid off, promotional stuff on ourselves? Why isn't that back-of-the-book material?

The book is slick, maybe in breathtaking color, but it may not lay flat open on a table and there isn't enough blank space for notes, so it is soon written all over in margins or stuffed full of loose pages of notes.

An easy way to find out how a manual is used is to pick one up after a few days of training. Or do a quick survey among a few trainees about what would make it a better training tool.

Manuals seem to follow an unwritten format the training world over. The language in them is getting better all the time, but some manuals still read like they were done by the authors of how-to-assemble instructions.

It is logical to follow the sequence of the curriculum in arranging the material, but it seems odd to identify every unit by day and time as some manuals do. If the schedule is changed, everything is out of kilter.

If blank pages are not practical, leave wide margins and lots of white space for scribbling. Graphics should be the same as the major visuals in presentations. It's safe to put correct answers to test questions in the back of the book; for some inexplicable reason, trainees seldom look ahead.

The appendix is salutary, and not because of our footnotes and references and bibliographies. Participants really go for articles, exhibits, model legislation, work samples, checklists, and other detailed material they don't have time to read during training but want to take with them.

I once interviewed a court administrator who had developed a handbook for jurors unlike any other. He did it by alerting his staff to keep track of all the questions that jurors asked, over a period of time. Then he put together a manual that answered the most-asked questions. It had earthy stuff like what to do in the middle of a trial if you have to go to the bathroom and where to park you car and whether you can ask questions of the judge or not, in addition to the standard content. Training manuals might be improved by such a process.

Developing a manual evolves as training is designed and developed. It is handy to keep a separate file of material that is to go into the manual. Of course, one person should be responsible for assembling the contributions of others and putting them in shape. A good move that is often overlooked is the recruitment of an editor, someone who knows training but is not involved in the present project, who can copyread the material with something closer to the reader's perspective.

By all means, provide each trainee with a stick-on name tag for her copy of the manual. A convenience, if you can manage it, is a mail slot set of shelves outside the training room where people can stow their stuff between sessions, receive telephone messages, program changes, and handouts.

If you are called upon to develop a trainer's manual, here's a tip: A painless way to get verbatim texts of lectures is simply to record them during presentations and have them transcribed. They must be edited by the trainers who did them, to take out all those embarrassing hums and ahems and lousy jokes.

Are you as bothered as I am by those trainer's manuals that don't include all the material from the participant's manual, but only make cross references to it? Try juggling back and forth between the two manuals and you'll see why a trainer's manual ought to be the participant's book plus scripts and instructions.

Handouts. A trainer friend of mine always included a note in the invitations to training to "bring an empty briefcase because we'll load you with material." And then he did.

If volume equals learning, trainers like that one are masters. Handouts are probably the worst offenders in this flow of paper that can become a flood. Distributing too much material is counterproductive. Soon, trainees can't discriminate what is important from what is supplemental, what is worth reading and what is not.

Most handouts belong in the manual, either in the appendix or with the curriculum unit they supplement. The exceptions are those handouts immediately needed that would have lost something if distributed earlier. Case studies, quizzes, checklists, and other action materials are best handed out at the moment they are to be used. They should be pre-punched for inclusion in the ring binder handbook, titled, and dated.

No need to caution any experienced trainer not to try to talk to trainees after you distribute a handout; they are too busy reading to pay any attention to you. If it is something you couldn't get into the manual and you don't plan to use it, hold distribution until the end of your session, or put it on a table in back and tell them to pick it up on the way out. The same caution goes for making reference to handouts that are in the manual. Don't mention them during the session unless you are prepared to interrupt yourself while they look it up.

The better handouts are usually those you develop yourself, especially those of some practical value. I once did a distribution study over several workshops of about ten different handout items—newspaper clips, journal articles, an outline for writing a proposal, suggestions for steps to be taken after training, a reference list, and requests for further training. I put equal numbers of each on a table at the rear and at the end of my session, described each piece and offered them to the participants. After they had gone, I counted each pile. The ones I expected to get heavy play—scholarly treatments of the topic—were the most passed over. The ones most taken were the proposal outline and suggestions for action steps, handouts I had developed that were of practical application to the training.

Study. Even when training is done in groups, learning is an individual affair. We need to protect the private learning process.

In development of training, time should be built in for individual study. If your session calls for individual work before returning attention to the group—taking a test, reading, reviewing a checklist—every trainee must be given time to finish, even if it holds up the others. Think of the time takers not as slow learners, but as more thorough.

Schedule study assignments just before lunch or at the end of the day, so trainees can go off by themselves. Setting makes a difference on private study. In a custom-designed training center, we had breakout rooms of different decoration, more to satisfy the architect's whims than training needs. The rooms of sumptuous furnishing were not as practical for study as one we called the "sterile" room, because of its stark white walls and uninteresting furniture. Over repeated use, we noticed more concentration and less conversation in that room. That center, by the way, was designed with groups in mind, and when we gave out individual assignments, the trainees were hard put to find places to get away from each other.

Individual differences have to be taken into account. In any group, there's the slow starter, the early finisher, the one who can't stand to be watched, another who is never sure of the assignment, others who simply can't stand to work alone.

Look at note taking. You know how pointless it is to tell learners they don't have to take notes because it is all in the handout—they'll take notes anyhow. Note taking is not only individual, it is habitual. Some take notes that follow content closely. Others use a kind of shorthand. Some make immediate application of the subject matter to their own experience and jot down terms and symbols that have meaning only to themselves. Others are summarizers,who wait for segments of content to be disclosed before writing anything down. Doodling and pencil fondling are part of concentration for some. And there are those who never take a note, and, according to them, retain it all.

If you ever peek at learners' notes, you can see the diversity. For one thing, their notes don't stick to your outline, which casts doubt on how much help it is to distribute it. They may catch your point but put it in their own terms or record only what is relevant to them. They often write those incongruous thinking-out-loud jottings or drawings—just like you do on the flip chart—that have meaning only when connected with what was said at the time.

Training involves the individual alone, alone in a group, and together with a group. Who knows for sure where or in which combination learning occurs? The best we can do is protect all possibilities.

Action plans. A popular device, with apparent good reason, is the action plan that asks the trainee what he is going to do with what he has learned after training is over. Action plans also can be used for needs assessment and evaluation of training.

Two or three things ought to be kept in mind in developing action plans. First, they should be introduced at the beginning of training, to alert the trainee that what goes on throughout is offered for her use later. This is a good discipline; trainees pay more attention when they are thinking about using the content.

Secondly, action plans ought to be as simple and open-ended as possible. Mine have evolved from highly structured formats down to simple statements like, "What are you going to do?" or "What action do you plan to take?" and then "What steps do you plan to implement this action?" and "By when?"

Also, some reminders of the resources that have become available by the time the trainees start to do their plans seem to help——mention their notes, their exchanges with others, the training materials, and anything else that links what they intend to do with what they have just been through.

If you use action plans for summative evaluation, you can ask that they be handed in when finished, together with names and addresses, and promise that you will return them by mail. Then, make copies for evaluation purposes, and mail them back two or three weeks after training. It is possible to use carbon backed forms and collect the carbon copy but, having done it both ways, I found that sending the action plans out a few weeks after training served as a reminder of the action they pledged to take. You can accompany the plan with a letter of encouragement.

Following up on those action plans months later to gather data for a summative evaluation is another prompter, and can bring letters and calls asking for assistance or information.

METHODS FOR TRAINERS

Skits, satire, analogies.   Being the performers that they are, trainers are closet thespians, and that hidden talent can be uncovered in the cause of training. The acting doesn't have to be polished; in fact, the flubs of improvisation give it a kind of humble believability.

Skits can be put on by trainers to introduce sessions, demonstrate correct and incorrect behavior, illustrate problems, or wake up trainees. A skit is an excellent way to warm up a cold audience, and it also goes a long way toward exorcising any lingering pomposity on the part of trainers.

A satire—maybe a monologue—on the occupational type or types that make up the participant group, however exaggerated, is an almost certain smash hit if they see themselves in it. And if they tend to take themselves too seriously, they need it.

The beauty of satirical skits is that they can convey messages that need to be stressed without offending or triggering defense mechanisms. I saw a mock hearing of a budget presentation before a legislative committee that was hilarious in a directed manner. The trainer-actors exaggerated the critical foibles, even to the point of lifting the vocal volume on crucial statements. It was a side-splitter, but when debriefing came, the observers were unhesitating about detecting the mistakes that had been made and what should have been said.

When trainees are stiff and stodgy, I have found nonsense to be a fine loosening device. If the trainer isn't afraid to play the fool, participants can let go of some of their anxiety. At the end of this chapter, I've included an Ignorance Aptitude Test that I have used this way.

Analogies are a bit more subtle and require a perceptive audience. Myths or fables—like Aesop's—are an oblique but telling way to communicate some truth. Illustrating a concept through the antics of incongruous characters like animals or children can make them unforgettable. But if you have to explain the point, forget it.

Dramatic devices take some preparation. No script is necessary, but performers need to know what characters they are to improvise and the objective of the drama. A rehearsal or two helps.

Panel discussions.   Here we are talking about panels conducted by trainers, sometimes erroneously referred to as team teaching.

Panels are frequently used, and almost as frequently misused. Putting too many people on a panel, letting one person dominate, using too much time for preliminary statements are some of the misuses.

A panel discussion is an excellent mode for delineating the various sides of an issue, expanding a knowledge base, or simply providing a change of pace. Content experts who are tempted to speechify irrelevantly by themselves get down to cases as part of a panel where their views can be questioned by others.

Some separation makes a better discussion, such as setting up the ground rules and deciding on the content to be covered, so the members don't repeat each other or go astray. A skilled moderator is essential, not merely to facilitate but to probe and provoke debate.

A good use of a panel is to present an overview of the training, with each trainer outlining his pieces, with a hint of the good things to come.

Of course, participants can be used on panels, especially practitioners who can give in-person case histories.

Interviews.   A seldom used gem of a method of getting the most out of a visiting expert is having a trainer interview her. Set it up like a television interview, with the two of you up front (or theater-in-the-round style). Forget the opening statement by the expert; after reciting her background, get right into the questions that are on the minds of the audience. Find out what they want to know ahead of time.

Interviews may be the only way to get some superbusy persons to contribute to your program. Visit them in advance on their own premises and record the interviews. They will accept those kinds of arrangements many times when they wouldn't come to the training event. (It's cheaper, too, if they are high-fee types). Your interview can be played again and again through several events.

I've used taped interviews with big-shot government bureau chiefs to let those who deal with them from a distance get a look at them and find out what kind of guys they are. Some bureaucrats work for years without ever seeing their bosses—who will say a lot of inane promotional things and may be paternalistic and stuffy. Just tape more than you need and edit out the guff—unless, of course, he's *your* boss.

Lectures.   It's ludicrous to describe how to develop a lecture—lectures are the first thing a trainer learns to do, and then spends the rest of her career learning *not* to do them.

Here are some reminders: When you are going over your material, trying to decide what to keep and what to leave out, tell yourself that not *everything* your listeners will learn about this topic has to come from you. That helps you keep what's salient and leave the rest behind.

Even if you write your lecture first, talk it out some time—to yourself, your spouse, your bathroom mirror, a tape recorder—before you settle on the final version. Time segments of the lecture, not just the entire thing, so if you have to cut, you will know how much time you are saving. Don't save all the good stuff for the end; it might get lost for posterity if you get verbose in the middle. Always leave a little time unfilled at the end, besides the time allowed for questions. That keeps you from rushing. But have filler material in mind, in case you are so thorough and fascinating that no questions come.

Don't assume that just because you have covered some point that it has been heard, let alone learned. If it's vital, repeat the point in different form—illustrations, anecdotes, analogies.

Be anecdotal. Avoid abstractions if you can, by dealing in persons or illustrations from reality. By all means use levity, but make it relevant— that keeps listeners on your hook waiting for your next jewel, and they may pick up some learning in between. Beware of entertaining without informing.

Don't overlook suspense as an interest-keeping device; raise questions that you don't answer right away or that require some learning to answer. Leave something for your listeners to do, to struggle with.

Some lecturers get hung up on outlines and alliteration. I submit that neither contribute much to learning. They serve only that immediate recall that fades away with time. Usable content doesn't have to come out in A-B-C or P-P-P form.

In my journalistic first career, I had the happy opportunity to interview John Mason Brown, a book critic and television personality who was at that time the most-in-demand lecturer in America. Brown gave only one lecture each season, repeated again and again to delighted and well-paying audiences. Then he spent the summer deciding what to lecture about next season, shaping it in his mind. His development process may have accounted for his success. He used index cards, one for every concept, thought, illustration, anecdote, quotation, or joke. He deliberately mixed the cards to separate heavy content from light content. He believed in giving his listeners "rest stops" every so often. After a profound or complex statement, he inserted a card with something easy—a joke, ad lib, or piece of nonsense—that required no mental exertion. He called it "letting them up" after intense concentration.

When he went on the circuit, he experimented with the placement of his cards through the first several appearances. If something died or didn't bring the reaction he wanted, he tossed it out or put it where it would work. By the time he had his lecture set, he threw away all the cards, because by then he had the thing memorized.

No wonder he had such a national reputation—except with those folks who caught him at the front end of the tour and didn't get as much for their money.

AUDIO-VISUAL METHODS

Charts, posters, photos Any day now we'll see it, a consultant trainer's business card reading: "Have Flip Chart; Will Travel." Or the old-pro trainer's retirement party, where he will be presented, not a gold watch, but a golden easel and a set of engraved markers.

The flip chart is, indeed, the tool of our trade. It is to the trainer what the blackboard was to the schoolteacher. Maybe because it is *not* a blackboard, with all those childhood associations.

Flip charts are so utilitarian, so mobile. They stand not behind and away, hard and impersonal, but right there among us, gently prompting, part of us. The only thing wrong with flip charts is that you can't carry them; they flip and flop and fall all over. There are cases to carry them in that help some, except then you feel like some furtive art thief on the lam.

Flip charts bring out something in trainers. They make lecturing easier, with those faint lecture notes scribbled on the corners, and they give your hands something to do, drawing those Freudian symbols and curlicues than mean so much to observers. They make some trainers get playful, secretly arranging the initiation of a fledgling trainer so that right in the middle of her nervous first presentation, she flips the page and finds the big, bold words DROP DEAD—or something more shocking. Other trainers go creative, like one who greeted the awed participants with hanging flip charts—suspended from the ceiling with string, wafting quietly.

Flip charts take preparation, whether they are predrawn or used as you go. You need to decide how and when you plan to use them, but you can put off preparing them to the last, until the content is firmly set.

If you just want something to write on while you talk, then it's a question of whether one is enough. Two or more—five or six are not unheard of—let you move from one to the other, or flip over predrawn concepts on one chart, while using the other for spontaneous thoughts.

There's the Surround System of displaying charts, in which each page is ripped off after it's been covered, and then posted on the wall, literally surrounding the trainees with the subject. And the Unveiling: several predrawn charts posted around the room with a blank page covering each, so that you move from chart to chart, ripping away the cover and unveiling the content, concluding with your full presentation exhibited in all its glory. Some advice on style: When you rip off covering pages, do it with a flourish of confident abandon, letting the sheet float gracefully to the floor.

One of the best times I ever had with flip charts—impressive and maybe even effective—was with a unit on the dynamics of change. I did it in the big training room of a Seattle hotel. My content included about twenty axioms for action, prescriptions for implementing change. Before the session, I drew a chart for each concept and posted them with push-pins high up on three walls of the room, covered with blank sheets for the Unveiling. My procedure was to move to each chart, reveal its axiom and explain it briefly, give an example from my experience and solicit an example from the participants. After I had done four or five, the group caught on to the procedure. I transferred the entire operation over to them, selecting volunteers to go up, unveil the next axiom, explain it, give an example, and ask for one from the others. Starting on one side of the room and working all the way around to the other, the participation kept shifting to trainees seated in different parts of the room. Attention was rapt, following that steady trail around, until it broke into a crescendo of laughter when the very last chart came up blank. Gremlins had been up later than I was the night before.

Participants quickly get comfortable with flip charts, and no break-out room should be without one. Many hotels and training centers are equipped, but an advance look is in order. I've had some relics dragged out in some highly advertised places, or found immovable chart mountings flat against some faraway wall. In one training center, shiny silver pegs were installed around the room to hold heavy flip chart mounting boards against the wall. They were almost never used—too out of vision, too perpendicular to work on.

If you prepare your charts in advance, or they are prepared by the art department, remember the admonitions against small lettering and charts "too busy" with content. Consider color, too, for its emphasis and contrast. The best color combination for clear vision and psychological impact is blue lettering on a persimmon yellow background, or so I was told at the annual audio-visual institute at Indiana University.

Don't letter on the lower fourth of the sheet, unless you're going to post the charts up high. That part can't be seen from the back of the room unless you do.

Placement of charts is a part of preparation. Make sure your training room has wall space to post charts on. Hotels sometimes think they are giving you a big break by booking you into the ballroom or some other exotic setting with statues and paintings—or worse, by putting you in a room with those corrugated folding doors that can't hold a chart, or noise either.

Check the lighting on your chart. What at first seems to be the best placement may put the chart in shadows. Track lighting is supreme, let's you focus a spot right on the chart. When you think you have the right placement, walk to the farthest corners of the room and see if you can read the chart, sitting down. Adjust until you can.

Charts can become posters, left up throughout training, calling continuous attention to objectives, content, mission statements, figures, and such.

Photographs are used in training to show equipment, step-by-step procedures, sites, episodes, clients, and other visual information. They can be posted, passed around, or included in exhibits or manuals. Big blowup photographs that illustrate the theme of training can keep its purpose before the participants.

One use of photographs that some find frivolous but that I strongly endorse is the class photo. Don't smirk. Try taking a group photo of all the participants, early in the event so it can be finished before the last day, and distribute one to each. They're like certificates; scoffed at, but everybody wants one. They also become a record of who attended that you're apt to use more often than your participant list.

Slides, overhead transparencies. Slides are almost as versatile as flip charts and do heavy duty in training. Slides can project anything that can be photographed or drawn and can bring illustrations into the classroom that might otherwise only be talked about.

Slide/sound shows can have almost as much dramatic impact as films or video tapes, are much cheaper to produce, and require much less sophisticated equipment. They can be used with groups and viewed by individuals on automatic rear screen projectors.

With all this potential, it seems a sin to use slides to project short-form phrases or subject matter outlines—what amounts to flashing lecture notes on the screen while the trainer talks along in the dark, equal to forcing everybody to watch a Teleprompter. The words and figures up there had better be pretty significant to compensate for all that is lost—eye contact, awareness of trainee responses, the direct engagement of speaker and listener.

Slides can be appropriately used for words-only projection, such as presenting case-problem data. I lost an argument against using slides to present information for a series of small group tasks and became a convert when I saw them at work. In the first round, members of the group had to make individual decisions on what they saw on the screen. In the next round, they had only headings of the information available and had to reach a consensus on what to look at next, an exercise in rank ordering. The final round, they could only see a limited amount of the slides, further tightening the priority setting. Later, after they had finished the task, they were permitted to see any slides they had not voted to inspect. All this was possible because the slides were coded and could be displayed when requested, a kind of instant retrieval feature.

Slide shows can be as simple as the one you put on in your living room with all that film you shot on your summer vacation or as stupendous as the multi-projector extravaganzas with split screens and evolving images. Costs vary accordingly. One of my daughters used to earn easy A's on school projects by doing slide shows that cost less than her allowance. She had learned a process of making slides from cutout magazine pictures and words, soaking off the layer of color print onto the plastic film part of shelving paper. Then she mounted the plastic slides in paper holders—all for a few cents a slide.

Developing something less than an award winning slide show can be simple, but time consuming. All you really need are photographs made into slides and a script. You need a shooting scenario to make sure you get the slides you need—overshooting is smart. Then you need a story board—cards with space marked off for the visual and the wordage to go with it. Story boards force you to keep your dialogue or narration brief and matched to the slide.

If you have a scene that photographs can't readily capture, try art work. I had that problem showing an assault victim in several scenes—the assault, in the hospital, in court. An artist's drawings portrayed those scenes better than photographs would have, and saved all the problems of trying to enact them. Cartoons can serve the same purpose, if appropriate.

If you find you have too much narration for one slide, to avoid keeping that one slide on through a long speech, try moving from your overall shot to one or more close-up details of it, or the same shot from a different angle.

Of course, music and sound effects add impact, but they also run up the cost. If you can afford to go first class, go to a sound studio to do your sound mixing.

Overhead transparencies are a favorite with many trainers, but not for me. I find them cumbersome, too prone to cover loads of content in one dizzy transparency, sometimes unreadable, and diverting of attention to the confounded projector. I've also noticed that devotees seem to overdo it, with transparencies in session after session.

Every audio-visual medium has strengths and weaknesses and the trainer needs to know these. Using a medium strong in one capability for some other purpose—such as projecting lecture outlines on slides—is a waste of the medium.

An example of a medium that, in my opinion, is not worth the effort, and the huge outlay of money, are those multi-image slide shows with banks of countless projectors, wide split screens, bombastic music, dazzling color, computer cueing, and control by a trainer with a "pickle switch." The very impact is their undoing—massive overkill. The effect is so fascinating that's all you retain. One that I viewed was expensive beyond belief and when I inquired about how it was used, the answer was that some big company commissioned it for a Sunday morning meeting during a three-day sales conference to blast their salesmen into consciousness and out of their morning-after hangovers.

Films, video-tapes produced by others.   There are times when an audio-visual medium is the only medium, when the trainees have to *see* and *hear* in order to understand. A case in point was an enlightening video tape produced by an audio-visual director I worked with about the physical barriers that block people who are handicapped. Only if you *see* the struggle that a person in a wheel chair goes through to get from an automobile into some building can you feel and understand how many impediments stand in the way.

What has to be remembered is that film or tape cannot do it all, alone. It must be supplemented with other methods, or used as a supplement. No less an expert than Walt Carroll, who has screened 2,500 audio-visual media for the Training Film Profiles published by his firm, Olympic Media Information, has said, "Audio-visual off-the-shelf materials are simply the occasion for learning, not the cause of it."

No trainer needs to be told that training films are not primarily entertainment, in the genre of movies or television. You know the false expectations encountered with trainees reared on so much easy-to-take entertainment. Without downgrading the media you use, something should be done to prepare participants for what they are to view, so they are not in the mind set for *Casablanca* or *The Empire Strikes Back*.

"Mediated training"—as some now term it—comes in many modes, many variations of quality. In the Develop Phase, mediated training is largely screening and selecting, an eye-straining, time-eating function. Catalogues and media-selection publications are available, along with training film festivals. People who know caution against assuming that what is new is what is best—the oldies-but-goodies media have proven effectiveness. I have found television networks to be a good source of programs of timely content. Most have viewer service departments that will send you a script, free or at minimal cost, for review before you commit to buy.

Producing video-tapes.   Just between us, haven't you always kind of hankered to direct a movie? I have. There's a bit of Cecil B. De Mille in most of us. You watch a television show—or a training tape—and say, "I could do as well as that," and then look around quickly to see if anybody overheard.

And why not? There are good and sufficient reasons for the trainer to produce. For one, commercial products available never seem to quite fit your needs. By producing your own, you get what you want.

Another, the equipment may be at hand, and needing to be used to justify its purchase. Or it can be hired, complete with operating crews if you don't have an A.V. staff.

Above all, who knows more about the instructional design that is imperative for a training tape? We've said there's a distinct difference between a film or tape produced for training and one produced for entertainment. That distinction can get lost in many subtle ways when standard production approaches are carried over into training films.

The typical television program or movie requires no *active* response from the viewer. Comparison has been made between reading and watching television for the different brain functions involved. A printed page must be *acted upon* by the neurological circuits of the brain. Television does the acting, presenting sequences of image and sound to the brain already processed. No real work is demanded of the viewer to make a movie work, unless we decide intentionally to exert critical intelligence on it—to analyze it or extract something from it.

Viewers of a television program may learn from it, or be moved or entertained, but usually not because they intend or actively sought that end. Their responses are generalized, almost accidental.

The programs we see on our screens are not after a specific response, except for commercials. A news show or documentary may seek to inform, but in no more specific manner than enlightening the electorate. Entertainment aims at a nonspecific emotional reaction—laughter, tears, fear, wonder—or, as one producer of a TV movie said, "If this can just move a man to move closer and hold his wife's hand, I'll be satisfied."

Because training strives for a particular response, its media must require learners to act upon them in some way. Information is paced so that it can be internalized; questions are asked for learners to ponder; a film is stopped for discussion; trainees are told to watch for certain action or developments; viewers go to other materials to use what they have taken from the media.

Writers, producers, directors, actors, and production crews do not always understand these demands of training audio-visuals, even those who produce for the training market. It has been my experience that people whose occupations involve continuous use or interaction with equipment tend to imperceptibly acquire the dimensions and limitations of that equipment. Thus, a cameraman sensitive to the constraints of his instrument can give you forty-seven reasons why you cannot get this or that shot on tape. A director whose preference is for a beautifully composed picture or some ingenious special effect will spend agonizing time striving for that result to the neglect of others. The lighting is never right for the lighting specialist. The sound person always wants another take. Even acting talent gets lost in this melange of mechanics. Admirable as this perfectionism might be in some circumstances—a $40 million movie—it can dominate and extinguish the instructional mandate of a training production. Someone—the trainer—must demand that learning prevail.

To do this, the trainer *must* control the content and how it is presented. The primary place to exercise that control is the script. Serving as producer is further assurance. The surest guarantee is for the trainer to write and produce.

In this section, I'm going to give a crash course in writing and producing television tapes. Not everything you need to know, but enough to start you on your way to fame and fortune. I'm centering on video tape because of its utility and popularity; film is a more complicated technology. The nomenclature for both is almost interchangeable; training film has become the generic term for both.

Everything involves a script, but scripts do not always precede production. I've seen scripts described as prescript, quasi-script, and postscript—apt definitions. The prescript is done before anything else, setting out words and action with precision. The quasi-script is what I call a scenario, the order of speech and action is only outlined—perhaps with opening and closing lines spelled out in exact words—but most of the speech is extemporaneous. The postscript is primarily an editing script, written after shooting has been done of events or performances that cannot be exactly predicted. Many major productions are postscripted. Woody Allen's comedies are largely assembled from raw footage of scenes that he improvises as he goes along.

If your content and objectives demand precision—careful following of a step-by-step procedure or faithful adherence to technical terms—then the safest course is a prescript. You may not wish any more personal involvement than control over the script. In such case, farm out the script to a production crew or company and sit back and wait for the first cut. Then rant and rave if they have not followed the script.

Scripts are also documents to submit for approval of those who have to approve, but there are clunkers to this, which I will get to later.

You are aware that scriptwriting is not the same as writing ordinary prose. Words are to be spoken and heard, rather than read, which exerts a special simplicity on the writing that is not instantly acquired. The coordination of audio and video—sound with images—is a delicate maneuver. Above all, a *visual* sense is obligatory.

My first assignment in scriptwriting was for a prime time show to be aired on a leading television station. It was a rare opportunity to promote the organization I was serving as public relations director, but I had never *seen* a television script, let alone written one.

I invaded the library, borrowed an armload of books, and boned up on scriptwriting. I learned the format and a lot of other things I didn't know, and plunged. I have since burned that script because it was so awful—so wordy. Yet the show that came out of it was, by all counts, a surprising success.

What made it that was a fine producer and a patient director. I thought I was being visual in my script, but they took my concepts and turned them into visualizations that I never dreamed of—and they turned my verbosity over to a couple of fine television performers who scanned my speeches, then gave them in plain English. And all of it was done with great care not to tread on my tender ego.

If you've never written a script, or your skill could stand some honing, there are a number of good books and articles. Better yet, study scripts of effective training tapes, or slide shows. You'll get a notion of it that way, but this is one of those learn-by-doing skills; you have to see your script take form to find out what works and what doesn't.

Let's say you want to do more than write the script; you want to produce, maybe even direct. Or yours is a lonely operation where if you don't do it, nobody else will. That's no trouble; roles often overlap and the writer-producer-director process I'm going to describe fits all.

Concept paper. In the parlance of Hollywood productions, this is known as a "treatment," but whatever the name, it is simply a planning document, an outline of the "concept" or "project." It is brief—as brief as a page or two—so that busy executives of the industry can make quick decisions about the box-office worth of the idea. You'll have some financial backing to seek, as well, but your backer is apt to want more than a bare suggestion before granting approval, so the concept paper should be fairly detailed.

Because this is the starting point and your arrangements cannot be firm, the paper is bound to be tentative. It is your best shot at answering the question: What do you have in mind for this training tape?

The concept paper should cover your intentions and recommendations on:

- *Objectives* Not merely the learning objective of the curriculum that the tape will serve, but the more limited objectives of the tape. How the tape will be used and what other methods will be keyed to it.

- *Audience* A description of the primary viewers, why the tape will be helpful to them, and how it will be aimed directly at their needs.

- *Time*   How long will the tape run and where will it be used in the training program?

- *Perspective*   From what viewpoint will you approach the subject; the learner's view, a spectator's, a client's or an objective documentary any-person view?

- *Approach*   Your strategy for the tape, such as using it as a case study, giving viewers a feel of a situation, following the steps of a skill, making comparison to present practices, and so on.

- *Flow*   An outline of the content and how it will be covered, including some suggestions on sequencing.

- *Scenes and locales*   Where do you plan to shoot? Studio or remotes? What sites and what will you shoot at each site?

- *Talent*   Who will appear in the tape and in what roles? What groups will appear? Professionals or amateurs? Who will narrate or do voice-over?

- *Graphics*   What art work will you need; title cards, diagrams, still photos, transitions, illustrations, credits, and so on?

- *Crew and equipment*   Who will do what in production? In-house A.V. staff or hired crew? Do you have equipment or will you rent it? Studio bookings, postproduction work, and other special arrangements.

- *Cost*   A budget should accompany the paper, but put it on the last page so the boss can get fired up about your idea before she sees how much it will cost. Don't be too conservative; A.V. productions have a way of busting budgets because of forgotten costs or unforeseen events.

- *Problems or questions*   Special conditions that could cause trouble, like lining up a certain expert, getting permission to shoot at some location, scheduling, whatever.

- *Production steps*   Assuming approval, when could you start and how long will it take? Think of phases—preproduction, production, and postproduction—and mention anything that could foul up your schedule.

If it is not impolitic, circulate the concept paper widely, to all who might eventually be involved in production. Some will not read it, or only glance through it, but you may get suggestions. And you will have put them on notice.

Shooting schedule.   After you've received a go-ahead on the concept paper, with whatever adjustments are made necessary by the comments received, you need a production schedule to work from. This issues from arrangements you make for shooting locations, studio, talent, crews, equipment, and so on.

The shooting schedule is primarily a logistical instrument that helps you coordinate your work, make travel arrangements, book talent, and appraise all concerned.

If your plan calls for remote shooting, I strongly advise advance visits to the sites to look things over, obtain permissions, set up dates, and make other preliminary arrangements. Such visits save money by shortening the time on site with a crew, when time is very expensive.

Scenario. At the same time that you are doing the shooting schedule, you will be working on the scenario (you wanted to produce, write, and direct, remember). This is a working script, not exact in speaking parts, to guide you and others on what you want to shoot, where, with whom, and how.

The scenario is used when the action is spontaneous, such as an actuarial, or when action is largely improvised with some direction, like taping a worker performing, the comments of a "talking head," or actors doing a scene. In-house productions generally use amateurs, such as your own staff members or people being themselves. They are not always comfortable with a script but can perform remarkably well, given some direction and as many retakes as necessary.

The scenario will tell you what actors you need and your casting comes from that. Rehearsals may be necessary if the action is complicated or lengthy, but I have found people given very short notice can bring it off if they have a clear understanding of what is expected.

Some of the graphics you will need will issue from the scenario and you may want to make preliminary sketches of them or order those you are certain will not be changed.

The scenario will also tell you needs like the amount of tape stock, music and sound effects, lighting and special equipment, costumes and props, and back-up sites in case one falls through.

Share copies of the scenario with the production crew, but don't be surprised if they don't read it until a day or two before you go out on a shoot, if then. One way to get their attention is to call a production meeting to go over the scenario, so that they can raise their objections and give their suggestions ahead of time, and not while you are shooting.

If you decide not to direct, then you should go over the scenario in full with the director, so he knows what you want.

Shooting. Few events short of war demand as much definition of authority and coordinated execution of separate assignments as the shooting of a film. The too-many-cooks syndrome can turn a shoot into havoc and run costs up outrageously. The director must be the boss and her decisions, right or wrong, must be followed implicitly.

Discussions can and should be held before a scene is shot, because it is never exactly as you expected it to be and input from those most critically involved can keep you from wasted effort. But when shooting starts, the director must be in charge. For example, if the talent—especially eager but inexperienced volunteers—get directions from more than one person, they get caught in a maddening crossfire.

It was once my unhappy assignment to try to repair a training tape that was months overdue, had far exceeded its budget, and was in such miserable shape that it was headed for the trash can. I discovered that no less than three people had taken a stab at directing, without official sanction, sometimes at the same shoot. No less than twelve times more tape had been shot than normal and most of it was unusable.

To prevent that sort of thing, I've found it useful to lay down some "rules for the shoot," especially when working with a strange crew. These may differ from tape to tape and you could make up your own, but the shoot goes much more smoothly if there is clear and advance understanding of the ground rules.

Shooting from a scenario, what you're after is raw footage that will later be edited into the final production. Overshooting is permissible, to get the best you can. The safeguard in video tape equipment is instant replay; if you don't get it right the first time, you can do it over. Just be sure you slate each take and mark the good one. When you surmise that the performance isn't going to get better, no matter how many more takes you do, quit.

Every writer-producer-director has watchwords that grow out of mistakes from the past. Here are some of mine:

- Keep technical people by your side when scouting scene locations. What looks perfect to you may have horrible problems for the crew. I dearly loved settings in offices with a big picture window looking out over a magnificent landscape, but the vidicons go berserk in all that light.

- Set up lighting and equipment before bringing the talent onto the set, so they don't stand around and get restless or distracted. But bring them in a few minutes before you are ready to shoot, so they can get used to the atmosphere.

- Warm up the talent with an easy, over-the-top run-through, paying little attention to their speaking parts, more to their comfort level. When they are not aware of it, turn on the camera and shoot a few minutes of the warm-up, then show it to them. They'll get a feel for how they are projecting and their self-critical attitude will be diminished knowing it was only a warm-up.

- If you have trouble getting people to speak naturally to that fearsome camera, try giving it a name—Old Mr. One-Eye, Ignorant Ike, Larry Ikagami, or something more ridiculous. I've hung name cards beneath the lens; silly, maybe, but it makes the camera less threatening.

- Before you get into serious shooting, put your hosts—the ones who provided your site and are hanging around—on camera in an off moment, then let them see themselves on the monitor. That's all the payoff they'll need.

- Don't let talent get into the habit of viewing every take, especially the bad ones. Use the monitor to point out errors they might not be aware of, but always let them see when they have done well. The old positive re-enforcement.

- If there are kids around, apt to be noisy or interfering, put them on tape and let them see themselves. They'll behave like angels after that.

- Don't let actors slate (announce the number) their own takes. It reminds them of the number of bad ones.

- "Quiet on the set" or "Stand by" are legitimate warnings given when you are ready to start. Chatter must cease, so everybody can concentrate.

- If an actor can't handle some jawbusting term, let her change it into her own words. If they insist on trying to get it right the way it was, there's not much you can do. I had a man doing voice-over who used nineteen takes to get the correct pronunciation of "investigative."

- When the talent gets into one of those nothing-works streaks—and they will—don't think that taking a break will rectify things. They will just worry more. If you can, go to a different piece of action or speech and come back to the botched one afterward.

- Let the actors make up their own cue cards; it helps them memorize. But remind them to write big and use trigger terms.

- Insist that the technical people do their jobs and not anybody else's, and be on hand when they are needed. But listen when they have something to say, even if you don't always follow their advice. Experienced professionals can save the day for you sometimes, or let you flounder.

- If you are shooting documentary style, be prepared for action and scenes that are different from what you perceived. You don't know what is there until you get there. You have to adjust *your* thinking, not the reality. Think of it as cinema verité.

- Try to line up a principal contact person at each location, one who can be around or reachable when you need help.

- Be wary about using substance experts or practitioners as narrators. Don't get committed to using them that way until you have auditioned them in some manner. They might be tops in their field but narration before a camera is a unique skill they may not possess. It is unfair to them, as well as your production, to put them in a role they will mess up, no matter how eager they are.

- Shoot plenty of cutaways, short takes of anything and everything on the scene around your primary setup, that you'll need for bridges and back-up. Street scenes, people working, computers running, hallways, names on doors, buildings, products, coffee cups, books on shelves—you never know when a cutaway will save you when you have an editing problem. And record some ambience audio— sounds in the plant, the hum of conversation and the clatter of type- writers, birds singing. But be aware of what any audio engineer will tell you—natural sounds don't always sound natural in reproduc- tion.

- Besides slating takes and marking the number of them on your sce- nario, be sure to label each box of tape stock with the site of the shoot, the scenes and people taped, and the box number. Knowing where to find sequences saves a lot of time later.

- Take a small tape recorder along on shoots. It may come in handy, for things like rehearsing speeches by talking heads before the cam- era is set up. Doing remotes at scattered sites with different actors, I played audio recordings so they could hear what went on in the scene just preceding theirs so they could link to it.

- Don't be hesitant about using background music, it adds impact. But please, something besides a guitar player doing folk tunes. I use a lot of classical music; it has great short passages for any mood, or jazz. Look out, though, you'll have a permission problem with most popu- lar and copyrighted music. You can buy original music for scoring, but don't use it in tape after tape; you'll stick yourself with a theme that will bore you.

- In training tapes, your intent is to capture action or content that means something to trainees. Don't get carried away trying to com- pose pretty pictures or show off how original you can be. If you can do both, fine, but it is the impact on learning that matters most.

- Keep fun in your shoots. Save your outtakes for a comedy show at the office party. Slate and mark the most embarrassing and hilarious ones. They'll happen. In the midst of shooting in a supersecret computer center, we began picking up police calls on the monitor. It was not only funny but it loosened up what had been a stiff and not-so-wonderful performance.

Final or editing script.   Under this production procedure, most of the footage has been shot before the final script, or postscript, is prepared. Action has been improvised and speeches have been extemporaneous. Now you can get exact wordage, by transcribing the audio from final footage.

The final script serves several purposes—it's the format that brings everything together, tells you what you still need, and where to put it. It's a document to submit for final approval and you can't edit without it.

First comes the eye-bugging and time-weary task of viewing and marking the raw footage. This is when you find out how much overshooting you've done and where you have forgotten to mark the good takes. I use a mark-up script, blank script sheets to record counter numbers, tape-box numbers, segment times, opening and closing phrases of speeches, and quick notations of the video action. Use a stop watch to time segments and it's a good idea to tape usable speeches on a small recorder to hear them again if you're in doubt, without having to use the video machine again.

Your typist will love you if you ask for only transcriptions of the audio segments you expect to use, underlined and accented with start and finish counter numbers on the mark-up script. Some writers insist on transcriptions of all the raw footage, good takes and bad; I've never understood why.

Even before you get the transcriptions, sit down with your copy of the mark-up script and call upon the Muses. Here is where you need all your artistic judgment and knowledge of training. You must make hundreds of decisions—what to keep and what to throw out, where it should be placed. Draw on your sense of flow, of viewer responses, learning objectives, and the tape's connection with the rest of training.

Gradually, you'll see where you need graphics, where music or sound effects should come, where you need voice-overs and cutaways. You may have some reshoots to do, where something didn't come out right. And you may have put off shooting your narrator's opening and closing gambits, which you can now prepare with precise language.

I do a handwritten script—it's easier to change and start over. When you get back the transcribed audio, you can paste in the speeches and have the final script typed.

Before you submit the final script for approval, start on a rough edit. This is a throw-together of footage you intend to use, with shots of roughed-out flip charts substituting for the final graphics, and voice-overs and narration audio recorded by yourself, if need be. The idea is to *see* what it is going to look like rather than visualize it from the script. A rough edit can show you, literally, where changes need to be made.

Submitting a final script for approval is both necessary and risky. That risk can be reduced if, back when you were getting approval of the concept paper, you negotiated a condition that final script approval would be done by a single person. A committee reviewing your script can kill you; the only redeeming possibility is that they will disagree with each other and cross each other out. Most people think they know something about show business—they watch television, don't they? They will nit-pick a script and offer strange "suggestions," always followed by the de-murrer, "Of course, you know best." Some image-conscious executive will discover negative connotations that nobody else sees. And once in a while, you'll get some comments for genuine improvements, or they will catch something you completely overlooked.

Your rough edit can help with picky reviews. Let the authorities view it, so they can get a visual idea of the production and not depend entirely on the script. Apologize mildly for the roughness of the edit, but the rougher it is, the better. They will recognize that it is not a finished product and soften their criticism. Usually, they don't stay to the end, but rush off to some meeting tossing back some remark like, "Looks good. Keep it up."

Having survived final script approval, you now put it all together. Shoot your final scenes, do your voice-overs, put in the graphics and begin editing—probably in some editing house with all that exotic equipment like character generator, sound mixer, color correction, computerized editing machine, credit crawls, and technical people who treat you as if you really know what you are doing.

When you are sitting there in the dim light of the editing room with all those screens blinking, surrounded by switches and terminals and compliant technical staff—when you begin to think seriously about ordering a director's chair with your name on the back—then you know that it was all worth it.

VTR in the classroom. The camera and television monitors can be used as live training tools. Role plays, interviews, group discussions, simulations, games, evaluations, skill practice, and other activities that haven't occurred to me or you yet can be taped. Tapings can be short, such as in role play, or extended for almost the duration of training time.

VTR is valuable whenever recording for playback will add to learning.

Here are some suggestions:

- Don't make a big deal over the equipment so that you exaggerate its presence. Expect people to be curious and keep your A.V. people nearby to answer questions and protect the hardware. VTR is not a novelty anymore, but its presence in the classroom arouses reactions like, "Show time!"

- Allow time, preferably before the session starts, for people to appear on camera and see themselves in the monitor. Some will act foolish, some will be embarrassed, a few who have done it will regard it as old stuff. A little exposure knocks the edge off anxiety.

- Use natural light whenever possible. Hot, bright lights can be uncomfortable and distracting and throw eerie shadows around the room.

- Don't force anyone to appear on camera; ask for volunteers. When some start, others will follow. Expect unnatural behavior and posturing at first, but be patient; it will usually subside. Recognize, though, that a few people will never adjust to being on camera.

- Prepare people with a full explanation of what to expect and a brief run-through. Adopt a casual manner yourself to take some of the gee-whiz out of being taped.

- When playback time comes, put the monitors where they can be seen by all, not just the principals. Take a tip from the airlines—place your monitors in tandem order, one up front, others deeper into the audience down the middle aisle. Or variations of that if you are in a theater-in-the-round arrangement. More people can see and hear that way than if you put all the monitors in front, even if they're on high racks.

- If you are taping extended sessions, such as a mock proceeding, consider scheduling your playback review in evenings. You may prefer to do essential playback immediately and then show the entire tape in the evening for optional viewing.

- Be aware of mixing commercially produced films in your curriculum with your own video taping. The contrast in quality can cheapen the effect of your work.

TELECONFERENCES

After some early claims heralding the teleconference as the mode of the millennium that would bring people close together without spending time and money on travel to the traditional out-of-town meeting, teleconferencing has settled back into a more realistic perspective as a delivery mechanism of considerable untapped potential and unacknowledged limitations.

The teleconference is, indeed, a way to cut travel costs, and it can link people in instant communication by satellite anywhere in the nation or the world. A satellite "footprint" on earth offers enormous coverage and the number and networking of receiving stations has so proliferated that millions can be reached simultaneously. That very expanse is an impediment if the intention is two-way communications or "interactive television." How many people can talk at once, or get a chance to talk at all? Even for a reduced number of participants, the two-way technology still has bugs in it.

I don't share the simplistic complaint that the teleconference is an inadequate training medium because "you can't pick up the nonverbals" or that all is lost without live contact between people. What about the telephone, our most common communications instrument? Every day we are in electronic contact with countless other people, not the least concerned that never do we *see* the persons we talk with.

After reading a rash of articles that declared teleconferencing would revolutionize training, and noticing all the workshops being offered to tell you how to get in on the revolution, I assumed the state of the art to be very advanced. When I did some teleconferences, though, I felt as if I was out on the frontier, pioneering in an unexplored wilderness.

As a training method, teleconference awaits the attention of some consummate trainers who can invent nontraditional ways to exploit its possibilities. Most training teleconferences now are little more than lectures with some tortured questions and answers at the end, or a panel discussion with phoned-in questions, with maybe a video tape once in a while.

The potential of the medium is certainly there. I sensed it while doing some planning conferences on American Bell's Picturephone system. That is true two-way, interactive television, with all the accouterments of training. Groups up to twenty assemble in telephone company conference rooms in several cities and can be united audio-visually through two TV screens at the front of the room, one for the outgoing picture, one for incoming. Five cameras operate under automatic control. If a person speaks, her voice-actuated mike focuses the camera on the speaker. If there is a fifteen second silence, the camera pulls back to a long shot, or can be controlled by the conference leader from an easy-to-operate console. Other cameras can pick up displays of an overhead projector or a slide carousel. A tripod mike can pan to a chalkboard. Video tape can be played and anything on the incoming screen can be copied and made available in ten seconds.

The ease of interaction is astonishing; repeatedly people remarked of it seeming as though conferees half way across the country were "right in the next room." As a planning conference, with the need for exchanges of information and views, the Picturephone conferences did all that a live meeting might have done, maybe a bit more, at much less cost. The unexpected bonus is an intense level of concentration—no idle chatter or rhetorical questions, all business. You'd think each participant was paying for the call.

The stricture of Picturephone is that only the Bell system's meeting rooms are equipped for such conferences and those are not in all major cities. Some of our people drove one hundred miles to get to the conference site near them. The day will come when sites will be more numerous and convenient and it is not hard to envision big companies outfitting their conference rooms around the country for teleconferencing.

There are several format options for teleconferences dictated by the technology. There is one-way video (such as closed circuit viewing of a surgical operation), one-way video-audio (the boss addressing the branch offices on the company network, with no talking back), two-way audio (the old-time party line or what today we call the conference call), two-way video-audio (Picturephone), and the most common mode for satellite television conferences, one-way video and two-way audio (television transmission and a long-lines telephone hookup).

Variations with other media are possible. A surprisingly efficient example was a tie-up with training expert Robert Mager conducted at one of the annual audio-visual institutes at Indiana University. Mager had prepared a video tape, in that unique one man home studio of his in California, that was shown to us. Then we talked with him live in a two-way telephone connection. The effect of first seeing him and then talking to him seemed to mesh, so it had that right-in-the-room feeling.

You can add facsimile machines to audio conferences to provide graphics and text, or link teleprinters and computers to show visuals and produce copies. Bell has an electronic blackboard that picks up an instructor's chalk strokes, converts them to data signals, and transmits them to television monitors in remote classrooms.

Still, all these modes are only delivery mechanisms. Their usefulness for training depends on the content they carry. On that, the hardware is way out ahead of the software.

Although teleconferencing is advertised as simple and easy, done properly it requires a heavy investment in preproduction planning and preparation. Not only do you have the usual front-end work, but you must be concerned about meeting sites, local facilitators, time-zone differences, studio, technicians, set design, equipment checks, call-in procedures, booking signal time, contracts and subcontracts, uplinks, downlinks, ground lines, and gremlins. The equipment can and does break down. And as nonbroadcast television, you don't get the priority treatment that steady customers do.

The development phase depends on the length of your teleconference. They can vary from one hour to several days. For a two-day workshop transmitted on television by satellite, I task loaded the services of twenty-three people. I also scripted all eleven hours of air time, first with a scenario and then with a continuity script. To give you an idea what that is like, I've added the scenario at the end of this chapter.

Teleconferencing is still new enough and varied enough that it is unwise to strike any standard procedure for development. I have seen attempts at this, but they are usually traditional training processes superimposed on teleconferences. That's appropriate, up to a point. New technologies call for new use patterns and they are slow in coming. If you can remember the early days of television, it first followed radio formats in programming, until those unique to the new medium could be dreamed up.

What follows are some matters to think about if you are developing a teleconference:

- Adding up all the unfamiliar cost items of a teleconference may give the impression it is inordinately expensive. It is not, if you calculate the per-participant cost of a large audience. It is expensive if the number of sites and participants is small.

- Consider producing video tapes in advance to show on the teleconference. They can be brief nuggets to slip in here and there or augment a presentation. I did an eight minute orientation tape describing the satellite transmission system and a promotion tape about the sponsoring agency. We used them to open the show and then repeated them at fill times, like lunch hour, when you are still on the air even if everybody has gone out to eat.

- You can video tape content presentations, thereby increasing their quality, and transmit them at scheduled times with the presenter standing by to handle call-in questions.

- A good teleconference mix is content presented from the originating studio, with two-way discussion, and then group work at the outlying sites, as you might do in a customary seminar.

- Teleconferences can originate from several places, so that each may contribute in a true two-way video-audio connection. However, each originating site requires a studio, equipment, and crew—which runs up the cost.

- Local groups taking part in a teleconference should be programmed with as much care as you would any participant group. A local facilitator is a must, with group leaders as needed.

- In addition to mailings of materials to local facilitators, a conference call with them a week or so before the teleconference is a good move, for last minute briefing and to get them into the feeling of long-range telecommunication.

- Trainers should have a technical rehearsal, at least a walk through, to get accustomed to studio performance.

- Some thought given to set design is worthwhile and not necessarily expensive. Talk to the studio staff about design that projects well on the screen.

- A problem with one-way video, two-way audio teleconferences is what to put on the screen while a phone-in caller is talking. Keeping the camera on the leader in the studio slights the participant, who becomes a voice from far off heard while viewers are looking at the leader. I tried site graphics—slides with state or city names and geographic illustrations like maps, palm trees, cactus, mountains, and such, appropriate to the site. With this backdrop, the participant's name can be supered on the screen if you have a rapid operator on the character generator.

- Teleconference courses with weekly air times have given students a telephone number to call at certain hours throughout the week to discuss the subject with the professor.

- In producing a teleconference, you are dependent on numerous sub-contractors, even if you use a central-source broker. Be aware of the conditions of those contracts, in case of breakdowns. So-called redundancy systems—back-up transmission—are still rare. Look into disrupted service insurance.

- You should have a glitch plan, in case things go wrong. Example: by prior understanding, if you lose your video signal, inform the viewers by audio. If you lose audio, let them know by video cards. If you lose both, sue.

MUSIC, ART, LITERATURE

If we mean what we say about a holistic approach to training, should that not involve all the senses? Why not use music, art, literature as aids to learning?

No one thinks twice about hearing music as background in a video tape or slide show. Lecturers spice their speeches with ribald poetry. A giant reproduction of the company logo often stares down at participants.

Scholarly presentations are carefully footnoted in homage to the literature.

How about more intentional, direct use of the arts, where fitting? In a workshop on stress management, when we are striving to bring home the feeling of stress through some exercise, why not some pulsing, pounding, stressful music? In our bibliographies, why not include some work of fiction that evokes the emotion of some working environment?

Use of the arts need not be stuffy; they can lift and give substance, break through routine.

You would know best whether your circumstances can stand such a departure, but here are some examples of what I have tried:

- In sessions for poverty workers, Edwin Markham's once widely known poem, "The Man With the Hoe," was read and distributed, and a print of Millet's classic painting that inspired the poem was on display.

- For an awareness-building session for Girl Scout leaders, a recording of Helen Reddy's song, "I Am Woman," was used as a theme.

- In a training festival where compressed time demonstrations necessitated quick movement of participants from room to room, the hurry-up rhythm of Reznicek's "Donna Diana Overture" prodded them along.

- Elgar's "Pomp and Circumstance March" is the traditional graduation theme. Playing parts of it when the trainees march up to receive their certificates always brings laughter and a light moment.

IGNORANCE APTITUDE TEST

This is a bit of nonsense that can be used, if you have the nerve, to loosen up a tight audience. Merely ask the questions and wait for answers. It takes only a few minutes.

Every question has a logical answer, regardless of how simple or silly it may sound.

1. If I went to bed at 8:00 P.M. and set the alarm to get up at 9:00 A.M., how many hours of sleep would this permit me?
2. Do they have a Fourth of July in England?
3. How many birthdays does the average man or woman have?
4. Why can't a person living in Winston-Salem, North Carolina be buried west of the Mississippi River?

5. If you had one match and entered a room in which there was a kerosene lamp, an oil heater, and a wood burning stove, which would you light first?
6. Some months have thirty days, some have thirty-one; how many months have twenty-eight days?
7. If a doctor gave you three pills and told you to take one pill every half hour, how long would they last?
8. A man builds a house with four sides to it, and it is rectangular in shape. Each side has a Southern exposure. A big bear comes wandering by. What color is the bear?
9. How far can a dog run into the woods?
10. What four words appear on every denomination of U.S. coins?
11. I have in my hand two U.S. coins which total fifty-five cents in value. One is not a nickel. What are the two coins?
12. A farmer had seventeen sheep. All but nine died. How many did he have left?
13. Divide 30 by ½ and add 10. What is the answer?
14. Two men play checkers. They each played five games. Each wins the same number of games. How can you figure this?
15. Take two apples from three apples and what do you have?
16. How many animals of each species did Moses take on board the Ark?
17. A woman gives a beggar fifty cents. The woman is the beggar's sister but the beggar is not the woman's brother. Why?
18. Write the six letters contained in the word meaning a dumb person.
19. If daddy bull eats ten bales of hay and baby bull eats four bales of hay, how many would mommy bull eat?
20. What word is misspelled on this test?

ETHICAL DILEMMAS

Questionnaire

Please read each of the questions that follow and mark your answers next to the questions. Then, transfer your answers to the answer sheet, which follows this questionnaire. This way, we can collect everyone's responses, compile them, and get a picture of the way others in the workshop group responded to compare with your own answers, on the questionnaire proper, which you should keep.

Try to answer every question "Yes" or "No," and briefly state your reason for answering the way you did. If you absolutely cannot answer "Yes" or "No," give your reasons why you cannot.

Do *not* sign your name on the answer sheet.

1. The Board of Directors of the Chamber of Commerce has an annual weekend outing at a resort some miles from your city. During the weekend there are golf, tennis, swimming, card games, dinner dances with entertainment, and numerous cocktail parties. During the day, there are sessions at which the Chamber Board reviews progress for the past year and discusses plans for the coming year.

    For several years, the city has contributed $100,000 annually for the support of the Chamber.

    You are invited to the Chamber's weekend outing with all expenses paid by the Chamber. *Do you accept the invitation and go for the weekend?*

    (_____) Reason:
    Yes
    (_____)
    No

2. You have been asked to speak to a Sunday brunch meeting of the Board of Aldermen of a smaller city across the river, which is the state line, from the city of which you are chief administrative officer. They want you to tell them about your budget reduction program, in anticipation of a Proposition Thirteen kind of measure that is pending in the legislature of their state.

    At the conclusion of your appearance, the chairman hands you an envelope containing an honorarium check for $250 and explains that "This is in appreciation of you giving up your Sunday morning." *Would you accept the honorarium?*

    (_____) Reason:
    Yes
    (_____)
    No

3. For many years, you and Frank Jordan have been close friends. You went to high school together and were college classmates. You were best man at each other's weddings. Your wives are good friends. For the past ten years, Frank and his wife have taken you and your wife to dinner on your birthday. It is just something he insists upon

doing and it has become something of a tradition. He can well afford it; Frank owns the largest plumbing supply business in the state and does more than $500,000 in business each year with the city.

You have been an insurance agent all your professional life. Last year, you ran for a seat on the City Council and you were elected. You have been named chairman of the Council committee which oversees procurement contracts, including plumbing supplies.

Your birthday is coming up in a couple of weeks. Frank has called you to remind you that he and Mrs. Jordan have a special treat for your birthday dinner this year. He has made reservations at a fancy new restaurant that everyone is talking about. *Do you accept?*

(_____) Reason:
  Yes
(_____)
  No

4. For some time, police officers on three adjacent beats have met each day for a coffee break at a restaurant near a point where the three beats intersect. They usually have coffee and danish, and occasionally a piece of pie.

   You are newly assigned to one of the beats. When you go for the coffee break the first day, and you walk up to pay the check, the proprietor says, "No charge. I am glad to have you officers around." The others leave without paying. *Do you pay your check?*

   (_____) Reason:
     Yes
   (_____)
     No

5. Henry Settles is a man who has worked in your department for a long time. He is conscientious, in fact, maybe too conscientious, in the view of many of his fellow workers. He is always at work on time, always puts in all his hours, and works hard. But he expects others to do the same and frequently complains about others who are tardy or who take long lunch hours or call in sick when almost everyone knows they are not sick.

   Recently, Henry reported to you that some employees were using City automobiles to drive to pro football games in a city about one hundred miles away. You put a stop to that, but Henry has been personna non grata with many of the employees of the department since. Henry is a probable candidate for a new position, one that would mean a promotion for him. *Do you promote Henry?*

(____)   Reason:
Yes
(____)
No

6. A new civic plaza is in the plans to restore the downtown area of your city. The bond issue for development that was passed three years ago is already too little to assure completion of the project, because of inflation. A developer who wants to erect a high-rise office building and mall near the civic plaza offers to buy a large tract of undeveloped land in the plaza area and donate it to the city, in exchange for permission to build his proposed building higher than the present zoning restrictions will permit.

He has made this offer to you and it is up to you to decide whether to communicate the offer to the City Council. *Do you pass on the offer to the Council?*

(____)   Reason:
Yes
(____)
No

7. A few days before Christmas, a package arrived at your office. Inside is a card from the vice-president and general manager of a large corporation in your city. The company has never done any business with the city. The card says, "You are doing a great job for our city and we just wanted you to know that we appreciate it. We hope you will accept this token of our gratitude."

You open the package and find a beautiful crystal vase which you estimate to be worth seventy-five to one hundred dollars. *Do you accept the vase?*

(____)   Reason:
Yes
(____)
No

8. Your favorite brand of Scotch is Chivas Regal, but you don't buy it too often because it is so expensive. You have told this to the liquor dealer from whom you buy your booze. It's a kind of a joke. "Think rich and drink cheap," you sometimes remark when you buy a less expensive brand.

The liquor dealer gets in trouble for making book and his license is in jeopardy. You have nothing to do with the hearing on suspension of his license, but the next time you go to buy liquor, you discover when you get home that the sack containing your liquor includes a fifth of Chivas Regal which you didn't order or pay for. *Do you return the Scotch?*

(____) Reason:
Yes
(____)
No

9. A physician friend of yours asks if you would be interested in investing in a Doctors Building which a group of physicians are planning to erect in the city of which you are manager. No decisions involving your job are expected as part of the investment; the doctors are simply selling shares in their venture. It will be next to a shopping center in a rapidly growing part of town.

You stand to more than quadruple the $25,000 cost of a share in a short time; maybe make even more than that. You have the money. *Would you invest in the Doctors Building?*

(____) Reason:
Yes
(____)
No

10. Hazel Stevens is a valued employee. She has worked for you for years and she is the kind of worker you can depend upon to put in extra time and effort when it is needed. She is always there in a crisis and several times she has handled situations that would have been uncomfortable for you. You really owe her a lot.

Recently, Hazel came to you and admitted that for some time, she has been "borrowing" money from the petty cash fund, writing false receipts to cover it. It was never much; usually ten or fifteen dollars, and she always repaid it. But her conscience has bothered her so much that she had to confess.

Under your personnel policies, her action is clearly a cause for dismissal. *Do you fire her?*

(____) Reason:
Yes
(____)
No

11. In the space for this item on the answer sheet, would you briefly describe an ethical dilemma which you have encountered in your experience? It may be some situation which caused you considerable distress in making a decision or it may be something which has happened with some regularity. Tell us what the dilemma was, what you did about it, and what resulted from your decision—on the answer sheet.

ETHICAL DILEMMAS

Answer Sheet

Check the appropriate "Yes" or "No" box for each question and in the space indicated briefly set out the reason for your answer.

1. (＿) Reason:
   Yes
   (＿)
   No

2. (＿) Reason:
   Yes
   (＿)
   No

3. (＿) Reason:
   Yes
   (＿)
   No

4. (＿) Reason:
   Yes
   (＿)
   No

5. (＿) Reason:
   Yes
   (＿)
   No

6. (___) Reason:
    Yes
    (___)
    No

7. (___) Reason:
    Yes
    (___)
    No

8. (___) Reason:
    Yes
    (___)
    No

9. (___) Reason:
    Yes
    (___)
    No

10. (___) Reason:
     Yes
     (___)
     No

11. Your Ethical Dilemma:

MPI SATELLITE WORKSHOP

February 25-26, 1981

Scenario

EST

Wednesday

12:30 P.M.   On air—Bars and tone
              Site technicians begin signal check

12:39 P.M.   Title card—tone continues
              Managing the Pressures of Inflation—A workshop

| 12:40 P.M. | Time Signal—Tone continues |
| | 20 Minutes to Start (graphic or character generator) |

| 12:41 P.M. | Open camera—Tone or ambience audio |
| | Video of studio audience gathering |

| 12:45 P.M. | Time Signal |
| | 15 Minutes to Start (graphic or character generator) |

| 12:46 P.M. | Open camera—Tone or ambience audio |

| 12:47 P.M. | Credit card |
| | A Presentation of the National Institute of Justice |

| 12:48 P.M. | Roll NIJ promotion tape |

| 1:00 P.M. | Title and credit cards repeat |
| | Managing the Pressures of Inflation—A Presentation of NIJ |

1:01 P.M.	Program start—Two shot of Soady and Pesce
	Soady introduces self, welcomes participants for NIJ, explains why workshop being conducted this way, introduces Pesce as workshop leader
	Pesce makes opening comments, refers to uniqueness of workshop by satellite, intros satellite tape

| 1:06 P.M. | Roll satellite tape |
| | Tape explains satellite transmission |

1:12 P.M.	Roll call of sites
	Pesce asks sites to report in, site facilitators call in, spend two minutes each describing their audiences
	Site graphics and name tags for facilitators on video as they report in by predetermined order

1:30 P.M.	State reports on impact of inflation
	Pesce calls for state report from Florida, spokesperson gives five minute report, Pesce calls for state report from Louisiana, spokesperson gives five minute report
	Video on site graphic and name tag of spokesperson
	Video also on Pesce writing down highlights of reports

| 1:40 P.M. | Workshop overview and problem statement |
| | Pesce links state reports to agenda of workshop, describes flow, introduces trainers, makes reference to handbooks, stresses time observance |

Trainers move to camera position for one-shots when introduced by Pesce; name tags on screen

Ed gives statement of problem of inflation

2:00 P.M.   BREAK
Can reroll NIJ promotion tape during break

2:15 P.M.   Cutback Management
Levine gives presentation
Name tag on Levine
Slide graphics on ten paradoxes

3:00 P.M.   Random questions/comments from sites
Levine invites questions from sites (could take starter question from studio audience), graphic giving phone numbers on screen, site graphics ready for use during questions.

3:27 P.M.   Wrap-up
Pesce shuts off questions, leads into group work by local participants at sites, reminds of starting time tomorrow, signs off

3:29 P.M.   Closing graphic
Pressures?
Responses?
Consequences?

3:30 P.M.   Fade to Black

3:45 P.M.   Site participants break into small groups for group discussions
Studio audience meets with Levine

5:00 P.M.   Site groups reconvene for discussion reports

5:15 P.M.   Adjourn

EST   *Thursday*
8:30 A.M.   On air—color bars and tone
Site technicians begin signal check

8:40 A.M.   Time signal—tone continues
20 Minutes to Start

8:41 A.M.   Bars and tone

8:45 A.M.   Time signal—tone continues
15 Minutes to Start

8:46 A.M.	Open camera—tone or studio ambience
8:55 A.M.	Time signal 5 Minutes to Start
9:00 A.M.	Title and credit cards Managing the Pressures of Inflation—A Presentation of . . .
9:01 A.M.	Introduction Pesce gives good morning, reviews day ahead, asks first site to call in, leads in to group reports from sites. Phone numbers on screen
9:05 A.M.	Site reports on group work Site spokespersons report on group work of previous afternoon, five minutes each, sites report in predetermined order, site graphics on screen Pesce anchors calls, writes highlights on chart
9:49 A.M.	Pesce summarizes, introduces next session
9:50 A.M.	Police Program Models Wasserman makes presentation
10:30 A.M.	BREAK Can roll NIJ promo tape
10:45 A.M.	Police Program Models (continued) Wasserman resumes, plays MCI, MPO tape segments
11:15 A.M.	Police Program Models (continued) Martin makes presentation
12:00 NOON	LUNCH MPO VTR rolls during lunch
1:30 P.M.	Police Program Models (continued) Wasserman and Martin take questions, comments at random from sites Phone numbers on screen Site graphics for callers if possible
2:15 P.M.	Planning for Cutback Management Pesce makes presentation Graphics as predetermined
3:15 P.M.	Wrap-up Soady makes summary speech, gives credits and acknowledgements

Pesce concludes television segment of workshop, leads in to group work, hands off to local facilitators

3:25 P.M.   Slide graphic on five critical questions

3:30 P.M.   Fade to Black

3:45 P.M.   Site participants hold group discussions
Studio audience meets with Wasserman, Martin

5:00 P.M.   Site groups reconvene for reports, conclusion

5:30 P.M.   Adjourn

15

Deliver

Now that the gestation period is concluding and the brain child is fully developed, it is time to deliver it. Yes and no. In training, delivery is not necessarily the end of development.

A pilot test may have been the first delivery, or an in-house rehearsal, or even an extensive walk through. If the training is to be repeated for several groups, the first delivery is more of a shakedown.

The Deliver Phase is also a time of polishing, adjusting, refining. The results of the first time out may send you back to redefine, redesign, or redevelop some units. That is always a reluctant decision. All the work you've put in already is an overwhelming rationalization for going ahead with a flawed piece as it is. You tell yourself, "I'll fix it later." But a sour curriculum piece is like a rotten apple, it can spoil the rest, especially if it is critical to the flow of the others.

True, some units are made worse by tampering, but there's always enough that still needs work. The consummate trainer is forever conjuring how to turn a fair-to-middling piece into a winner.

From here on, I'll take up some of the concerns usually associated with the delivery of training.

SITES, FACILITIES

Long before you are ready to deliver, you will have arranged for your training site, if you have that choice. And you may not have gotten what you wanted. Every trainer has tales to tell about the improbable places in which she has plied her trade, made picturesque by the passing of time.

No question about the influence of environment. That was brought home to me years ago during a visit to the Southern Police Institute at the University of Louisville. The Institute was set up under a Ford Foundation grant shortly after the Supreme Court decision requiring the desegregation of public schools, to train law enforcement officers of the South, where trouble was expected. The second floor of a building was refurbished in a startling motif. Deep-pile blue carpeting was laid, the walls painted in soft pastels and covered with tasteful paintings. The large classroom was paneled in oak and huge, leather covered overstuffed chairs provided for each participant. It was the ambience of an oil-company board room.

When I expressed amazement, the rationale was explained. One of the overriding purposes of the training was to imbue the officers with a sense of pride and professionalism, to strengthen them in their sworn duty to enforce the law, in spite of anticipated pressures to prevent it.

Their training started with a presentation on the history of law enforcement. Until then, some of the deputies and marshals were not aware that policing *had* any history.

Many came from county seats where the sheriff's department might be in a dismal courthouse basement, next to the men's room, or from a small town where the police station is in an abandoned building beside the town dump. Imagine the impact when they joined fellow officers in a place of dignity and respect and learned they were part of a long tradition of peacekeeping.

"They are never the same afterward," said the Institute's director.

In choosing a site for training, advance inspection is almost mandatory. People from a logistics or conference management department may have some idea of training requirements, but they must juggle so many variables—cost, availability, location, schedule—that take on more importance than the purpose of the booking. I'll wager you know what it's like to arrive to find yourself assigned a long, narrow room split by two big pillars, or one that the hotel claims can accommodate 200 that you'd need a shoehorn to squeeze forty people in. If you have to rely on others to pick your places, by all means give them a little training on what you require, with a handy checklist to go by.

Different topics and different participant groups take different facilities. The all-purpose facility is a nice idea, but it is apt to provide much of what you don't need and little of what you do.

The "ideal" training center is supposed to be every trainer's dream. With exceptions, that's about what it is—a dream. I've toured a few, worked in a couple, and read about others. In those articles about what a training center ought to be, ever notice that the experts quoted are people in the business of designing training centers? They often look askance at architects, perhaps for good reason, but they can also be condescending about trainers. One remarked huffily about the "bias" of HRD professionals. And why is it that stories about some company's new, expensive, custom-designed training center never mentions any mistakes that might have been made, or bugs that had to be worked out?

The feature I find missing in any real or imagined ideal training center is the freedom for trainees to make it their own. Every comfort, every convenience is provided *for* them, by others, with a sameness of standards the military services might envy. Where is individuality admitted; where is each participant's separate path to learning facilitated? It seems to me a training facility ought to furnish more than so much table space and seats for each learner, but give him a chance to act upon his environment— change it around, do things with it, mess it up. By anticipating the trainee's every need, we can subtly divest her of her own personality and the chance to make her own training experience. Maybe that's why training that is undertaken under adverse circumstances, in a less than ideal setting where everybody must pitch in and make the best of it, is sometimes surprisingly successful. In making a contribution, the participants take ownership.

So if you can't find the ideal training center, you come as close as you can, trading off the shortcomings for something you need more. And whether it be hotel, conference center, schoolroom, college campus, camp, office, or cruise ship—there is always some drawback.

Hotels are getting better at providing for training, but they have a long way to go. Hotels still seem to regard every meeting as either a banquet or a conference. Try getting some conference arrangement besides U-shaped, green draped tables with water pitchers. What trainer hasn't walked into a room he ordered set up theater style to find all those hardback chairs lined up in military precision, almost daring to be moved? Chairs are for sitting, not stacking, and until hotels find out about those easy-on-the-end, tiltback, swivel, roll-around kind, the trainer should do a sit test to feel what punishment he's going to subject participant posteriors to.

Lighting is often poor in hotels, and in some conference centers. Layered lighting that can be dimmed is desirable, but focusing is also needed—on charts, displays, speakers, and chalkboards. As one who goes for frequent changes in room arrangement and just as frequent cleanups, I have trouble with the hotel practice of setting up once a day and cleaning up only after meals. Giving diagrammed instructions ahead of time—to the custodial staff, not the sales people—helps in some places, but usually I take their morning setup and do the rest myself. I like old hotels that have seen better days; they're so glad to have you, they'll do almost anything for you.

Now about learning climate—climate in the literal sense. Should you go to a resort? Should you get away from the distractions of the big city? Is there such a thing as too much comfort? The definitive answer to all these questions is: It depends. If your training calls for the total concentration of a "cultural island," then choose that out-of-the way conference center. If a resort setting will attract your clients, or they need relaxation, that's a good choice. If your trainees must be bright-eyed and bushy-tailed each morning, avoid the big cities with their nightly temptations.

When training is in a twenty four hour residential setting, attention must be given to after-hours activities, of course. Tutoring and elective sessions draw better, but recreation is needed, too, more than the inevitable card games and quaffing. Organizing is not as important as making opportunities available, and furnishing equipment. Volleyball games are fun and you'd be amazed at how much activity a simple frisbee can stimulate. It only takes a bat and ball to start a softball game. A table tennis or pool table can lead to a tournament. Watch out for touch football games, though, unless you've got insurance covering the players.

Exercise, even standing and stretching once in a while, can legitimately be said to contribute to learning.

EXECUTION

A training event is made up of a lot of little things. Any one of them alone may be inconsequential, but together they have a cumulative influence for good or ill. All the small parts contribute to learning, setting an atmosphere of respect for participants, serious attention, orderly flow, easy interaction, and trust.

A training event is also a microcosm of life—a compressed, somewhat accelerated span of time in which behavior is intensified. Especially in long-term, residential events, relationships form quickly, reactions are rapid. The learner prone to withdraw will do so immediately; the abrasive one will be heard from sooner. Irritations are more manifest but subside suddenly. Groups that flare into fierce rivalry end up as partners in a love feast.

This paroxysm of minor details wrought large in effect bids the trainer to overlook nothing. Some system is needed to assure that all those items that can cause damage if ignored are covered. A checklist is essential. A number are available from hotel chains, conference management publications, and training periodicals, but because every event is different and the variables are unique to your operation, it is smart to use the published lists to make up your own. Be sure to include those items that don't seem important enough to be included; those are the ones you forget.

Besides knowing what is to be done, it's necessary to know who is to do it. There's an administrative role connected with training delivery that is better assigned than assumed. If training is done by a team, the team leader performs the administrator's duties. And time must be allotted for those chores, which means lessening the training load of the leader. A familiar problem is the small crisis that breaks out when the leader is up front doing her presentations.

A good scheme, if you can afford it, is to assign a secretary or administrative assistant to be conference manager. I can testify to the invaluable assistance of such a person, performing many functions better than the team leader can. Chances are, some secretary has done heavy duty getting the training ready to deliver, yet many organizations stop short of permitting that secretary to attend the session, or cast her in a purely registration clerk role. It's a false economy. Not only can she take a load off the trainers, but she can serve as hostess, a touch that gives the event a little class.

Here are some other recommendations on a few of the details that go into the execution of training:

- Arrive early, the day before training begins if possible. You need to case the place and make sure you've gotten what you ordered. Check the rooms, the first day setup, the light switches and plugs, the room climate. Test the equipment. Meet the staff at the site you'll be depending on. Early arrival may leave you time to meet and greet the folks when they arrive.

- Go out of the training room, come back in and give yourself a participant's first impression. Sit down at one of the seats and forget you're a trainer. Is the scene foreboding or unfriendly? Is there too much head table, the podium too dominant? Imagine what it would be like to spend numerous hours in that setting. Make the changes that occur to you.

- Registration can be made easy. Know who your participants are before they arrive, have their names and addresses typed out so all they have to do is sign in and correct any mistakes. Trainees can automatically be assigned to color groups at registration, too. Preassign each and stick a small colored dot by the name; also put color dots on the trainee's name tag and manual. Then put large color signs on the tables and walls where the group to which each belongs is seated.

- If your site has labyrinthine passages and incomprehensible floor numbering that makes finding the way to breakout rooms an exploration, don't depend on directions or hall signs. Have your group leaders escort them to the breakouts the first time. Once is usually enough.

- There's no rule that says training must begin with introductions, orientation, housekeeping, and other opening exercises that we think put the participants at ease. Why not plunge right into the first session, particularly if it is a getting acquainted piece or a really first-rate opening unit? That will allay anxiety about as quickly as all that customary wind-up we go through, which could bring them to the point of wanting to shout, "Get on with it!"

- Whenever you get around to them, don't slight housekeeping announcements as being mundane. They tell people what they need to know to operate in the coming time—the schedule, eating arrangements, location of rest rooms, fire precautions, coffee breaks, materials, expense vouchers, telephone messages, who to see for what.

- Outsiders who are not active participants can have a distracting, even intimidating influence. The ideal but not always plausible rule is to ban them altogether. If you can require that all who attend become active participants, that helps. The in-and-out observers, who show up just to have a look, can be deterred by a rule against such practice if the rule is interpreted as being in the best interests of training. Spread that word among authorities who like to fulfill their oversight responsibility by taking a quick look. It works sometimes.

- Latecomers can be brought up to date by assigning a trainer to give them a miniview of what they have missed, give them their materials, and even let them screen any audio-visuals they've missed. Take them aside and spend some time with them, so they have a reasonable chance to catch up. The temptation is to penalize those who show up late, but it is not always their fault.

- Humor has a place in training but dirty stories are something else. I'm no prude but I have been appalled by the vulgarity of some stories told by trainers. The off-color joke is apparently assumed to have universal appeal, but there are always persons who are offended or disgusted. The sexist story is not made acceptable by an opening admission that it is probably sexist, or by a later apology "to the ladies." Shaggy dog stories are good, and corny ones, too—the cornier the better. They take the trainer out of that stuffy stance he can project, even unknowingly. The best stories, of course, are those that make some point about the subject matter, directly, not just dragged in through some strained connection.

- Booze seems to go with the territory in training, especially away from the office. The rule of reason ought to apply here, because drunk or hung over trainees don't learn much, despite the great time they think they are having. Drinking during sessions should never be tolerated (I've had it happen) and imbibing ought to be put off until the happy hour at the end of the day; martini luncheons make for sodden afternoon sessions.

  Learning seems to be stimulated by spirits, however, in those after-hours critiques in the cocktail lounge, where participants share what they *really* think about the training, and trainers. Joining in on one of these exchanges can be a revealing evaluation.

Cash bars are the general order, because they hold down expenses. It can be justified for the team leader to keep an after-hours hospitality suite going; I've found it a good cover for troubled participants to unload problems they might otherwise keep to themselves.

- The farewell party or dinner is a staple, sometimes including the presentation of awards and some choice after-dinner speechmaking. These can be memorable occasions; I can freshen the dim memory of a past training group by recalling their final party. It is unwinding time for everybody and by then the trainees feel such camaraderie you'd think they'd spent four years of college together.

    Fun gifts—those silly articles that poke fun at the foibles of the unsuspecting—are characteristic of going-away time. We found them so entertaining that my team made them part of our planning, with a place on the PERT chart and an assignment for someone. To leave no one out, we systemized our collection of nefarious data. Group leaders kept an eye out for peculiarities in their groups and we devoted a team meeting to compiling such trivia. Then the duty trainer went out to the dime stores to select something appropriate.

    Participants ought to have a right to defend themselves against such a conspiracy, and I found that the way to do this was to drop a hint to three or four of them about what we were plotting to do. They never failed to pass the word and on the occasion of gift giving, they had some hilarious surprises for us.

    I have never found a training group so serious or sober that they failed to be delighted by the silliness of fun gifts.

- Interruptions are the bane of training. They break concentration and throw everybody off track. A way to minimize them is to discourage the acceptance and delivery of telephone messages. Some participants—especially the executive class—carry on as if they are still running the office back home, giving what is left over of their attention to the training. An announcement that only emergency messages will be delivered and a request that all calls be confined to after hours will help some. But those who can't exist out of telephone contact will pick up messages at noon and during breaks, and often be late getting back. It is almost a no-win situation.

- Emergencies can occur in the course of training. You may be called upon to notify a participant of the illness, accident, or death of a loved one, or pass along that urgent "Call home" message. It's a tragic time for them and a frustrating one for you, because you feel so helpless.

Your good instincts come forth then. Of course, don't deliver shocking messages to them while they are in a group. Draw them outside, be gentle in passing the word and offer condolences. Try to *be* of help, instead of offering it. They are stunned and confused and need time, perhaps by themselves. Keep someone hovering nearby, perhaps checking with them occasionally. Collect their materials, pave the way for their easy departure if that is necessary, and realize that training is of no consequence to them now.

If they stay, don't embarrass them with an announcement to the rest of the group of what has happened. That can bring more expressions of concern than they can handle. Let a few participants who have been close to them know, for the support they can provide. Then go on with the training, showing your care by no more painful reminders.

PRESENTATIONS

Most of us could do a better job of lecturing than we do. One reason we don't is that we focus too much on one or the other of the two central elements—content or delivery. It is easy to do. *What* we say is of undeniable importance, but *how* we say it is also important.

Another tendency is to reach a certain level of competence in delivering lectures and to become satisfied, assuming that improvement would require more effort than we have time for. It doesn't have to be all that difficult to keep improving; all it takes is some intentional effort.

Improving the content of a lecture is a matter of time and practice. As you prepare—when you are selecting the points and concepts you want to include—make a point right then to put them down in speakable language. Say it to yourself, out loud, before you write it down. So often, we pick up language that we know isn't vocal, from sources that are in written style, and promise ourselves that sometime later we will translate it into verbal style. And then never do.

Even if you can't keep at it through the preparation of an entire presentation, do it whenever you think about it. Gradually, it becomes a habit.

After you've gotten down what you want to say, practice speaking it out, even if it only means reading your lecture aloud. Keep moving toward the outline that you know you're going to use when you deliver it, and go back to your literal text only when you can't remember.

Then get yourself an audience, any kind of audience, even if you have to visualize one. I knew a preacher who used to practice his sermons on a dog and another who spent Saturday nights in the empty sanctuary of his church, delivering what he'd say the next morning to an imaginary

congregation. Talking to a tape recorder is good, especially playing it back
and noticing the phrases you trip over and the concepts that don't make
sense.

What you're after is a shakedown of the content—the words you are
using. Don't bother about your delivery now; concentrate on finding language that communicates.

Improving your delivery can come imperceptibly and surely if, each
time you give a lecture, you concentrate on just one aspect of your delivery—projecting your voice to the back of the room one time, slowing
down or pausing another time, keeping eye contact a third time. Make a
note to yourself on a card that you keep before you on the lectern; you'll
forget about it most of the time, but once in a while you'll notice it and
remember.

Pick out your weaknesses and try to correct them, one at a time.
Over a period of time, you'll be improving, while hardly noticing how
much.

Here are some other thoughts on presentations:

- If you feel anxious before you go on, welcome to the club. You know
  that as soon as you get into it, you'll be fine. To get over those opening fidgets, *master* your opening—the first few minutes worth. Know
  exactly what your first two or three sentences are going to be—that
  gets you started. Also know how you intend to end—the clincher or
  fitting denouement. If you are certain of the beginning and the end,
  the middle comes easier.

- Of course, before you can start, you have to get their attention,
  which is not always easy. There are numerous devices. There's the
  equipment check: "Testing. Testing. One, two, three, four." (Never
  more than four.) Or glowering in stern silence until the miscreants
  quiet down. A simple, "Let's get started," or "Could I have your attention?" sounds pleading. For raucous disturbers, I favor the Navy
  command, ominously given: "Now hear this!" Some trainers just
  start talking, then back up and start over when all is quiet. Having
  somebody slam the door loudly in back works sometimes.

- Don't step on your own lines or give away everything you've got at
  the beginning. That quick capsule of what's coming may lead some
  to take a nap. Keep them in suspense about the startling disclosures
  to come.

- We all know the lectern is a crutch, something to hide behind. It is
  also very handy for holding notes, propping up weak knees, and for
  clinging to. To get free of the lectern, accept it as your home port that
  you can leave and come back to any time you feel insecure. As an

incurable pacer, I pass by the lectern repeatedly, drawing sustenance each time.

- The trainer who is heavily dependent upon notes (if you want to panic him, hide his notes) may hardly ever refer to them. It wouldn't do much good; chances are they are scrawled small and incomprehensible. All that matters is their presence. If you *use* notes, cards with key phrases printed large work better and can be carried around. One of those typewriters with extra large letters makes notes readable at a glance.

- It's an old trainer trick to use visual aids as notes—the flip charts, transparencies, slides. Trouble is, you get into the habit of talking to the aids, not the people. You also leave the impression that the aids are the whole show.

- When you time segments of your lecture, rank order them so that if you get pressed for time at the end, you cut out the low-priority stuff. Of course, have a couple socko segments on hand if you should run short.

- Unless there's good reason to run straight through your lecture, pause at the end of various segments for questions, rather than waiting until the end. Listeners may forget their questions if they have to wait. The pauses are good for you, too—breathing space and a gauge of how you are coming across.

- Don't be afraid of silence. Cramming the air with words is not necessarily communicating. Use silence for emphasis and sinking-in time for hard-to-grasp thoughts. And to collect yourself.

- If you get lost or your mind goes blank in the middle (it happens), turn to someone in the audience and ask a question, any question. While it is being answered, race back mentally to find your place or consult your notes. Then gratefully acknowledge the answerer who saved you, and go on.

- If you encounter disruptions, such as the hum of conversation in the back of the room—stop, walk in deliberate silence over to a chart or something on the side, then walk back. Silence accentuates the disruption and brings it to an end faster than any word from you.

- Be careful about following the advice to pick out one person in the audience and talk to him. That person may be utterly unrepresentative of the rest. Shift eye contact from person to person and don't forget those in the back.

- Use a lot of "you angle" in your lecture, statements that address all as one person. Try to overcome the one to thirty or one to seventy-five ratio that exists between you and the audience by addressing them as one.

- Never give the same lecture twice in the same way. If you do, you are not adjusting to the uniqueness of the new audience.

- If you flub, make the most of it by some amusing comment on your human frailty. This may or may not amuse the listeners, but it helps you stay in command.

- The most troubling tone for lecturers—and their audiences—is monotone. Worse, it flattens out your content so that minor points are equal to major ones. Changes in volume, pauses, movements are vehicles of emphasis. Lowering the voice can give stress as well as raising it.

- This might not be your style, but you might try the politician's trick of playing the audience by addressing persons in it by name—"Isn't that right, Harry?" or "Patricia, you remember that time, don't you?" The old pol is trying to give the impression he's on a first name basis with everybody there, even if he knows only a few. Used judiciously, the ploy can wake up a slumbering audience.

- If you have a scratchy throat or laryngitis, try what singers do: carry a small creamer-size container of honey to the podium with you. Take it just before you start speaking. It will usually keep you clear until you finish. Adding a little lemon helps, too.

- When giving task instructions, ask a trainee to repeat her understanding of what is expected. Correct and repeat if necessary. Don't be afraid of sounding too simple; there is always someone who needs clarification and repetition.

- In taking questions from the group, repeat the question before you answer it, to make sure you've got it right and so everybody can hear it. Don't comment on the quality of the question, just answer it.

- When you are pressed for time and you inevitably fall into that just-one-more-question phase, remind yourself of the lengthy cogitation that may have gone on in the mind of the questioner. At the moment, his question looms larger than your entire lecture. Contract with the group for ample time to adequately deal with those last questions. They'll love you for it.

- If you have to use a public address system, consider the disadvantage of the questioner if his voice is not amplified and yours is. Step away from the mike, walk out into the group, when taking questions.

- Be aware of the cumulative effect of lectures, how they have a way of losing something by repeated use. A lecture on Day One is a lot easier for a listener to take than one given on the last day of training.

GUIDING GROUPS

Every training group has a dynamic of its own, an always new and different mix of personalities. The interplay of individual characteristics is so variable that it slips beyond the reach of static rules of group process.

The trainer, too, is an inconstant variable in the group mix. Yet most treatises on group process seem to assume that the trainer is unfailingly the same—always the paragon of maturity, skill, and patience.

First-rate trainers differ from each other, and have a right to their differences. Trainers have needs and limits of their own, skills of uneven distribution, and an undeniable claim to their own authenticity. They should not be expected to function as personless facilitation machines.

I have come to this conclusion after my share of exposure to group process theory and more than my share of work with groups. I have watched trainers with deserved reputations as magnificent facilitators break every rule in the book. And I've sat as a participant squirming with discomfort in sessions with trainers who stridently followed the conventions. My resentment mounted at the sense of being manipulated, at the artificial interest, the unnatural control over spontaneous emotions, and the knowledge that whatever my behavior might be, it could be classified under some label. I can't help but believe that other participants might feel the same.

I question whether full participation is always tantamount to learning, or only the triumph of group think. Why must some trainees, who prefer not to participate, perhaps because they learn more by listening, always be drawn out or be categorized as withdrawing and resisting? Some people who participate the most don't appear to learn much that is new—their contributions only rehash and re-enforce what they already know. Ironically, I've noticed some dominators—whom we are admonished to divert and contain because they obstruct others—being ultimately taken to the hearts of the group members because of their leadership.

My plea is for naturalness in the group leader, so that naturalness can be encouraged in group members. Every trainer brings her unique personality to interaction with a group and must work out those practices that are both natural to her and responsive to trainees. By being genuine, she achieves a respect that is not possible when trying to play a role. Furthermore, she is a more accurate representative of the real world in which the trainee must learn to function. This is not laissez faire for the trainer; on the contrary, she must persist in finding the approach that best serves the group within the repertoire of her own skills.

I have never considered myself a very good facilitator. In groups, I can't keep track of who is "gate keeping" and who is "resisting." My interventions never seem to come at the right time. I can be directive or nondirective, but not always when I am supposed to be. I talk; I offer my opinions. I don't always look the participants straight in the eye and I don't give a lot of re-enforcement. I never pay any attention to body language. I get very bored with participants at times and I don't always hide my impatience with stupid questions. I am not always thrilled by group discussions.

Strangely, though, my groups seem to perform as well or better than others in the same workshop. They seem to enjoy themselves and my marks on participant evaluations are consistently high. The group task always gets done and they make me proud when they report on their work. Maybe that is because I am "task oriented," which I realize is a pejorative label.

The function of groups seems to fall into two categories—where the purpose of the group is to learn group work or the purpose is to learn the content. They call for different kinds of group leadership. In the first, the leader pays far more attention to personal and process elements; in the second, the leader pays most attention to the task and the content.

I broke in during the 1960s training poverty workers, who were imbued with the necessity of challenging the power structure. When they came to training, *we* trainers were the power structure and confrontations were as common as coffee breaks. Their ultimate objective was to take over the training session, and once in a while they did. We invited confrontations by our practice of offering to negotiate the curriculum, in the interest of having them take ownership of it. When we gave them an overview at the beginning, they didn't have enough information or cohesiveness to take us on. But by the third or fourth day, they had gotten themselves together enough to mount a challenge. It was so predictable we got up a pool to bet on the day and the hour the seminar would "blow." A shrewd trainer could advance or retard the time by adroit but not altogether orthodox measures, to win his bet.

We learned quickly how to handle such challenges. When they rose up, stopped everything, and demanded changes, we were sweetly compliant. We put up the curriculum schedule and went through it, unit by unit, listing their objections. Here and there we gave in, after a decent interval of stalling, and added some new unit or altered an existing one. Invariably, they threw out a unit or two; what they didn't know was that we had put some pieces there for that purpose. From that point on, everything was roses.

It was manipulation, pure and simple. We outsmarted them. Clever trainers can usually outsmart participants, who are not experts in their own training and are in a poor position to seek something other than what they are offered. And trainers can do it all without violating process.

It could be that my approach to group work is a reaction to the dishonesty I have experienced in practice by the book. Let me describe how I deal with a group, and you make up your own mind.

When my participant group convenes for the first time, I move to establish control, as surreptitiously as possible. Sitting at the head of the table or standing at what is the command post while they gather indirectly communicates that I am the leader. Then through humor—remarks about our common situation, the appearance of the room, the session we have just left, the weather—I make my presence known by being the first to talk in a tone that all can hear. I then switch moods, talk rather seriously for a moment about the work before us.

Next, I let them talk, through some kind of getting-acquainted exercise or by asking questions. Their responses may be frivolous banter, but they come at my cue. I want each one to talk, to exercise her vocal chords, to get the feeling of speaking out. I make harmless comments, engage in brief digressions, talk more than seems necessary. I am setting a norm of talking, by talking. I learned as a reporter that the easiest way to get a news source to talk was to talk a lot yourself.

Then I set the task, repeating instructions, answering questions, making certain all understand. At that point, I get out of the way and let them go, put them on their own to do what they are supposed to do.

In those opening moments, I have tried to erect a structure and a tone for the group's future functioning. Nondirective trainers may not agree, but I find that groups yearn for structure and participate more freely and comfortably within a framework.

In succeeding group meetings, my control will gradually diminish, so that somewhere along about midpoint in training, the group moves almost on its own. From time to time, I will need to give instructions for new tasks or answer questions, and I will guide discussions, but my "air time" all but fades away. As the natural leadership of the group emerges, I will make excuses to leave the room, so they can take over.

My abdication of control is not always smooth, but I believe in facilitating by exception—taking an active role only when necessary. What you do *not* do, I have found, is as important as what you do.

You could call this manipulative indirection. I push the task by time reminders and other promptings, but I avoid much singling people out for personal references. I leave it to them to make their own contributions. No interventions like, "What is going on here?" If some trainee hangs back, I leave him alone, except that I may chat with him during a break, but not about his nonparticipation. I seldom call on anybody; they may not be prepared to recite and if a response is extracted, it is usually not genuine. Occasionally, I will obliquely invite a comment: "I'll bet Joan would love to see that happen at her place." If distractions occur, I try to change course, turning the subject to something so different the fuss seems incongruent. The same with a dominator who needs to be saved from himself by a change of subject. If one participant attacks another, I do not support or control either, but switch to some "we" configuration that lifts them out of their adversarial stance and into a less loaded subject they can share.

There's a lot of avoidance in this approach, but years of group work have taught me to believe in it. Maybe I am not alone in observing that trainers who are so adept at handling group tensions always *have* group tensions, as if they were looking for trouble, even unconsciously stirring it up. For me, patience works better. More than once I have gotten ready to administer the big fix to some conflict only to discover it had worn itself out. People don't need to be told when they are overacting; they need a way out. Time is their best out and if you draw attention to what they are trying to escape, they won't be a bit grateful.

A skill that is not fully appreciated in group facilitation, one I am trying to acquire, is asking provocative questions. One of the most skillful group leaders I know has a knack of posing hypothetical problems, drawn from his own experience, but uncannily appropriate. They not only stimulate interest but they peel back new layers of learning.

I never summarize at the end of a session. The practice smacks of presumptiveness, telling people what they have learned. A recap of what has been covered is legitimate, I suppose, but it is still telling people what they already know.

This side trip into my group-leadership style may have merely convinced you that yours is better. It is, to be sure, because you know what works best for you. Keep that in mind through these other observations on guiding groups:

- The trainer's responsibility has to be to the entire group, not any individual member. The disrupter has a right to your attention only until the rest of the group begins to suffer. If it gets to the point of him or them, you have to go with them.

- Ambiguity and confusion are part of learning. The trainees will exhibit enough of this; the leader shouldn't add to it. She must tolerate the craziness that precedes learning, serve as the steadfast anchor for the flounderers.

- Check your pace as you go along. I became aware of this sitting in with another trainer who moved at breakneck speed, dragging the group along. Later I noticed times when I got hyper and rushed, infecting the group. Once I caught myself, I could slow down.

- A hard thing to handle is the "wait time" between a question and its answer, recommended to be at least six seconds. Silence is awkward but thinking is going on.

- The best question of all is the "dumb question," because it truly seeks an answer and is asked at some risk. That question, though, may be on the minds of many others, who were not brave enough to take the risk.

- Please pardon this, but my pet peeve is the trainer response to a learner that begins, "What you are saying is. . . . " I've heard some strained rationalizations that this was paraphrasing or seeking clarification. Sounds to me, as it must to the participant, that he's being told he didn't know what he said.

- To tell a trainer that serving as a scapegoat for participant hostility goes with the job doesn't make it any easier. Keeping your cool takes a lot of tongue biting. The usual prescriptions—go outside for a drink, cool off, get a grip on yourself—usually work. But I've discovered that, after getting accustomed to group hostility, when I went through a season of placid workshops, I actually missed the excitement. A little hostility adds vitality, shows there's some spirit in the group. Far worse are those sessions in which the only reaction is sweet cooperation.

- If you encounter repeated group resistance or a prevalence of hostility in certain curriculum units, the problem may not be facilitation failure. The design of the piece may be flawed with irrelevant case material or make-work exercise. Back to the designing board.

- Training groups vary rather widely in their receptiveness. Some will lull you to sleep with their dullness. If you're lucky, once in a while you'll get a supersharp outfit that puts you to the test. This happened to me once in Wisconsin, where they still believe in the work ethic. I was a substitute trainer and hadn't done my homework well. They finished the group work way ahead of time and took me beyond my depth in the case material. I was up working far into the night trying to stay ahead of them. It was an awakening experience.

EVALUATION

The use and abuse of evaluation is an ad nauseam debate in which everybody agrees how right and true and essential evaluation is, but as one debater put it, "Evaluation is seldom done, hard to do, and the results are rarely really useful." My concern is not to add to the debate but to look at how evaluation might be helpful to the trainer looking to improve.

Evaluation of trainer performance is not the same as evaluation of training. A so-called results evaluation that tries to measure learning may show a course to be a whacko success or a dismal flop, with hardly a hint as to the trainer's part in the outcome. Was it the design, the delivery, the topic, the participants, the timing, or some other of a clutch of variables that made it work or not work? Data, hard or soft, may be used to prove most anything, but it doesn't help the trainer much.

An unfortunate starting point is the grim acknowledgement that most evaluations are not very reliable. Every trainer has a story to prove it. I recall a public official who made himself obnoxious to everybody in his group, then rated our entire workshop zilch on every evaluation question. But wait. He was first in line to request that we come out to his jurisdiction and put on a repeat of the workshop for his staff. And we did.

Who hasn't smiled to find one's training piece mentioned in answers to the question, "What was of most value to you in this workshop?" And then blanched to find the same piece listed in the "least value" category by some other participant. Where does it leave you?

A trainee who gets ticked off at something can kill you on an evaluation, to get even, maybe out of defensiveness, like one I had who repeatedly missed sessions or was late and then dumped on us with low scores. Variables that have little or nothing to do with learning have inordinate bearing on evaluations. We used to find that if the participants came down hard on the meals and accommodations, they would always go easy on the training.

Yes, we are talking about participant evaluations, those happiness quotients that are notoriously subjective and questionable, yet—somebody tell me why—continue to be the most frequently used form of evaluation.

Summative evaluations offer the most usable data, but their results come in too late to be of much help in revisions. For that matter, most evaluations get fed back too late to be very useful, despite those flow charts that show evaluation darting back to hook up with the front end of the training cycle.

All too often, evaluation scores serve some ax-grinding purpose—to justify a budget, to decide whether to discontinue the training or not, to keep the sponsors happy—that discolors their measurement of learning. When I once suggested changing to a one-to-ten Likert rating scale would give a better idea of where to make improvements, I was told frankly by the head of the consulting firm that our present one-to-five scale would better hide our weaknesses from our government sponsor.

No wonder trainers shudder about evaluation and sometimes get accused of not cooperating properly in accumulating data. Still, in spite of all the suspicions and shortcomings, I believe most trainers would agree that it is better to have evaluations than not. Without them, you are flying blind.

THE TRAINER'S PART

Trainers ought not *do* evaluations, that is, prepare instruments—unless there is no one else to do them. It's a simple case of conflict of interest; you can't be very objective about judging your own product. The trainer might have a part in framing instruments, such as including items for his own benefit.

Relations between trainers and evaluators are not always cordial. If they get too cozy, somebody is not doing his job. The incordiality usually begins when the evaluator complains that the trainer's objectives are not quantified enough to measure. I recommend you respond thusly, with a nice smile: "Oh. How did you intend to measure them?" Odds are, all that quantification will go for naught, if the objectives are measured at all.

Worse, however, is the way some evaluators slip out of their role and into the trainer's. They get paid for criticisms of training and easily fall into the presumption that they "know training." Some do, but their function is contaminated when they go beyond their data to offer advice. If the trainer encourages this, the collusion serves neither.

I have tried, with no encouragement, to go after microevaluations. Within a curriculum piece, you may have an exercise or case study or some other part you are not sure about. Why not an item on the evaluation form to detect the worth of that single part? Most measurements are too general to assist the trainer.

If participant evaluations are all you've got to go on, ever think of a brief introduction to them at the beginning of training? Talking about the seriousness of the evaluations can take some trainees out of the temptation to become overnight training experts when you put that form before them on the last day. With advance notice, they'll work hard to give fair and helpful feedback.

Verbal evaluations are about as useful to the trainer as written ones, even if they are subjective and not codified. The spontaneous open-endedness of a group critique brings out information you would never have thought to ask for in paper-and-pencil instruments. I am partial to checkpoints every other day or so throughout a training event—twenty or thirty minutes to stop and inquire, "How are we doing?" They give you a gauge of how on-target you are and where midcourse corrections are needed.

Occasionally, I have buttonholed four or five participants at the end of a session and put questions to them about some new tack I am trying with an old piece. That feedback usually told me what I wanted to know.

The presentation of evaluation results needs some care. It is standard practice to grab up the completed forms as soon as they are collected and rifle through them, because you can't wait to see how you did. You don't get a comprehensive picture that way, and if the reviews aren't all you expect, kiss it off with, "Aw, what do they know." A better scheme is to save all forms, or have them collected by the evaluator who is instructed to "protect the data." Then have them compiled and analyzed before the trainers see them for the first time. If you debrief after a training event, put it off until the evaluation report is ready, or have it presented verbally by the evaluator.

Debriefings tend to resort to anecdotal information if more objective and comprehensive data are not available. Trouble is, revisions are often based on this slim evidence.

Evaluators should stick to reporting the data and leave interpretation of it to the trainers. But evaluators can provide unexpected service with their data. Doing a pilot one time that included tryouts of some substance experts as trainers, we were faced with one who antagonized the participants in some way every session he did. We all agreed he had to go, but the boss couldn't get up the guts to tell him. At debriefing, the evaluators came in prepared with scores on flip charts and presented their findings with admirable straightforwardness. The proof was there in the figures, for all to see, where the expert had affronted the customers. He stared at his scores for a moment and then said quietly, "I guess this just isn't my cup of tea."

————————PART FOUR CHECKPOINT————————

1. *Item:* Almost any generic planning technique can be applied to training production—PERT, Critical Path, six-step, seven-step, ten-step, etc. Most experienced trainers follow some sort of plan, often an amalgam of several others.

   Judgment: What plan to you follow in producing training?

   Reasons:

2. *Item:* The people to be trained are not often the ones who originate the idea of training.

Judgment:

Agree		Neutral		Disagree
1	2	3	4	5

Reasons:

3. *Item:* How often do you hear some trainee remark, "My boss ought to have this training?" It's a valid comment and reflects the desirability of clustering participants—the boss *and* workers, whole departments, work units.

Judgment:

Agree		Neutral		Disagree
1	2	3	4	5

Reasons:

4. *Item:* The ideal design is one that, besides achieving the goal, is almost trainer proof and has structure that is unnoticeable.

Judgment:

Agree		Neutral		Disagree
1	2	3	4	5

Reasons:

5. *Item:* Training is not filling time slots. The schedule should fit the training, not the training fit the schedule.

   Judgment:

	Agree	Neutral	Disagree	
1	2	3	4	5

   Reasons:

6. *Item:* If possible, the design team should include someone to represent the trainees. Letting the participants speak for themselves can do much to keep the design relevant.

   Judgment:

	Agree	Neutral	Disagree	
1	2	3	4	5

   Reasons:

7. *Item:* Supported by study, the trainer is the ultimate judge of the content to be supplied, what the trainee needs to learn.

   Judgment:

	Agree	Neutral	Disagree	
1	2	3	4	5

Reasons:

8. *Item:* The very writing of objectives is arbitrary and inexact. It is the quantification that makes them so ludicrous. Who is to say that if the participants list six of the causes of inflation or identify nine ways to skin a cat that they have learned?

Judgment:

Agree		Neutral		Disagree
1	2	3	4	5

Reasons:

9. *Item:* I don't find the standard academic outline—with its alphabetical and numerical format—to be very useful because it forces a rank ordering of content by significance or chronology.

Judgment:

Agree		Neutral		Disagree
1	2	3	4	5

Reasons:

10. *Item:* The worst advise ever given to trainers is that hoary platitude: "Tell 'em what you're gonna tell 'em, tell 'em, and then tell 'em what you told 'em."

Judgment:

Agree		Neutral		Disagree
1	2	3	4	5

Reasons:

11. *Item:* The question that always occurs to me—and makes me wonder why it seems to occur to nobody else—is why we trainers put all our faith in one-shot training? One conference, one workshop seems to be all we ever devote to one subject, however complex.

    Judgment: Why do you think there's so much one-shot training?

    Reasons:

12. *Item:* Appended to the chapter on design was a list of Ninety-Two Ways To Train. It listed and described methods, devices, processes, and techniques for training.

    Judgment: How would you rate this list?

Useful		Neutral		Useless
1	2	3	4	5

    Reasons:

13. *Item:* The strongest admonition I can offer about giving assignments before, during, and after training is: Don't be afraid to do it.

Judgment:

Agree   Neutral   Disagree

1   2   3   4   5

Reasons:

14. *Item:* Time should be built in for individual study. If your session calls for individual work before returning attention to the group— taking a test, reading, reviewing a checklist—every trainee must be given time to finish, even if it holds up the others.

Judgment:

Agree   Neutral   Disagree

1   2   3   4   5

Reasons:

15. *Item:* When trainees are stiff and stodgy, I have found nonsense to be a fine loosening device. If the trainer isn't afraid to play the fool, participants can let go of some of their anxiety.

Judgment:

Agree   Neutral   Disagree

1   2   3   4   5

Reasons:

16. *Item:* Some lecturers get hung up on outlines and alliteration. I submit that neither contribute much to learning. Usable content doesn't have to come out in A-B-C or P-P-P form.

    Judgment:

	Agree		Neutral		Disagree
	1	2	3	4	5

    Reasons:

17. *Item:* I find overhead transparencies cumbersome, too prone to cover loads of content in one dizzy transparency, sometimes unreadable, and diverting of attention from my thoughts and the audience to the confounded projector.

    Judgment:

	Agree		Neutral		Disagree
	1	2	3	4	5

    Reasons:

18. *Item:* In the production of training tapes, the trainer *must* control the content and how it is presented.

    Judgment:

	Agree		Neutral		Disagree
	1	2	3	4	5

Reasons:

19. *Item:* Teleconference awaits the attention of some consummate trainers who can invent nontraditional ways to exploit its possibilities. Most training teleconferences now are little more than lectures with some tortured questions and answers at the end, or a panel discussion with phoned-in questions, with maybe a video tape once in a while.

Judgment:

Agree		Neutral		Disagree
1	2	3	4	5

Reasons:

20. *Item:* If we mean what we say about a holistic approach to training, should that not involve all the senses? Why not use music, art, literature as aids to learning?

Judgment: Have you used music, art, or literature in training?

Reasons:

21. *Item:* The feature I find missing in any real or imagined ideal training center is the freedom for trainees to make it their own. Every comfort, every convenience is provided *for* them, by others, with no chance to act upon their environment—change it around, do things with it, mess it up.

Judgment:

	Agree		Neutral		Disagree	
	1	2	3	4	5	

Reasons:

22. *Item:* There's no rule that says training must begin with introductions, orientation, housekeeping, and other opening exercises. Why not plunge right into the first session?

Judgment: Why not?

Reasons:

23. *Item:* I question whether full participation is always tantamount to learning, or only the triumph of group think. Why must some trainees, who prefer not to participate, perhaps because they learn more by listening, always be drawn out or be categorized as withdrawing and resisting?

Judgment:

	Agree		Neutral		Disagree	
	1	2	3	4	5	

Reasons:

24. *Item:* Clever trainers can usually outsmart participants, who are not experts on their own training and are in poor position to seek some-

thing other than what they are offered. And do it all without violating process.

Judgment:

Agree		Neutral		Disagree
1	2	3	4	5

Reasons:

25. *Item:* I believe in facilitating by exception—taking an active role only when necessary. What you do *not* do is as important as what you do.

Judgment:

Agree		Neutral		Disagree
1	2	3	4	5

Reasons:

26. *Item:* I never summarize at the end of a session. The practice smacks of presumptiveness, telling people what they have learned.

Judgment:

Agree		Neutral		Disagree
1	2	3	4	5

Reasons:

27. *Item:* The trainer's responsibility has to be to the entire group, not to any individual member. The disrupter has a right to your attention only until the rest of the group begins to suffer. If it gets to the point of him or them, you have to go with them.

Judgment:

Agree		Neutral		Disagree
1	2	3	4	5

Reasons:

28. *Item:* Everybody agrees how right and true and essential evaluation is, but as one debater put it, "Evaluation is seldom done, hard to do, and the results are rarely really useful."

Judgment:

Agree		Neutral		Disagree
1	2	3	4	5

Reasons:

29. *Item:* In spite of all the suspicions and shortcomings, it is better to have evaluations than not.

Judgment:

Agree		Neutral		Disagree
1	2	3	4	5

Reasons:

30. *Item:* Verbal evaluations are about as useful to the trainer as written ones, even if they are subjective and not codified.

    Judgment:

	Agree		Neutral		Disagree
	1	2	3	4	5

    Reasons:

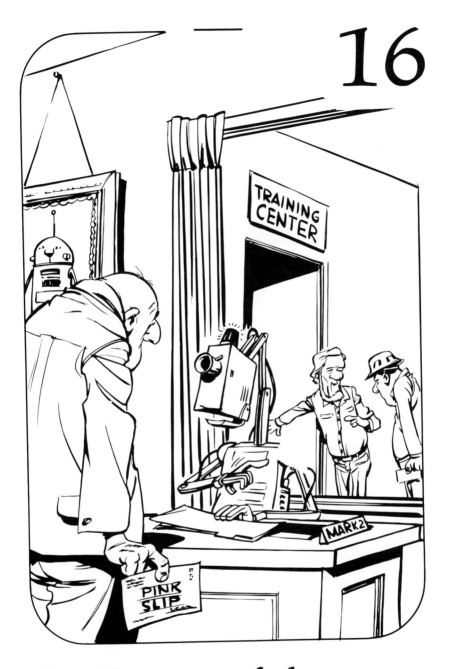

The Trainer of the Future

What will you be doing ten years from today?

Interesting question. One you don't think too much about, unless you get asked it in a job interview or you reach some milestone in your life that causes you to think ahead.

Suppose you were approached as part of a Delphi study that asked you to look ahead ten years, maybe fifteen or twenty, and predict what the practice of training will be then, and what your part in it will be. How would you respond?

You might want to write a large "It depends" on the question of your personal plans. And what they might well depend upon is your prediction of the future direction of training.

The future belongs to those who prepare for it, we are told, and that surely will be true about training. It doesn't take a crystal ball to perceive that training will change in the future.

The two biggest changes likely are in the environment in which training operates and in the technology with which it is delivered—changes in Content and Process.

In the next decade, training will have to cope with an environment that is changing, but not completely changed—part past, part present, part future.

The new directions in our society are the subject of much attention, in newspapers and magazines, on television and radio, and in books, such as John Naisbitt's best-selling *Megatrends* (Warner Books, New York, 1982). They tell of the movement from an industrial society to an information society, in which what is mass produced is not things but information and services, powered and linked by communications technology. The marketplace is to move from a national to a global economy, with international interdependence replacing competition. High technology, led by the computer, will perform work formerly done by human hands. Population will shift from the Northeast and Midwest to the Sunbelt. Great demographic changes will occur in the work force—mounting need for technically skilled workers, the emergence of more women, minorities, foreign born, middle-aged and older workers, increasing mobility of the labor force, and work relationships that are less hierarchical.

These transformations will not come without distress—severe displacement of employes in labor-intensive manufacturing industries and the dislocation of people without the skills required in the new economy. The educational system will be wrenched to prepare young people for the era of high technology.

Evolving changes in the kinds of work to be done will bring continuous changes in the subject matter of training. Retraining experienced workers out of one skill and into another will be an increasing demand.

To deliver this growing load of training, high tech sets out a vast electronic smorgasbord, with choices almost as bewildering. Training will be delivered more to individuals than groups, more at home or in the work place than in the classroom, more by package than in person, more from distant originating sites.

Not all the new modes of instructional technology will prove out. Some will await further state-of-the-art development to bring down costs. Others will simply not live up to their advertised claims, when users begin to focus more on how to utilize a device than merely how it works. The literature of change speaks of the adoption of innovation as gradual and uneven, with acceptance grouped among "innovators, early adopters, early majority, late majority, and laggards." Even if some innovation makes its way through to adoption by the late majority, the process can take years. Some innovations never make it past the early adopters.

If Naisbitt is right in his assertion that trends are initiated from the bottom up (and fads from the top down), then trainers could have much to say about what technology survives. An apt term for the next decade might be *shakedown*.

Divining the future is hardly a science, but a popular pursuit nonetheless, fed by our appetite for horoscopes, preseason sports predictions, political prognostications, stock market forecasts, and prophecies about what will happen in the new year or next decade. For all our fascination with advanced readings, it is remarkable how rarely we check out the accuracy of the predictions. Only when decisions based on them go sour are projections seriously questioned. Witness the widespread shutdown of nuclear energy plants with losses of billions of dollars by utilities that gambled on projections of future energy consumption and on equally wrong estimates about how much consumers would conserve energy.

Your Delphi projection of training's future would probably combine what you have heard and read with your own past and present experience. So it is with mine, which is colored by an experience in the early 1960s with a rather radical experiment using new technology as a delivery system.

A 26,000-FOOT TRANSMITTING TOWER

When early television was still searching for a rapid, efficient way to link up local stations for network transmission, numerous alternatives were being considered. Westinghouse Corporation came up with a dilly—transmit the television signal from an airplane. To demonstrate, Westinghouse outfitted a war surplus B-17 with television transmitters and telecast a World Series baseball game from Boston to Cleveland. This was at a time when television reception was limited to the range of a local station and the search for a medium for network feeds was urgent, so the idea was not entirely implausible. (In fact, it was the forerunner of transmission by satellite).

Airborne television, as it was called, lost out when the coaxial cable was settled upon as the way to link stations into a network.

Some years later, a Westinghouse engineer who had worked on airborne television was observing the schools of Hagerstown, Maryland, one of the first systems to have closed circuit television. He got to thinking—why couldn't airborne television be joined to systems like this to transmit the best in quality instruction from some central place?

The idea found its way to the Ford Foundation, then in full support of educational television. Ford underwrote a demonstration, located at Purdue University in Indiana, largely because the Midwestern terrain was free of obstructions to the television signal and because Purdue has an airport and a school for pilots.

The project became know as the Midwest Program on Airborne Television Instruction (MPATI) and was governed by a consortium of schools. Essentially, the delivery system was a DC-8 that hovered (flew lazy eights) for five hours each school day over Montpelier, Indiana and telecast instructional programs over two UHF channels, using video tape recorders on board and a transmitting antenna lowered from the belly of the plane. Ultimately 1,200 schools and colleges in six states picked up the signal with antennae on their roofs and distributed it to classrooms through closed circuit systems.

Because television is a line-of-sight broadcasting (contrasted to radio, which is skip signal), the higher the tower, the greater the range. The plane was, in fact, a 26,000-foot tower and transmitting station.

My tenure as an MPATI staff member yielded a number of conclusions that bear on my purview of future training technology. I found, for instance, that the medium of television, itself, is neutral. At first I was skeptical. I didn't want *my* kids taught by some boob tube. Later I learned that what mattered was not the mode, but what came from it.

For some inexplicable reason, television has characteristics that person-to-person teaching does not. A teacher in a class with thirty children is in a one to thirty relationship with them, but they respond in a one to one manner to the teacher on the television screen. They would talk back to the set, write letters to the teachers. One boy wrote a science teacher: "You understand me better than any teacher I ever had."

From this I concluded:

High tech media are only media; the content they deliver gives them validity.

In those days, instructional television was primarily a camera pointed at a teacher. MPATI broke out of that bind. Its productions made unprecedented use of graphics, set design, and action. Many lessons were remote productions—a social studies course went to thirty locations to show a day in the life of a governor, how automobiles are manufactured, the Cleveland Symphony, a railroad marshalling yard, growing tobacco, going to college at Antioch and Michigan. We had Robert Frost reading his own poetry, Basil Rathbone reciting Edgar Allen Poe, an act from Thornton Wilder's "Our Town." I visited a grammar school in a rural area where the kids chatted easily with migrant laborers in Spanish they had learned from airborne television. MPATI quality of instruction was as leading as its delivery system.

Conclusion:

The potential of new training technologies will not be realized without quality production of the content they carry.

Somewhat reluctantly, we discovered that the teacher in the classroom was essential to learning; the tube couldn't carry the lesson alone. Through briefings and lesson guides, classroom teachers learned to prepare students for a telecast and to process the learning after the set was shut off. Evaluations submitted by classroom teachers after every lesson were taken seriously by curriculum designers and producers.

Instructional media of the future will require the guidance and stimulation of user leaders.

As a breakthrough experiment, MPATI had to deal with equipment problems, fear of its cost and operation. The cost problem was dealt with by school discounts from major manufacturers. Operating problems were met by sending technicians to instruct local maintenance people—sometimes school custodians backed up by technical service people in the community. Problems with the hardware diminished gradually, but never went away.

In fantasies of the high tech future, equipment never fails. In harsh reality, malfunctions and breakdowns are common.

Perhaps the most telling latter day application of the MPATI experience was its classic demonstration of the hardware outrunning the software. At the time, ground based ETV stations were just getting started. States were setting up instructional networks. They were so preoccupied with funding and installing the hardware that they all but forgot the software. Came the day when they could turn on the power, the question became: "Now that we've got the air, what will we put on it?"

MPATI became a sudden mecca for ITV networks and stations outside our viewing area looking for program content to fill their schedules. We did a land office business renting our tapes.

Hardware without software is not half a system, it is no system at all.

Even the demise of MPATI affords a high tech lesson. The experiment found itself in competition with the burgeoning ground based ETV stations (now called public television). MPATI needed more channels—simultaneous transmission of lessons to students in primary, secondary and college level institutions takes a lot of air time. Our license application for six more channels to expand and become self-supporting was lobbied to death by the competition. So, after several years as a daring new concept in delivering high quality education to learners in remote villages and hamlets, MPATI faded from existence and now is only a chapter in college audio-visual textbooks.

New technologies compete with each other and kill each other off. Some will not live out the decade.

Twenty years after my adventure with airborne television, when I undertook a new adventure delivering training via a much higher flying transmitter—the satellite—it was with a rather pronounced sense of déjà vu. At the threshold of the new era of high technology, I found glitches and equipment failure as frequent as ever, dubious content quality hidden under the novelty of the medium, continued dependence on flesh-and-blood local leaders, counterproductive competition among distributors, and software that had almost lost sight of the hardware up ahead. The state of the art in making use of an exciting new technology seemed almost static.

ONE SMALL STEP AT A TIME

Wise counsel for the consummate trainer facing the future might be not "wait and see"—training has far too much at stake for that—but "proceed with caution."

Many concerns arise that must be addressed by trainers, to protect learning and learners from those less mindful. Trainers will have to be the stewards of quality, else technology can bog down into garbage in, garbage out. Need and use should dictate the development of new features of technology, not the sales gimmickry now so evident. The complexity of new devices must be straightforwardly recognized, not masked by a user-friendly label on instruments that take a good long time to make friends with. When new features of technology emerge, it may be up to trainers to array them in combinations to fit training's purposes.

In the coming shakedown years, trainers will need to experiment with new technologies and to lead their organizations to explore possibilities that have not occurred to manufacturers. Media, however exciting it might be, cannot be permitted to dominate content, because what people must learn in coming years may shift more rapidly than delivery methods.

Your Delphi projection may be less tainted with nostalgia than mine, but I do not foresee as quick or drastic a revolution as has been foretold. Some trends may turn into fads. Advances occurring in some places, although avidly reported by the media, may be slow spreading to other places and by that time the fickle media will have moved on to newer excitement. A sizable amount of the goods we consume will continue to be manufactured and not all of it by robots. The majority of the population will not join the migration to the growth areas, particularly when they discover how uncrowded it has become at home. Although the computer is already a cradle-to-grave presence in our lives, performs weddings, makes dolls, serves as scapegoat for our mistakes, and will one day mature from "friendly" to "affectionate," an incredible number of people will live perfectly happy and productive lives without tapping the keys on a box and peering at a dimly lit screen full of graphs and swirls and graceless digital figures.

Naisbitt acknowledges the genuine likelihood of a backlash to technology in his conception of high tech-high touch—the desire of people to be together, to go to the office rather than work at home, to browse through the crowded shopping malls to see and feel merchandise rather than punch an order into their home terminals. He flatly predicts that teleconferencing will never make it, because talking with people via television cannot begin to substitute for the high touch of a meeting. One day going off to a training event with live participants and live trainers may be a treat.

Change will come and the change that comes in training can be influenced profoundly by trainers if they practice their craft proactively in the coming years, when they will be needed as never before. The skills necessary in the next decade will not be altogether different, but some will be crucial. Some special requirements of the trainer of the future:

- She must be solidly grounded in the "old" approaches to learning—those processes of proven empirical worth—and be committed to keeping the needs of the learner in the forefront.

- He must master the new technologies to a level of sophistication that enables him to convert them to the most effective use for learning, even if this requires breaking new ground. His judgment must prevail in matching the "old" with the "new" to blend them if possible or to reject what does not serve learning.

- The trainer of the future must be a superior design specialist, whose capability ranges over content of long-standing need and that which is not known yet and the entire repertoire of methodology. She will be able, with help from programmers, to design software for customized training without waiting for it to become available on the market.

- The future trainer must be an innovator—a blend of guts and creativity that empowers him to lead, not follow, to resist faddism and gimmickry and to assert his dominance in the field he knows best.

In an era of confusing change, many human beings get lost. As we move away from the industrial nation we have been to a society in which technology performs much of the labor, millions of people will be hurt. Until our economy and national policy find a place for those who have lost their livelihood and their hope, their survival could depend upon the contribution that can be made by the consummate trainer—you.

About the Author

Ora Spaid's first calling was to journalism, inspired while a nickel-a-column-inch stringer writing high school sports for a newspaper in his home town of South Bend, Indiana. First he worked in the factories of the Studebaker and Bendix corporations and then attended Notre Dame and Michigan State universities. At the outbreak of World War II, he enlisted in the Army Air Corps and served as a navigator in the European theater, then resumed his training and was graduated from the Medill School of Journalism at Northwestern University.

His first job was editor of a small daily newspaper in McCook, Nebraska, and then he spent twelve years as a reporter and editor for *The Courier-Journal* in Louisville, Kentucky.

He left journalism for educational television, to be public relations officer for the Midwest Program on Airborne Television Instruction at Purdue University. In another career change, he moved to Asheville, North Carolina to set up an agency under the Ford Foundation's gray-areas program, the forerunner of the nation's War on Poverty. During four years there as director of a community action agency, Spaid repeatedly requested training in management. When none was forthcoming, he proposed a program to train persons in his circumstances, which took him to Washington, D.C. to establish an organization to train poverty leaders—his back door entry into training. The organization grew and gained a reputation for innovation, but was unable to weather a change in political climate.

For some time, Spaid worked as an independent consultant, serving a variety of clients with training, writing, and editing. Then he joined a client, a consulting firm that trained leaders in the field of criminal justice for the Justice Department.

Spaid now lives and writes in the picturesque old river town of Madison, Indiana.

266

Index